THE FREEMASON'S MONITOR

OR ILLUSTRATIONS OF FREEMASONRY
(1818)

Contained herein is the complete rituals, explanations, signs, prayers, charges, remarks, ceremonies, teachings and all information of the first three degrees.

Thomas Smith Webb

ISBN 1-56459-443-6

Request our FREE CATALOG of over 1,000

Rare Esoteric Books

Unavailable Elsewhere

Alchemy, Ancient Wisdom, Astronomy, Baconian, Eastern-Thought, Egyptology, Esoteric, Freemasonry, Gnosticism, Hermetic, Magic, Metaphysics, Mysticism, Mystery Schools, Mythology, Occult, Philosophy, Psychology, Pyramids, Qabalah, Religions, Rosicrucian, Science, Spiritual, Symbolism, Tarot, Theosophy, *and many more!*

Kessinger Publishing Company
Montana, U.S.A.

SANCTION.

GRAND-ROYAL ARCH CHAPTER OF THE STATE OF RHODE ISLAND.

Providence, July 7, A. L. 5802.

THE subscribers, having been appointed a committee to examine a publication by companion THOMAS S. WEBB, entitled, "THE FREEMASON'S MONITOR," beg leave to report, that, having attended to the subject of their appointment, they are of opinion, that the said publication is replete with useful Masonic Information, and is fully entitled to the sanction of this grand chapter.

JOHN CARLILE, *R. A. K.*
WM. WILKINSON, *R. A. S.*
JER'H F. JENKINS, *R. A. T.*
NATHAN FISHER, *R. A. C.*
JOSEPH TILLINGHAST, *R. A. C.*

Whereupon resolved unanimously, That this Grand Chapter recommend the aforesaid work to the attention and study of all the members of the fraternity to whom the same may come.

EXTRACT FROM THE RECORDS,

AMOS T. JENCKES, *Grand Secretary.*

PREFACE.

The following work, although chiefly intended for the use of the ancient and honourable society of Free and Accepted Masons, is also calculated to explain the nature and design of the Masonic Institution, to those who may be desirous of becoming acquainted with its principles, whether for the purpose of initiation into the society, or merely for the gratification of their curiosity.

The observations upon the first three degrees are many of them taken from Preston's '*Illustrations of Masonry,*' with some necessary alterations. Mr. Preston's distribution of the first lecture into six, the second into four, and the third into twelve sections, not being agreeable to the mode of working in America, they are differently arranged in this work.

It is presumed that all regular Lodges, and Royal Arch Chapters, will find it a use-

1 *

ful assistant and *Monitor ;* inasmuch as it contains most of the Charges, Prayers, and Scripture Passages, made use of at our meetings, and which are not otherwise to be found, without recourse to several volumes. This often occasions much delay in the recitals, produces many irregularities in their distribution, and sometimes causes important omissions.

The whole are here digested and arranged in such order, through the several degrees, from the *Entered Apprentice* to the *Royal Arch Mason,* that they may be easily understood ; and, by a due attention to their several divisions, the mode of working, as well in arrangement as matter, will become universally the same. This desirable object will add much to the happiness and satisfaction of all good Masons, and redound to the honour of the whole fraternity.

CONTENTS.

———◆———

PART I.

BOOK I.

CONTENTS.

PART II.

BOOK I.

BOOK II.

SKETCH OF THE HISTORY OF FREEMASONRY IN AMERICA.

THE
FREEMASON'S MONITOR.

PART FIRST.

BOOK I.

CHAPTER I.

Origin of Masonry and its general Advantages.

FROM the commencement of the world we may trace the foundation of Masonry.* Ever since symmetry began, and harmony displayed her charms, our order has had a being. During many ages, and in many different countries, it has flourished. In the dark periods of antiquity, when literature was in a low state; and the rude manners of our forefathers withheld from them that knowledge we now so amply share, masonry diffused its influence. This science unveiled, arts arose, civilization took place, and the progress of knowledge and philosophy gradually dispelled the gloom of ignorance and barbarism. Government being settled, authority was given to laws, and the assemblies of the fraternity ac-

---

* Masonry and Geometry are sometimes used as synonimous terms.

2

quired the patronage of the great and the good, while the tenets of the profeſſion were attended with unbounded utility.

Maſonry is a ſcience confined to no particular country, but diffuſed over the whole terreſtrial globe. Wherever arts flouriſh, there it flouriſhes too. Add to this, that by ſecret and inviolable ſigns, carefully preſerved among the fraternity throughout the world, maſonry becomes an univerſal language. Hence many advantages are gained: the diſtant Chineſe, the wild Arab, and the American ſavage, will embrace a brother Briton, Frank, or German; and will know, that beſide the common ties of humanity there is ſtill a ſtronger obligation to induce him to kind and friendly offices. The ſpirit of the fulminating prieſt will be tamed; and a moral brother, though of a different perſuaſion, engage his eſteem. Thus, through the influence of maſonry, which is reconcileable to the beſt policy, all thoſe diſputes, which embitter life, and four the tempers of men, are avoided: while the common good, the general deſign of the craft, is zealouſly purſued.

From this view of the ſyſtem, its utility muſt be ſufficiently obvious. The univerſal principles of the art unite men of the moſt oppoſite tenets, of the moſt diſtant countries, and of the moſt contradictory opinions, in one indiſſoluble bond of affection, ſo that in every nation a maſon finds a friend, and in every climate a home.

CHAPTER II.

The Government of the Fraternity explained.

THE mode of government obferved by the fraternity will beft explain the importance, and give the trueft idea of the nature and defign of the mafonic fyftem.

There are feveral claffes of mafons, under different appellations. The privileges of thefe claffes are diftinct, and particular means are adopted to preferve thofe privileges to the juft and meritorious of each clafs.

Honour and probity are recommendations to the firft clafs; in which the practice of virtue is enforced, and the duties of morality inculcated, while the mind is prepared for regular and focial converfe in the principles of knowledge and philofophy.

Diligence, affiduity and application, are qualifications for the fecond clafs; in which an accurate elucidation of fcience, both in theory and practice, is given. Here human reafon is cultivated by a due exertion of the rational and intellectual powers and faculties: nice and difficult theories are explained; new difcoveries produced, and thofe already known beautifully embellifhed.

The third clafs is compofed of thofe whom truth and fidelity have diftinguifhed; who, when affaulted by threats and violence, after folicitation and perfuafion have failed, have evinced their firmnefs and integrity in preferving inviolate the myfteries of the order.

The fourth clafs confifts of thofe who have perfeveringly ftudied the fcientific branches of the art, and exhibited proofs of their fkill and acquirements, and who have confequently obtained the honour of this degree, as a reward of merit.

The fifth clafs confifts of thofe who, having acquired a proficiency of knowledge to become teachers, have been elected to prefide over regularly conftituted bodies of mafons.

The fixth clafs confifts of thofe who, having difcharged the duties of the chair with honour and reputation, are acknowledged and recorded as *excellent mafters.*

The feventh clafs confifts of a felect few, whom years and experience have improved, and whom merit and abilities have entitled to preferment. With this clafs the ancient landmarks of the order are preferved; and from them we learn and practife the neceffary and inftructive leffons, which at once dignify the art, and qualify its profeffors to illuftrate its excellence and utility.

This is the eftablifhed mode of the mafonic government, when the rules of the fyftem are obferved. By this judicious arrangement, true friendfhip is cultivated among different ranks and degrees of men, hofpitality promoted, induftry rewarded, and ingenuity encouraged.

CHAPTER III.

The Importance of the Secrets of Masonry demonstrated.

If the secrets of masonry are replete with such advantages to mankind, it may be asked, Why are they not divulged for the general good of society? To which it may be answered: Were the privileges of masonry to be indiscriminately bestowed, the design of the institution would be subverted; and, being familiar, like many other important matters, would soon lose their value, and sink into disregard.

It is a weakness in human nature, that men are generally more charmed with novelty, than the real worth or intrific value of things. Novelty influences all our actions and determinations. What is new, or difficult in the acquisition, however trifling or insignificant, readily captivates the imagination, and ensures a temporary admiration; while what is familiar, or easily obtained, however noble and eminent for its utility, is sure to be disregarded by the giddy and unthinking.

Did the particular secrets or peculiar forms prevalent among masons constitute the essence of the art, it might be alledged that our amusements were trifling, and our ceremonies superficial. But this is not the case. Having their use, they are preserved; and from the recollection of the lessons they inculcate, the well informed mason derives instruction. Drawing

2*

them to a near inspection, he views them
through a proper medium; adverts to the
circumstances which gave them rise; dwells
upon the tenets they convey; and, finding them
replete with useful information, adopts them as
keys to the privileges of his art, and prizes them
as sacred. Thus convinced of their propriety,
he estimates the value from their utility.

Many persons are deluded by their vague
supposition that our mysteries are merely nomi-
nal; that the practices established among us are
frivolous; and that our ceremonies might be
adopted, or waved, at pleasure. On this false
foundation, we have found them hurrying
through all the degrees, without adverting to
the propriety of one step they pursue, or possessing a single qualification requisite for advancement. Passing through the usual formalities,
they have accepted offices, and assumed the
government of lodges, equally unacquainted
with the rules of the institution they pretended
to support, or the nature of the trust reposed in
them. The consequence is obvious; wherever
such practices have been allowed, anarchy and
confusion have ensued, and the substance has
been lost in the shadow.

Were the brethren, who preside over lodges,
properly instructed previous to their appointment, and regularly apprised of the importance
of their respective offices, a general reformation
would speedily take place. This would evince
the propriety of our mode of government, and
lead men to acknowledge, that our honours were
deservedly conferred. The ancient consequence

of the order would be reftored, and the reputation of the fociety preferved.

Such conduct alone can fupport our character. Unlefs prudent actions fhall diftinguifh our title to the honours of mafonry, and regular deportment difplay the influence and utility of our rules, the world in general will not eafily be led to reconcile our proceedings with the tenets of our profeffion.

CHAPTER IV.

GENERAL REMARKS.

MASONRY is an art equally ufeful and extenfive. In every art there is a myftery, which requires a gradual progreffion of knowledge to arrive at any degree of perfection in it. Without much inftruction, and more exercife, no man can be fkilful in any art; in like manner, without an affiduous application to the various fubjects treated of in the different lectures of mafonry, no perfon can be fufficiently acquainted with its true value.

It muft not, however, be inferred from this remark, that perfons, who labour under the difadvantages of a confined education, or whofe fphere of life requires a more intenfe application to bufinefs or ftudy, are to be difcouraged in their endeavours to gain a knowledge of mafonry.

To qualify an individual to enjoy the benefits of the society at large, or to partake of its privileges, it is not absolutely neceffary that he fhould be acquainted with all the intricate parts of the fcience. Thefe are only intended for the diligent and affiduous mafon, who may have leifure and opportunity to indulge fuch purfuits.

Though fome are more able than others, fome more eminent, fome more ufeful, yet all, in their different fpheres, may prove advantageous to the community. As the nature of every man's profeffion will not admit of that leifure which is neceffary to qualify him to become an expert mafon, it is highly proper that the official duties of a lodge fhould be executed by perfons whofe education and fituation in life enable them to become adepts; as it muft be allowed, that all, who accept offices and exercife authority, fhould be properly qualified to difcharge the tafk affigned them, with honour to themfelves, and credit to their fundry ftations.

CHAPTER V.

The Ceremony of Opening and Clofing a Lodge.

IN all regular affemblies of men, who are convened for wife and ufeful purpofes, the commencement and conclufion of bufinefs are accompanied with fome form. In every country of the world the practice prevails, and is deemed

effential. From the moft remote periods of antiquity it may be traced, and the refined im-
provements of modern times have not totally
abolifhed it.

Ceremonies, when fimply confidered, it is
true, are little more than vifionary delufions;
but their effects are fometimes important.—
When they imprefs awe and reverence on the
mind, and engage the attention by external at-
traction, to folemn rites, they are interefting
objects. Thefe purpofes are effected by judicious ceremonies, when regularly conducted and
properly arranged. On this ground they have
received the fanction of the wifeft men in all
ages, and confequently could not efcape the notice of mafons. To begin well is the moft likely means to end well; and it is judicioufly remarked, that when order and method are neglected at the beginning, they will be feldom
found to take place at the end.

The ceremony of opening and clofing a lodge
with folemnity and decorum, is therefore univerfally admitted among mafons; and though
the mode in fome lodges may vary, and in every *degree* muft vary, ftill an uniformity in the
general practice prevails in every lodge; and
the variation (if any) is folely occafioned by a
want of method, which a little application might
eafily remove.

To conduct this ceremony with propriety
ought to be the peculiar ftudy of every mafon;
efpecially of thofe who have the honour to rule
in our affemblies. To perfons who are thus
dignified, every eye is naturally directed for pro-

priety of conduct and behaviour; and from them, other brethren, who are lefs, informed, will naturally expect to derive an example worthy of imitation.

From a fhare in this ceremony no mafon can be exempted. It is a general concern, in which all muft affift. This is the firft requeft of the mafter, and the prelude to all bufinefs. No fooner has it been fignified, than every officer repairs to his ftation, and the brethren rank according to their degrees. The intent of the meeting becomes the fole object of attention, and the mind is infenfibly drawn from thofe indifcriminate fubjects of converfation, which are apt to intrude on our lefs ferious moments.

This effect accomplifhed, our care is directed to the external avenues of the lodge, and the proper officers, whofe province it is to difcharge that duty, execute their truft with fidelity, and by certain myftic forms, of no recent date, intimate that we may fafely proceed. To detect impoftors among ourfelves, an adherence to order in the character of mafons enfues, and the lodge is either opened or clofed in folemn form.

At opening the lodge, two purpofes are wifely effected: the mafter is reminded of the dignity of his character, and the brethren, of the homage and veneration due from them in their fundry ftations. Thefe are not the only advantages refulting from a due obfervance of this ceremony; a reverential awe for the Deity is inculcated, and the eye fixed on that object from whofe radiant beams light only can be derived. Here we are taught to adore the God of heaven, and to fupplicate his protection on our well meant endeavours. The mafter affumes his government in due form, and under him his wardens; who accept their truft, after the cuftomary falutations. The brethren then, with one accord, unite in duty and refpect, and the ceremony concludes.

At clofing the lodge, a fimilar form takes place. Here the lefs important duties of mafonry are not paffed over unobferved. The neceffary degree of fubordination in the government of a lodge is peculiarly marked, while the proper tribute of gratitude is offered up to the beneficent Author of life, and his bleffing invoked and extended to the whole fraternity. Each brother faithfully locks up the treafure he has acquired, in his own fecret repofitory; and, pleafed with his reward, retires to enjoy and diffeminate among the private circle of his brethren, the fruits of his labour and induftry in the lodge.

These are faint outlines of a ceremony, which univerfally prevails among mafons in every country, and diftinguifhes all their meetings. It is arranged as a general fection in every degree, and takes the lead in all our illuftrations.

Charge ufed at Opening a Lodge.

Behold! how good and how pleafant it is for brethren to dwell together in unity!

It is like the precious ointment upon the head, that ran down upon the beard, even Aaron's beard, that went down to the fkirts of his garment:

As the dew of Hermon, that defcended upon the mountains of Zion: for there the Lord commanded a bleffing, even life forevermore.

A Prayer ufed at Clofing the Lodge.

May the bleffing of Heaven reft upon us, and all regular mafons! may brotherly love prevail, and every moral and focial virtue cement us! *Amen.*

———◆———

CHAPTER VI.

Charges and Regulations for the Conduct and Beha-viour of Mafons.

A REHEARSAL of the ancient charges properly fucceeds the opening, and precedes the clofing, of a lodge. This was the conftant practice of our ancient brethren, and ought never to be neglected in our regular affemblies. A recapitulation of our duty cannot be difagreeable to thofe who are acquainted with it; and to thofe who know it not, fhould any fuch be, it muft be highly proper to recommend it.

ANCIENT CHARGES.

On the Management of the Craft in Working.

Mafons employ themfelves diligently in their fundry vocations, live creditably, and conform with cheerfulnefs to the government of the country in which they refide.

[The moft expert craftfman is chofen or appointed mafter of the work, and is duly honoured by thofe over whom he prefides.

[The mafter, knowing himfelf qualified, undertakes the government of the lodge, and truly difpenfes his rewards, giving to every brother the approbation which he merits.

[A craftfman, who is appointed warden of the work under the mafter, is true to mafter and fellows, carefully overfees the work, and his brethren obey him.]

The mafter, wardens, and brethren, receive their rewards juftly, are faithful, and carefully finifh the work they begin, whether it be in the firft or fecond degree; but never put that work to the firft which has been accuftomed to the fecond degree, nor that to the fecond or firft which has been accuftomed to the third.

Neither envy nor cenfure is difcovered among true mafons. No brother is fupplanted, or put out of his work, if he be capable to finifh it; as no man, who is not perfectly fkilled in the original defign, can, with equal advantage to the mafter, finifh the work begun by another.

All employed in mafonry meekly receive their rewards, and ufe no difobliging name. Brother or fellow are the terms or appellations they beftow on each other. They behave courteoufly within and without the lodge, and never defert the mafter till the work is finifhed.

Laws for the Government of the Lodge.

You are to salute one another in a courteous manner, agreeably to the forms established among masons;* you are freely to give such mutual instructions as shall be thought necessary or expedient, not being overseen or overheard, without encroaching upon each other, or derogating from that respect which is due to any gentleman were he not a mason; for though, as masons, we rank as brethren on a level, yet masonry deprives no man of the honour due to his rank or character, but rather adds to his honour, especially if he has deserved well of the fraternity, who always render honour to whom it is due, and avoid ill manners.

No private committees are to be allowed, or separate conversations encouraged; the master or wardens are not to be interrupted, or any brother speaking to the master; but due decorum is to be observed, and a proper respect paid to the master and presiding officers.

These laws are to be strictly enforced, that harmony may be preserved, and the business of the lodge be carried on with order and regularity. *Amen.* So mote it be.

Charge on the Behaviour of Masons out of the Lodge.

When the lodge is closed, you may enjoy yourselves with innocent mirth; but you are

---

* In a lodge, masons meet as members of one family; all prejudices, therefore, on account of religion, country, or private opinion, are removed.

carefully to avoid excefs. You are not to compel any brother to act contrary to his inclination, or give offence by word or deed, but enjoy a free and eafy converfation. You are to ufe no immoral or obfcene difcourfe, but at all times fupport with propriety the dignity of your character.

You are to be cautious in your words and carriage, that the moft penetrating ftranger may not difcover, or find out, what is not proper to be intimated; and, if neceffary, you are to wave a difcourfe, and manage it prudently, for the honour of the fraternity.

At home, and in your feveral neighbourhoods, you are to behave as wife and moral men. You are never to communicate to your families, friends, or acquaintance, the private tranfactions of our different affemblies; but upon every occafion to confult your own honour, and the reputation of the fraternity at large.

You are to ftudy the prefervation of health, by avoiding irregularity and intemperance, that your families may not be neglected and injured, or yourfelves difabled from attending to your neceffary employments in life.

If a ftranger apply in the character of a mafon, you are cautioufly to examine him in fuch a method as prudence may direct, and agreeably to the forms eftablifhed among mafons; that you may not be impofed upon by an ignorant, falfe pretender, whom you are to reject with contempt; and beware of giving him any fecret hints of knowledge. But if you difcover him to be a true and genuine brother, you are to respect him; if he be in want, you are to relieve him, or direct him how he may be relieved; you are to employ him, or recommend him to employment: however, you are never charged to do beyond your ability; only to prefer a poor brother, who is a good man and true, before any other person in the same circumstances.

Finally: These rules you are always to observe and enforce, and also the duties which have been communicated in the lectures; cultivating brotherly love, the foundation and capestone, the cement and glory, of this ancient fraternity; avoiding, upon every occasion, wrangling and quarrelling, slandering and backbiting; not permitting others to slander honest brethren, but defending their characters, and doing them good offices, as far as may be consistent with your honour and safety, but no farther. Hence all may see the benign influence of masonry, as all true masons have done from the beginning of the world, and will do to the end of time.

Amen. So mote it be.

CHAPTER VII.

Prerequisites for a Candidate.

By a late regulation, adopted by most of the grand lodges in America, no candidate for the mysteries of masonry can be initiated without having been proposed at a previous meeting of the lodge; in order that no one may be introduced without due inquiry relative to his character and qualifications.

All applications for initiation should be made by petition in writing, signed by the applicant, giving an account of his age, quality, occupation, and place of residence, and that he is desirous of being admitted a member of the fraternity; which petition should be kept on file by the secretary.

Form of a Petition to be presented by a Candidate for Initiation.

" To the worshipful Master, Wardens, and Brethren of —— Lodge of Free and Accepted Masons.

" The petition of the subscriber, respectfully sheweth, that, having long entertained a favourable opinion of your ancient institution, he is desirous of being admitted a member thereof, if found worthy.

" His place of residence is ——, his age —— years; his occupation ——.

(*Signed*) A. B."

After this petition is read, the candidate must be proposed in form, by a member of the lodge, and the proposition seconded by another member; a committee is then appointed to make inquiry relative to his character and qualifications.

Declaration to be affented to by a Candidate, in an adjoining apartment, previous to Initiation.

"Do you ferioufly declare, upon your honour, before thefe gentlemen,* that, unbiaffed by friends, and uninfluenced by mercenary motives, you freely and voluntarily offer yourfelf a candidate for the myfteries of mafonry?" I do.

"Do you ferioufly declare, upon your honour, before thefe gentlemen, that you are prompted to folicit the privileges of mafonry by a favourable opinion conceived of the inftitution, a defire of knowledge, and a fincere wifh of being ferviceable to your fellow creatures?" I do.

"Do you ferioufly declare, upon your honour, before thefe gentlemen, that you will cheerfully conform to all the ancient eftablifhed ufages and cuftoms of the fraternity?" I do.

After the above declarations are made, and reported to the mafter, he makes it known to the lodge, in manner following, viz.

"BRETHREN,

"At the requeft of Mr. A. B. he has been propofed and accepted in regular form; I therefore recommend him as a proper candidate for the myfteries of mafonry, and worthy to partake of the privileges of the fraternity; and, in confequence of a declaration of his intentions, voluntarily made, I believe he will cheerfully conform to the rules of the order."

If there are then no objections made, the candidate is introduced in due form.

* The ftewards of the lodge are ufually prefent.

CHAPTER VIII.

REMARKS ON THE FIRST LECTURE.

WE shall now enter on a disquisition of the different sections of the lectures appropriated to the several degrees of masonry, giving a brief summary of the whole, and annexing to every remark the particulars to which the section alludes. By these means the industrious mason will be instructed in the regular arrangement of the sections in each lecture, and be enabled with more ease to acquire a knowledge of the art.

The first lecture of masonry is divided into three sections, and each section into different clauses. Virtue is painted in the most beautiful colours, and the duties of morality are enforced. In it we are taught such useful lessons as prepare the mind for a regular advancement in the principles of knowledge and philosophy. These are imprinted on the memory by lively and sensible images, to influence our conduct in the proper discharge of the duties of social life.

THE FIRST SECTION

In this lecture is suited to all capacities, and may and ought to be known by every person who ranks as a mason. It consists of general heads, which, though short and simple, carry weight with them. They not only serve as marks of distinction, but communicate useful and interesting knowledge, which they are duly investigated. They qualify us to try and examine the rights of others to our privileges; while they prove ourselves; and, as they induce us to inquire more minutely into other particulars of greater importance, they serve as an introduction to subjects more amply explained in the following sections.

A Prayer used at the Initiation of a Candidate.

" Vouchsafe thine aid, Almighty Father of the Universe, to this our present convention; and grant that this candidate for masonry may dedicate and devote his life to thy service; and become a true and faithful brother among us! Endue him with a competency of thy divine wisdom, that, by the secrets of our art, he may be better enabled to display the beauties of brotherly love, relief, and truth, to the honour of thy holy name! *Amen.*"

It is a duty incumbent on every master of a lodge, before the ceremony of initiation takes place, to inform the candidate of the purpose and design of the institution; to explain the nature of his solemn engagements; and, in a manner peculiar to masons alone, to require his cheerful acquiescence to the duties of morality and virtue, and all the sacred tenets of the order.

Towards the close of the section is explained that peculiar ensign of masonry, the *lamb-skin*, or *white leather apron*, which is an emblem of innocence, and the badge of a mason; more ancient than the golden fleece or Roman eagle; more honourable than the star and garter, or any other order that could be conferred upon the candidate at the time of his initiation, or at any time thereafter, by king, prince, potentate, or any other person, except he be a mason; and which every one ought to wear with equal pleasure to himself, and honour to the fraternity.

This section closes with an explanation of the *working tools* and implements of an entered apprentice, which are, the *twenty-four inch gauge*, and the *common gavel*.

The *twenty-four inch gauge* is an instrument made use of by operative masons, to measure and lay out their work; but we, as free and accepted masons, are taught to make use of it for the more noble and glorious purpose of dividing our time. Its being divided into twenty-four equal parts is emblematical of the twenty-four hours of the day, which we are taught to divide into *three* equal parts, whereby we find eight hours for the service of God and a distressed worthy brother; eight hours for our usual avocations; and eight for refreshment and sleep.*

The *common gavel* is an instrument made use of by operative masons, to break off the corners of rough stones, the better to fit them for the builder's use; but we, as free and accepted masons, are taught to make use of it for the more

---

* "The most effectual expedient employed by Alfred the Great, for the encouragement of learning, was his own example, and the constant assiduity with which he employed himself in the pursuit of knowledge. He usually divided his time into three equal portions; one was employed in sleep and the refection of his body; another in the dispatch of business; and a third in study and devotion."

Hume's History of England.

noble and glorious purpose of divesting our
minds and consciences of all the vices and super-
fluities of life, thereby fitting our bodies, as
living stones, for that spiritual building, that
house not made with hands, eternal in the
heavens.

THE SECOND SECTION

Rationally accounts for the origin of our hieroglyphical instruction, and convinces us of the
advantages which will ever accompany a faithful
observance of our duty; it maintains, beyond
the power of contradiction, the propriety of our
rites, while it demonstrates to the most sceptical
and hesitating mind their excellency and utility;
it illustrates, at the same time, certain particulars,
of which our ignorance might lead us into error,
and which, as masons, we are indispensably bound
to know.

To make a daily progress in the art, is our
constant duty, and expressly required by our
general laws. What end can be more noble
than the pursuit of virtue? what motive more
alluring than the practice of justice? or what
instruction more beneficial than an accurate
elucidation of symbolical mysteries which tend
to embellish and adorn the mind? Every thing
that strikes the eye more immediately engages
the attention, and imprints on the memory serious and solemn truths: hence masons, universally adopting this method of inculcating the
tenets of their order by typical figures and allegorical emblems, prevent their mysteries from

descending into the familiar reach of inattentive and unprepared novices, from whom they might not receive due veneration.

Our records inform us, that the usages and customs of masons have ever corresponded with those of the Egyptian philosophers, to which they bear a near affinity. Unwilling to expose their mysteries to vulgar eyes, they concealed their particular tenets and principles of polity under hieroglyphical figures; and expressed their notions of government by signs and symbols, which they communicated to their Magi alone, who were bound by oath not to reveal them. The Pythagorean system seems to have been established on a similar plan, and many orders of a more recent date. Masonry, however, is not only the most ancient, but the most moral institution that ever subsisted; every character, figure and emblem, depicted in a lodge, has a moral tendency, and inculcates the practice of virtue.

The Badge of a Mason.

Every candidate, at his initiation, is presented with a lamb-skin, or white leather apron.

The *lamb* has in all ages been deemed an emblem of *innocence;* he, therefore, who wears the lamb-skin as a badge of masonry, is thereby continually reminded of that purity of life and conduct which is essentially necessary to his gaining admission into the Celestial Lodge above, where the Supreme Architect of the universe presides.

THE THIRD SECTION

Explains the nature and principles of our conftitution, and teaches us to difcharge with propriety the duties of our refpective ftations. Here, too, we receive inftruction relative to the form, fupports, covering, furniture, ornaments, lights and jewels of a lodge, how it fhould be fituated, and to whom dedicated. A proper attention is alfo paid to our ancient and venerable patrons.

From eaft to weft, freemafonry extends; and between the north and fouth, in every clime and nation, are mafons to be found.

Our inftitution is faid to be fupported by *wifdom*, *ftrength* and *beauty*; becaufe it is neceffary that there fhould be *wifdom* to contrive, *ftrength* to fupport, and *beauty* to adorn, all great and important undertakings. Its dimenfions are unlimited, and its *covering* no lefs than the canopy of heaven. To this object the mafon's mind is continually directed, and thither he hopes at laft to arrive, by the aid of the theological ladder, which Jacob, in his vifion, faw afcending from earth to heaven; the three *principal rounds* of which are denominated *faith, hope* and *charity*; and which admonifh us to have faith in God, hope in immortality, and charity to all mankind.

Every well governed lodge is *furnifhed* with the *Holy Bible*, the *Square* and the *Compafs*; the *bible* points out the path that leads to happinefs, and is dedicated to *God*; the *fquare* teaches us to regulate our conduct by the principles of morality and virtue, and is dedicated to the *Master*; the *compass* teaches us to limit our desires in every station, and is dedicated to the *Craft*.

The bible is dedicated to the service of God, because it is the inestimable gift of God to man; the square to the master, because, being the proper masonic emblem of his office, it is constantly to remind him of the duty he owes to the lodge over which he is appointed to preside; and the compass to the craft, because, by a due attention to its use, they are taught to regulate their desires, and keep their passions within due bounds.

The *ornamental* parts of a lodge, displayed in this section, are, the *Mosaic pavement*, the *indented tessel*, and the *blazing star*. The *Mosaic pavement* is a representation of the ground floor of king Solomon's temple; the *indented tessel*, that beautiful tesselated border, or skirting, which surrounded it; and the *blazing star* in the centre is commemorative of the star which appeared to guide the wise men of the east to the place of our Saviour's nativity. The *Mosaic pavement* is emblematic of human life, chequered with good and evil; the *beautiful border* which surrounds it, those blessings and comforts which surround us, and which we hope to obtain by a faithful reliance on Divine Providence, which is hieroglyphically represented by the *blazing star* in the centre.

The *moveable* and *immoveable* jewels also claim our attention in this section.

The *rough ashler* is a stone as taken from the quarry in its rude and natural state. The *per-*

4

fect aſhler is a ſtone made ready by the hands of the workman to be adjuſted by the tools of the fellow craft. The *treſtle-board* is for the maſter, workman to draw his deſigns upon.

By the *rough aſhler* we are reminded of our rude and imperfect ſtate by nature ; by the *perfect aſhler*, that ſtate of perfection at which we hope to arrive, by a virtuous education, our own endeavours, and the bleſſing of God ; and by the *treſtle-board*, we are reminded, that as the operative workman erects his temporal building agreeably to the rules and deſigns laid down by the maſter on his treſtle-board, ſo ſhould we, both operative and ſpeculative, endeavour to erect our ſpiritual building agreeably to the rules and deſigns laid down by the Supreme Architect of the Univerſe, in the book of life, or the holy ſcriptures, which is our ſpiritual treſtle-board.

By a recurrence to the chapter upon the dedication of lodges, it will be perceived, that although our ancient brethren dedicated their lodges to king Solomon, yet maſons, profeſſing chriſtianity, dedicate theirs to St. John the Baptiſt, and St. John the Evangeliſt, who were eminent patrons of maſonry ; and ſince their time there is repreſented in every regular and well governed lodge, a certain *point within a circle ;* the *point* repreſenting an individual brother, the *circle* repreſenting the boundary line of his duty to God and man, beyond which he is never to ſuffer his paſſions, prejudices or intereſt, to betray him, on any occaſion. This *circle* is embordered by two perpendicular, parallel lines, repreſenting

St. John the Baptift, and St. John the Evangelift, who were perfect parallels in chriftianity as well as mafonry; and upon the vertex refts the book of Holy Scriptures, which point out the whole duty of man. In going round this circle, we neceffarily touch upon thefe two lines, as well as upon the Holy Scriptures; and while a mafon keeps himfelf thus circumfcribed, it is impoffible that he fhould materially err.

This fection, though the laft in rank, is not the leaft confiderable in importance. It ftrengthens thofe which precede, and enforces in the moft engaging manner a due regard to character and behaviour, in public, as well as in private life, in the lodge, as well as in the general commerce of fociety. It forcibly inculcates the moft inftructive leffons. Brotherly love, relief, and truth, are themes on which we here expatiate.

Of Brotherly Love.

By the exercife of brotherly love, we are taught to regard the whole human fpecies as one family, the high and low, the rich and poor; who, as created by one Almighty Parent, and inhabitants of the fame planet, are to aid, fupport and protect each other. On this principle, mafonry unites men of every country, fect and opinion, and conciliates true friendfhip among thofe who might otherwife have remained at a perpetual diftance.

Of Relief.

To relieve the diftreffed is a duty incumbent on all men; but particularly on mafons, who

are linked together by an indiffoluble chain of
fincere affection. To foothe the unhappy, to
fympathize with their misfortunes, to compaf-
fionate their miferies, and to reftore peace to
their troubled minds, is the grand aim we have
in view. On this bafis we form our friendfhips,
and eftablifh our connexions.

Of Truth.

Truth is a divine attribute, and the foundation of every virtue. To be good and true, is
the firft leffon we are taught in mafonry. On
this theme we contemplate, and by its dictates
endeavour to regulate our conduct; hence, while
influenced by this principle, hypocrify and deceit are unknown among us, fincerity and plain
dealing diftinguifh us, and the heart and tongue
join in promoting each other's welfare, and rejoicing in each other's profperity.

To this illuftration fucceeds an explanation of
the four cardinal virtues—temperance, fortitude,
prudence and juftice.

Temperance

Is that due reftraint upon our affections and
paffions, which renders the body tame and gov-
ernable, and frees the mind from the allurements
of vice. This virtue fhould be the conftant
practice of every mafon, as he is thereby taught
to avoid excefs, or contracting any licentious or
vicious habit, the indulgence of which might
lead him to difclofe fome of thofe valuable fecrets, which he has promifed to conceal and
never reveal, and which would confequently

subject him to the contempt and detestation of all good masons.

Fortitude

Is that noble and steady purpose of the mind, whereby we are enabled to undergo any pain, peril or danger, when prudentially deemed expedient. This virtue is equally distant from rashness and cowardice; and, like the former, should be deeply impressed upon the mind of every mason, as a safeguard or security against any illegal attack that may be made, by force or otherwise, to extort from him any of those secrets with which he has been so solemnly entrusted, and which was emblematically represented upon his first admission into the lodge.

Prudence

Teaches us to regulate our lives and actions agreeably to the dictates of reason, and is that habit by which we wisely judge, and prudentially determine, on all things relative to our present as well as to our future happiness. This virtue should be the peculiar characteristic of every mason, not only for the government of his conduct while in the lodge; but also when abroad in the world; it should be particularly attended to in all strange and mixed companies, never to let fall the least sign, token or word, whereby the secrets of masonry might be unlawfully obtained.

Justice

Is that standard, or boundary, of right, which enables us to render to every man his just due,

4*

without distinction. This virtue is not only consistent with divine and human laws, but is the very cement and support of civil society; and, as justice in a great measure constitutes the real good man, so should it be the invariable practice of every mason never to deviate from the minutest principles thereof.

The illustration of these virtues is accompanied with some general observations peculiar to masons.

Such is the arrangement of the different sections in the first lecture, which, with the forms adopted at the opening and closing of a lodge, comprehends the whole of the first degree of masonry. This plan has the advantage of regularity to recommend it, the support of precedent and authority, and the sanction and respect which flow from antiquity. The whole is a regular system of morality, conceived in a strain of interesting allegory, which must unfold its beauties to the candid and industrious inquirer.

Charge at Initiation into the First Degree.

" BROTHER,

"As you are now introduced into the first principles of masonry, I congratulate you on being accepted into this ancient and honourable order; ancient, as having subsisted from time immemorial; and honourable, as tending, in every particular, so to render all men who will be conformable to its precepts. No institution was ever raised on a better principle, or more solid foundation; nor were ever more excellent rules and ufeful maxims laid down; than are inculcated in the feveral mafonic lectures. The greateft and beft of men in all ages have been encouragers and promoters of the art, and have never deemed it derogatory from their dignity, to level themfelves with the fraternity, extend their privileges, and patronife their affemblies.

"There are three great duties, which, as a mafon, you are charged to inculcate—to God, your neighbour, and yourfelf. To God, in never mentioning his name, but with that reverential awe which is due from a creature to his Creator; to implore his aid in all your laudable undertakings, and to efteem him as the chief good : to your neighbour, in acting upon the fquare, and doing unto him as you wifh he fhould do unto you : and to yourfelf, in avoiding all irregularity and intemperance, which may impair your faculties, or debafe the dignity of your profeffion. A zealous attachment to thefe duties will enfure public and private efteem.

"In the ftate, you are to be a quiet and peaceful fubject, true to your government, and juft to your country; you are not to countenance difloyalty or rebellion, but patiently fubmit to legal authority, and conform with cheerfulnefs to the government of the country in which you live.

"In your outward demeanour be particularly careful to avoid cenfure or reproach. Let not intereft, favour, or prejudice, bias your integrity, or influence you to be guilty of a difhonourable action. Although your frequent appearance at our regular meetings is earneftly folicit-

ed, yet it is not meant that mafonry fhould
interfere with your neceffary vocations; for
thefe are on no account to be neglected; neither are you to fuffer your zeal for the inftitution to lead you into argument with thofe
who, through ignorance, may ridicule it. At
your leifure hours, that you may improve in
mafonic knowledge, you are to converfe with
well informed brethren, who will be always as
ready to give, as you will be ready to receive,
inftruction.

"Finally: keep facred and inviolable the myfteries of the order, as thefe are to diftinguifh
you from the reft of the community, and mark
your confequence among mafons. If, in the
circle of your acquaintance, you find a perfon
defirous of being initiated into mafonry, be particularly attentive not to recommend him, unlefs
you are convinced he will conform to our rules;
that the honour, glory and reputation of the
inftitution may be firmly eftablifhed, and the
world at large convinced of its good effects."

CHAPTER IX.

REMARKS ON THE SECOND DEGREE.

MASONRY is a progreffive fcience, and is divided into two different claffes or degrees, for
the more regular advancement in the knowledge
of its myfteries. According to the progrefs we
make, we limit or extend our inquiries; and in

proportion to our capacity, we attain to a lefs or greater degree of perfection.

Mafonry includes within its circle almoft every branch of polite learning. Under the veil of its myfteries is comprehended a regular fyftem of fcience. Many of its illuftrations, to the confined genius, may appear unimportant ; but the man of more enlarged faculties will perceive them to be, in the higheft degree, ufeful and interefting. To pleafe the accomplifhed fcholar, and ingenious artift, mafonry is wifely planned ; and in the inveftigation of its latent doctrines, the philofopher and mathematician may experience equal delight and fatisfaction.

To exhauft the various fubjects of which it treats, would tranfcend the powers of the brighteft genius ; ftill, however, nearer approaches to perfection may be made; and the man of wifdom will not check the progrefs of his abilities, though the tafk he attempts may at firft feem infurmountable. Perfeverance and application remove each difficulty as it occurs; every ftep he advances, new pleafures open to his view, and inftruction of the nobleft kind attends his refearches. In the diligent purfuit of knowledge, the intellectual faculties are employed in promoting the glory of God, and the good of man.

The firft degree is well calculated to enforce the duties of morality, and imprint on the memory the nobleft principles which can adorn the human mind. It is therefore the beft introduction to the fecond degree, which not only extends the fame plan, but comprehends a more diffusive system of knowledge. Here practice and theory join, in qualifying the industrious mason to share the pleasures which an advancement in the art must necessarily afford. Listening with attention to the wise opinions of experienced craftsmen on important subjects, he gradually familiarizes his mind to useful instruction, and is soon enabled to investigate truths of the utmost concern in the general transactions of life.

From this system proceeds a rational amusement; while the mental powers are fully employed, the judgment is properly exercised; a spirit of emulation prevails; and all are induced to vie, who shall most excel in promoting the valuable rules of the institution.

THE FIRST SECTION

Of the second degree accurately elucidates the mode of introduction into that particular class; and instructs the diligent craftsman how to proceed in the proper arrangement of the ceremonies used on the occasion. It qualifies him to judge of their importance, and convinces him of the necessity of strictly adhering to every established usage of the order. Here he is entrusted with particular tests, to enable him to prove his title to the privileges of this degree, while satisfactory reasons are given for their origin. Many duties, which cement in the firmest union well informed brethren, are illustrated in this section; and an opportunity is given to make such advances in masonry as will always distinguish the abilities of those who have arrived at preferment. The knowledge of this section, is abfolutely neceffary for all craftfmen; and as it recapitulates the ceremony of initiation, and contains many other important particulars, no officer or member of a lodge fhould be unacquainted with it.

The *plumb*, *fquare*, and *level*, thofe noble and ufeful implements of a fellow craft, are here introduced and moralized, and ferve as a conftant admonition to the practice of virtue and morality.

The *plumb* is an inftrument made ufe of by *operative* mafons, to raife perpendiculars; the *fquare*, to fquare their work; and the *level*, to lay horizontals; but we, as free and accepted mafons, are taught to make ufe of them for more noble and glorious purpofes: the *plumb* admonifhes us to walk uprightly in our feveral ftations before God and man, fquaring our actions by the *fquare* of virtue, and remembering that we are travelling upon the *level* of time, to " that undifcovered country, from whofe bourne no traveller returns."

THE SECOND SECTION

Of this degree has recourfe to the origin of the inftitution, and views mafonry under two denominations, operative and fpeculative. Thefe are feparately confidered, and the principles on which both are founded particularly explained. Their affinity is pointed out by allegorical figures, and typical reprefentations. The period ftipulated for rewarding merit is fixed, and the inimitable moral to which that circumftance alludes is

explained ; the creation of the world is defcrib-
ed, and many particulars recited, all of which
have been carefully preferved among mafons,
and tranfmitted from one age to another, by
oral tradition.

Circumftances of great importance to the fraternity are here particularized, and many tradi-
tional tenets and cuftoms confirmed by facred
and profane record. The celeftial and terreftrial
globes are confidered ; and here the accomplifhed
gentleman may difplay his talents to advantage,
in the elucidation of the *Orders of Architecture*,
the *Senfes* of human nature, and the liberal *Arts*
and *Sciences*, which are feverally claffed in a regular arrangement. In fhort, this fection contains a
ftore of valuable knowledge, founded on reafon
and facred record, both entertaining and inftructive.

Mafonry is confidered under two denominations ; *operative* and *fpeculative*.

Operative Mafonry.

By operative mafonry we allude to a proper
application of the ufeful rules of architecture,
whence a ftructure will derive figure, ftrength,
and beauty, and whence will refult a due proportion and a juft correfpondence in all its parts. It
furnifhes us with dwellings, and convenient fhel-
ters from the viciffitudes and inclemencies of
the feafons ; and while it difplays the effects of
human wifdom, as well in the choice as in the
arrangement of the fundry materials of which
an edifice is compofed, it demonftrates that a

fund of science and industry is implanted in man for the best, most salutary, and beneficent purposes.

Speculative Masonry.

By speculative masonry we learn to subdue the passions, act upon the square, keep a tongue of good report, maintain secrecy, and practise charity. It is so far interwoven with religion, as to lay us under obligations to pay that rational homage to the Deity, which at once constitutes our duty and our happiness. It leads the contemplative to view with reverence and admiration the glorious works of the creation, and inspires him with the most exalted ideas of the perfections of his divine Creator.

In six days God created the heavens and the earth, and rested upon the seventh day ; the seventh, therefore, our ancient brethren consecrated as a day of rest from their labours, thereby enjoying frequent opportunities to contemplate the glorious works of the creation, and to adore their great Creator.

The doctrine of the spheres is included in the science of astronomy, and particularly considered in this section.

Of the GLOBES.

The globes are two artificial spherical bodies, on the convex surface of which are represented the countries, seas, and various parts of the earth, the face of the heavens, the planetary revolutions, and other particulars.

The fphere, with the parts of the earth delineated on its furface, is called the terreftrial globe;
and that, with the conftellations, and other
heavenly bodies, the celeftial globe.

The Ufe of the Globes.

Their principal ufe, befide ferving as maps to
diftinguifh the outward parts of the earth, and
the fituation of the fixed ftars, is to illuftrate
and explain the phenomena arifing from the
annual revolution, and the diurnal rotation, of
the earth round its own axis. They are the
nobleft inftruments for improving the mind,
and giving it the moft diftinct idea of any pro-
blem or propofition, as well as enabling it to
folve the fame. Contemplating thefe bodies, we
are infpired with a due reverence for the Deity
and his works, and are induced to encourage
the ftudies of aftronomy, geography, navigation,
and the arts dependent on them, by which fociety has been fo much benefited.

The orders of architecture come under confideration in this fection ; a brief defcription of
them may therefore not be improper.

Of ORDER in ARCHITECTURE.

By order in architecture, is meant a fyftem of
all the members, proportions and ornaments of
columns and pilafters ; or, it is a regular arrangement of the projecting parts of a building,
which, united with thofe of a column, form a
beautiful, perfect and complete whole.

Of its Antiquity.

From the firſt formation of ſociety, order in architecture may be traced. When the rigour of ſeaſons obliged men to contrive ſhelter from the inclemency of the weather, we learn that they firſt planted trees on end, and then laid others acroſs, to ſupport a covering. The bands, which connected thoſe trees at top and bottom, are ſaid to have given riſe to the idea of the baſe and capital of pillars; and from this ſimple hint originally proceeded the more improved art of architecture.

The five orders are thus claſſed: the Tuſcan, Doric, Ionic, Corinthian, and Compoſite.

The Tuſcan

Is the moſt ſimple and ſolid of the five orders. It was invented in Tuſcany, whence it derives its name. Its column is ſeven diameters high; and its capital, baſe and entablature have but few mouldings. The ſimplicity of the conſtruction of this column renders it eligible where ornament would be ſuperfluous.

The Doric,

Which is plain and natural, is the moſt ancient, and was invented by the Greeks. Its column is eight diameters high, and has ſeldom any ornaments on baſe or capital, except mouldings; though the frieze is diſtinguiſhed by triglyphs and metopes, and triglyphs compoſe the ornaments of the frieze. The folid compofition of this order gives it a preference, in ftructures where ftrength and noble fimplicity are chiefly required.

The Doric is the beft proportioned of all the orders. The feveral parts, of which it is compofed, are founded on the natural pofition of folid bodies. In its firft invention it was more fimple than in its prefent ftate. In after times, when it began to be adorned, it gained the name of Doric; for when it was conftructed in its primitive and fimple form, the name of Tufcan was conferred on it. Hence the Tufcan precedes the Doric in rank, on account of its refemblance to that pillar in its original ftate.

The Ionic

Bears a kind of mean proportion between the more folid and delicate orders. Its column is nine diameters high; its capital is adorned with volutes, and its cornice has dentals. There is both delicacy and ingenuity difplayed in this pillar; the invention of which is attributed to the Ionians, as the famous temple of Diana at Ephefus was of this order. It is faid to have been formed after the model of an agreeable young woman, of an elegant fhape, dreffed in her hair; as a contraft to the Doric order, which was formed after that of a ftrong, robuft man.

The Corinthian,

The richeft of the five orders, is deemed a mafterpiece of art. Its column is ten diameters high, and its capital is adorned with two rows of leaves, and eight volutes, which sustain the abacus. The frieze is ornamented with curious devices; the cornice with dentals and modillions. This order is used in stately and superb structures. It was invented at Corinth, by Callimachus, who is said to have taken the hint of the capital of this pillar from the following remarkable circumstance.—Accidentally passing by the tomb of a young lady, he perceived a basket of toys, covered with a tile, placed over an acanthus root, having been left there by her nurse. As the branches grew up, they encompassed the basket, till, arriving at the tile, they met with an obstruction, and bent downwards. Callimachus, struck with the object, set about imitating the figure : the vase of the capital he made to represent the basket ; the abacus the tile ; and the volutes the bending leaves.

The Composite

Is compounded of the other orders, and was contrived by the Romans. Its capital has the two rows of leaves of the Corinthian, and the volutes of the Ionic. Its column has the quarter-round, as the Tuscan and Doric order ; is ten diameters high, and its cornice has dentals, or simple modillions. This pillar is generally found in buildings where strength, elegance and beauty are displayed.

Of the Invention of Order in Architecture.

The ancient and original orders of architecture, revered by masons, are no more than

5*

three, the DORIC, IONIC and CORINTHIAN, which were invented by the Greeks. To these the Romans have added two: the Tuscan, which they made plainer than the Doric; and the Composite, which was more ornamental, if not more beautiful, than the Corinthian. The first three orders alone, however, shew invention and particular character, and essentially differ from each other; the two others have nothing but what is borrowed, and differ only accidentally; the Tuscan is the Doric in its earliest state; and the Composite is the Corinthian, enriched with the Ionic. To the Greeks, therefore, and not to the Romans, we are indebted for what is great, judicious and distinct in architecture.

Of the FIVE SENSES of Human Nature.

An analysis of the human faculties is next given in this section, in which the five external senses particularly claim attention; these are, hearing, seeing, feeling, smelling and tasting.

Hearing

Is that sense by which we distinguish sounds, and are capable of enjoying all the agreeable charms of music. By it we are enabled to enjoy the pleasures of society, and reciprocally to communicate to each other our thoughts and intentions, our purposes and desires; while thus our reason is capable of exerting its utmost power and energy.

The wise and beneficent Author of Nature intended, by the formation of this sense, that

we fhould be, focial creatures, and receive the
greateft and moft important part of our knowledge by the information of others. For thefe
purpofes we are endowed with hearing, that by
a proper exertion of our rational powers, our
happinefs may be complete.

Seeing

Is that fenfe by which we diftinguifh objects,
and in an inftant of time, without change of
place or fituation, view armies in battle array,
figures of the moft ftately ftructures, and all the
agreeable variety difplayed in the landfcape of
nature. By this fenfe we find our way in the
pathlefs ocean, traverfe the globe of earth, determine its figure and dimenfions, and delineate
any region or quarter of it. By it we meafure
the planetary orbs, and make new difcoveries in
the fphere of the fixed ftars. Nay, more: by
it we perceive the tempers and difpofitions, the
paffions and affections of our fellow creatures,
when they wifh moft to conceal them; fo that,
though the tongue may be taught to lie and
diffemble, the countenance would difplay the
hypocrify to the difcerning eye. In fine, the
rays of light, which adminifter to this fenfe, are
the moft aftonifhing parts of the animated creation, and render the eye a peculiar object of
admiration.

Of all the faculties, fight is the nobleft. The
ftructure of the eye, and its appurtenances, evin-
ces the admirable contrivance of nature for performing all its various external and internal
motions; while the variety difplayed in the

eyes of different animals, suited to their several ways of life, clearly demonstrates this organ to be the masterpiece of nature's work.

Feeling

Is that sense by which we distinguish the different qualities of bodies; such as heat and cold, hardness and softness, roughness and smoothness, figure, solidity, motion, and extension.

These three senses, *Hearing*, *Seeing* and *Feeling*, are deemed peculiarly essential among masons.

Smelling

Is that sense by which we distinguish odours, the various kinds of which convey different impressions to the mind. Animal and vegetable bodies, and indeed most other bodies, while exposed to the air, continually send forth effluvia of vast subtilty, as well in the state of life and growth, as in the state of fermentation and putrefaction. These effluvia, being drawn into the nostrils along with the air, are the means by which all bodies are smelled. Hence it is evident, that there is a manifest appearance of design in the great Creator's having planted the organ of smell in the inside of that canal, through which the air continually passes in respiration.

Tasting

Enables us to make a proper distinction in the choice of our food. The organ of this sense guards the entrance of the alimentary canal, as that of smelling guards the entrance of the canal for respiration. From the situation of both thefe organs, it is plain that they were intended by nature to diftinguifh wholefome food from that which is naufeous. Every thing that enters into the ftomach muft undergo the fcrutiny of tafting; and by it we are capable of difcerning the changes which the fame body undergoes in the different compofitions of art, cookery, chemiftry, pharmacy, &c.

Smelling and tafting are infeparably connected; and it is by the unnatural kind of life men commonly lead in fociety, that thefe fenfes are rendered lefs fit to perform their natural offices. On the mind all our knowledge muft depend: what, therefore, can be a more proper fubject for the inveftigation of mafons? By anatomical diffection and obfervation, we become acquainted with the body; but it is by the anatomy of the mind alone we difcover its powers and principles.

To fum up the whole of this tranfcendent meafure of God's bounty to man, we fhall add, that memory, imagination, tafte, reafoning, moral perception, and all the active powers of the foul, prefent a vaft and boundlefs field for philofophical difquifition, which far exceeds human inquiry, and are peculiar myfteries, known only to nature and to nature's God, to whom we and all are indebted for creation, prefervation, and every bleffing we enjoy.

Of the Seven Liberal ARTS and SCIENCES.

The feven liberal ARTS and SCIENCES are next illuftrated in this fection: it may not therefore be improper to infert here a fhort explanation of them.

Grammar

Teaches the proper arrangement of words, according to the idiom or dialect of any particular people; and that excellency of pronunciation, which enables us to fpeak or write a language with accuracy, agreeably to reafon and correct ufage.

Rhetoric

Teaches us to fpeak copioufly and fluently on any fubject, not merely with propriety, but with all the advantages of force and elegance; wifely contriving to captivate the hearer by ftrength of argument and beauty of expreffion, whether it be to entreat or exhort, to admonifh or applaud.

Logic

Teaches us to guide our reafon difcretionally in the general knowledge of things, and directs our inquiries after truth. It confifts of a regular train of argument, whence we infer, deduce, and conclude, according to certain premifes laid down, admitted, or granted; and in it are employed the faculties of conceiving, judging, reafoning, and difpofing; all of which are naturally led on from one gradation to another, till the point in queftion is finally determined.

Arithmetic

Teaches the powers and properties of numbers, which is varioufly effected, by letters, tables, figures, and instruments. By this art, reasons and demonstrations are given, for finding out any certain number, whose relation or affinity to another is already known or discovered.

Geometry

Treats of the powers and properties of magnitudes in general, where length, breadth, and thickness, are considered; from a *point* to a *line*, from a line to a *superficies*, and from a superficies to a *solid*.

A *point* is a dimensionless figure; or an indivisible part of space.

A *line* is a point continued, and a figure of one capacity, namely, *length*.

A *superficies* is a figure of two dimensions, namely, *length* and *breadth*.

A *solid* is a figure of three dimensions, namely, *length*, *breadth*, and *thickness*.

Of the Advantages of Geometry.

By this science, the architect is enabled to construct his plans, and execute his designs; the general to arrange his soldiers; the engineer to mark out ground for encampments; the geographer to give us the dimensions of the world, and all things therein contained, to delineate the extent of seas, and specify the divisions of empires, kingdoms and provinces; by it, also, the astronomer is enabled to make his observations, and to fix the duration of times and seasons, years and cycles. In fine, geometry is the foundation of architecture, and the root of the mathematics.

Music

Teaches the art of forming concords, so as to compose delightful harmony, by a mathematical and proportional arrangement of acute, grave and mixed sounds. This art, by a series of experiments, is reduced to a demonstrative science, with respect to tones, and the intervals of sound. It inquires into the nature of concords and discords, and enables us to find out the proportion between them by numbers.

Astronomy

Is that divine art, by which we are taught to read the wisdom, strength and beauty of the Almighty Creator, in those sacred pages, the celestial hemisphere. Assisted by astronomy, we can observe the motions, measure the distances, comprehend the magnitudes, and calculate the periods and eclipses of the heavenly bodies. By it we learn the use of the globes, the system of the world, and the preliminary law of nature. While we are employed in the study of this science, we must perceive unparalleled instances of wisdom and goodness, and, through the whole creation, trace the glorious Author by his works.

Of the Moral Advantages of Geometry.

From this theme we proceed to illustrate the moral advantages of Geometry; a subject on which the following observations may not be unacceptable.

Geometry, the first and noblest of sciences, is the basis on which the superstructure of masonry is-erected. By geometry, we may curiouſly trace nature, through her various windings, to her moſt concealed receſſes. By it, we diſcover the power, the wiſdom, and the goodneſs of the Grand Artificer of the Univerſe, and view with delight the proportions which connect this vaſt machine. By it, we diſcover how the planets move in their different orbits, and demonſtrate their various revolutions. By it, we account for the return of ſeaſons, and the variety of ſcenes which each ſeaſon diſplays to the diſcerning eye. Numberleſs worlds are around us, all framed by the ſame Divine Artiſt, which roll through the vaſt expanſe, and are all conducted by the ſame unerring law of nature.

A ſurvey of nature, and the obſervation of her beautiful proportions, firſt determined man to imitate the divine plan, and ſtudy ſymmetry and order. This gave riſe to ſocieties, and birth to every uſeful art. The architect began to deſign; and the plans which he laid down, being improved by experience and time, have produced works which are the admiration of every age.

The lapſe of time, the ruthleſs hand of ignorance, and the devaſtations of war, have laid waſte and deſtroyed many valuable monuments of antiquity, on which the utmoſt exertions of human genius have been employed. Even the Temple of Solomon, ſo ſpacious and magnificent, and conſtructed by ſo many celebrated artiſts, eſcaped not the unſparing ravages of barbarous force. Freemaſonry, notwithſtanding, has ſtill ſurvived. The *attentive ear* receives the ſound from the *inſtructive tongue*, and the myſteries of

6

mafonry are fafely lodged in the repofitory of *faithful breafts.* Tools and implements of archi-tecture are felected by the fraternity, to imprint on the memory wife and. ferious truths ; and thus, through a fucceffion of ages, are tranfmit-ted unimpaired the excellent tenets of our infti-tution.

Thus end the two fections of the fecond lec-ture ; which, with the ceremony ufed at opening and clofing the lodge, comprehend the whole of the fecond degree of mafonry. This lecture contains a regular fyftem of fcience, demonftra-ted. on the cleareft principles, and eftablifhed on the firmeft foundation.

Charge at Initiation into the Second Degree.

" BROTHER,

" Being advanced to the fecond degree of ma-fonry, we congratulate you on your preferment. The internal, and not the external, qualifications of a man, are what mafonry regards. As you increafe in knowledge, you will improve in focial intercourfe.

" It is unneceffary to recapitulate the duties which, as a mafon, you are bound to difcharge ; or enlarge on the neceffity of a ftrict adherence to them, as your own experience muft have ef-tablifhed their value.

" Our laws and regulations you are ftrenu-oufly to fupport ; and be always ready to affift in feeing them duly executed. You are not to palliate, or aggravate, the offences of your breth-ren ; but in the decifion of every trefpafs against our rules, your are to judge with candour, admonish with friendship, and reprehend with justice.

"The study of the liberal arts, that valuable branch of education, which tends so effectually to polish and adorn the mind, is earnestly recommended to your consideration; especially the science of geometry, which is established as the basis of our art. Geometry, or masonry, originally synonimous terms, being of a divine and moral nature, is enriched with the most useful knowledge: while it proves the wonderful properties of nature, it demonstrates the more important truths of morality.

"Your past behaviour and regular deportment have merited the honour which we have now conferred; and in your new character it is expected that you will conform to the principles of the order, by steadily persevering in the practice of every commendable virtue.

"Such is the nature of your engagements as a fellow craft, and to these duties you are bound by the most sacred ties."

CHAPTER X.

REMARKS ON THE THIRD DEGREE.

FROM this class the rulers of regular bodies of masons, in the first three degrees, are selected; as it is only from those, who are capable of giving instruction, that we can properly expect to receive it. The lecture of this degree, considered separately from the duties and ceremonies appertaining to the degree of presiding or past master, is divided into three sections.

THE FIRST SECTION.

The ceremony of initiation into the third degree is particularly specified in this branch of the lecture, and here many other useful instructions are given.

Such is the importance of this section, that we may safely declare, that the person who is unacquainted with it is ill qualified to act as a ruler or governor of the work.

The following passage of scripture is introduced during the ceremonies.

ECCLESIASTES xii. 1---7.

" Remember now thy Creator in the days of thy youth, while the evil days come not, nor the years draw nigh, when thou shalt say, I have no pleasure in them ; while the sun, or the light, or the moon, or the stars, be not darkened, nor the clouds return after the rain : in the day when the keepers of the house shall tremble, and the strong men shall bow themselves, and the grinders cease because they are few, and those that look out of the windows be darkened, and the doors shall be shut in the streets, when the sound of the grinding is low, and he shall rise up at the voice of the bird; and all the daughters of music shall be brought low. Also when they shall be afraid of that which is high, and fears shall be in the way, and the almond tree shall flourish, and the grashopper shall be a burden, and desire shall fail: because man goeth to his long home, and the mourners go about the streets: or ever the silver cord be loosed, or the golden bowl be broken, or the pitcher be broken at the fountain, or the wheel broken at the cistern. Then shall the dust return to the earth as it was; and the spirit shall return unto God who gave it."

The *working tools* of a master mason, which are illustrated in this section, are all the implements of masonry indiscriminately, but more especially the *trowel*.

The TROWEL is an instrument made use of by operative masons, to spread the cement which unites a building into one common mass; but we, as free and accepted masons, are taught to make use of it for the more noble and glorious purpose of spreading the cement of *brotherly love* and affection; that cement which unites us into one sacred band, or society of friends and brothers, among whom no contention should ever exist, but that noble contention, or rather emulation, of who best can work, or best agree.

THE SECOND SECTION

Recites the historical traditions of the order, and presents to view a finished picture, of the utmost consequence to the fraternity. It exemplifies an instance of virtue, fortitude, and integrity, seldom equalled, and never excelled, in the history of man.

6*

Prayer at raising a Brother to the Sublime Degree of a Master Mason.

"Thou, O God! knoweſt our down-ſitting and our up-riſing, and underſtandeſt our thoughts afar off. Shield and defend us from the evil intentions of our enemies, and ſupport us under the trials and afflictions we are deſtined to endure, while travelling through this vale of tears. Man that is born of a woman is of few days, and full of trouble. He cometh forth as a flower, and is cut down; he fleeth alſo as a ſhadow, and continueth not. Seeing his days are determined, the number of his months are with thee, thou haſt appointed his bounds that he cannot paſs; turn from him that he may reſt, till he ſhall accompliſh his day. For there is hope of a tree, if it be cut down, that it will ſprout again, and that the tender branch thereof will not ceaſe. But man dieth and waſteth away; yea, man giveth up the ghoſt, and where is he? As the waters fail from the ſea, and the flood decayeth and drieth up, ſo man lieth down, and riſeth not up till the heavens ſhall be no more. Yet, O Lord! have compaſſion on the children of thy creation, adminiſter them comfort in time of trouble, and ſave them with an everlaſting ſalvation. *Amen.* So mote it be."

THE THIRD SECTION

Illuſtrates certain hieroglyphical emblems, and inculcates many uſeful leſſons, to extend knowledge, and promote virtue.

In this branch of the lecture, many particulars relative to king Solomon's temple are conſidered.

The conftruction of this grand edifice was attended with two remarkable circumftances. From Jofephus we learn, that although feven years were occupied in building it, yet during the whole term it rained not in the day time, that the workmen might not be obftructed in their labour : and from facred hiftory it appears, that there was neither the found of the hammer, nor axe, nor any tool of iron, heard in the houfe, while it was building.

This famous fabric was fupported by fourteen hundred and fifty-three columns, and two thoufand nine hundred and fix pilafters ; all hewn from the fineft Parian marble. There were employed in its building three grand mafters ; three thoufand and three hundred mafters, or overfeers of the work; eighty thoufand fellow crafts ; and feventy thoufand entered apprentices, or bearers of burthens. All thefe were claffed and arranged in fuch a manner by the wifdom of Solomon, that neither envy, difcord nor confufion, were fuffered to interrupt that univerfal peace and tranquillity which pervaded the world at this important period.

The Pot of Incenfe

Is an emblem of a pure heart, which is always an acceptable facrifice to the Deity ; and, as this glows with fervent heat, fo fhould our hearts continually glow with gratitude to the great and beneficent Author of our exiftence, for the manifold bleffings and comforts we enjoy.

The Bee-Hive

Is an emblem of induſtry, and recommends the practice of that virtue to all created beings, from the higheſt ſeraph in heaven, to the loweſt reptile of the duſt. It teaches us, that as we came into the world rational and intelligent beings, ſo we ſhould ever be induſtrious ones; never ſitting down contented while our fellow-creatures around us are in want, when it is in our power to relieve them, without inconvenience to ourſelves.

When we take a ſurvey of nature, we view man, in his infancy, more helpleſs and indigent than the brutal creation: he lies languiſhing for days, months and years, totally incapable of providing ſuſtenance for himſelf, of guarding againſt the attacks of the wild beaſts of the field, or ſheltering himſelf from the inclemencies of the weather.

It might have pleaſed the great Creator of heaven and earth to have made man independent of all other beings; but, as dependence is one of the ſtrongeſt bonds of ſociety, mankind were made dependent on each other for protection and ſecurity, as they thereby enjoy better opportunities of fulfilling the duties of reciprocal love and friendſhip. Thus was man formed for ſocial and active life, the nobleſt part of the work of God; and he that will ſo demean himſelf as not to be endeavouring to add to the common ſtock of knowledge and underſtanding, may be deemed a *drone* in the *hive* of nature, a uſeleſs member of ſociety, and unworthy of our protection as maſons.

The Book of Constitutions, guarded by the Tyler's Sword,

Reminds us that we should be ever watchful and guarded, in our thoughts, words and actions, particularly when before the enemies of masonry; ever bearing in remembrance those truly masonic virtues, *silence* and *circumspection.*

The Sword, pointing to a Naked Heart,

Demonstrates that justice will sooner or later overtake us; and although our thoughts, words and actions may be hidden from the eyes of man, yet that

All-seeing Eye,

Whom the SUN, MOON and STARS obey, and under whose watchful care even comets perform their stupendous revolutions, pervades the inmost recesses of the human heart, and will reward us according to our merits.

The Anchor and Ark

Are emblems of a well grounded *hope*, and a well spent life. They are emblematical of that divine *ark* which safely wafts us over this tempestuous sea of troubles, and that *anchor* which shall safely moor us in a peaceful harbour, where the wicked cease from troubling, and the weary shall find rest.

The Forty-seventh Problem of Euclid.*

This was an invention of our ancient friend
and brother, the great Pythagoras, who, in his
travels through Asia, Africa and Europe, was
initiated into several orders of priesthood, and
raised to the sublime degree of a master mason.
This wise philosopher enriched his mind abun-
dantly in a general knowledge of things, and
more especially in geometry or masonry: on
this subject he drew out many problems and
theorems; and among the most distinguished,
he erected this, which, in the joy of his heart,
he called *Eureka*, in the Grecian language, signifying, *I have found it*; and upon the discovery
of which, he is said to have sacrificed a heca-
tomb.   It teaches masons to be general lovers
of the arts and sciences.

The Hour-Glass

Is an emblem of human life.   Behold! how
swiftly the sands run, and how rapidly our lives
are drawing to a close.   We cannot without
astonishment behold the little particles which
are contained in this machine, how they pass
away almost imperceptibly, and yet to our sur-
prise, in the short space of an hour, they are all
exhausted.   Thus wastes man! to-day, he puts
forth the tender leaves of hope; to-morrow,
blossoms, and bears his blushing honours thick
upon him; the next day comes a frost, which

---

* THEOREM.]   In any right-angled triangle, the square which is
described upon the side subtending the right angle, is equal to the
squares described upon the sides which contain the right angle.
Euclid, lib. i. *prop.* 47.

nips the fhoot, and when he thinks his greatnefs is ftill afpiring, he falls, like autumn leaves, to enrich our mother earth.

The Scythe

Is an emblem of time, which cuts the brittle thread of life, and launches us into eternity.—Behold! what havock the fcythe of time makes among the human race : if by chance we fhould efcape the numerous evils incident to childhood and youth, and with health and vigour arrive to the years of manhood, yet withal we muft foon be cut down by the all-devouring fcythe of time, and be gathered into the land where our fathers have gone before us.

The Three Steps,

Ufually delineated upon the mafter's carpet, are emblematical of the three principal ftages of human life, viz. youth, manhood, and age. In youth, as entered apprentices, we ought induf-trioufly to occupy our minds in the attainment of ufeful knowledge: in manhood, as fellow crafts, we fhould apply our knowledge to the difcharge of our refpective duties to God, our neighbours, and ourfelves ; that fo in age, as mafter mafons, we may enjoy the happy reflec-tions confequent on a well fpent life, and die in the hope of a glorious immortality.

Charge at Initiation into the Third Degree.

"BROTHER,

"Your zeal for the inftitution of mafonry, the progrefs you have made in the myftery, and your conformity to our regulations, have pointed you out as a proper object of our favour and esteem.

"You are now bound by duty, honour and gratitude, to be faithful to your trust; to support the dignity of your character on every occasion; and to enforce, by precept and example, obedience to the tenets of the order.

"In the character of a master mason, you are authorized to correct the errors and irregularities of your uninformed brethren, and to guard them against a breach of fidelity. To preserve the reputation of the fraternity unsullied, must be your constant care; and for this purpose it is your province to recommend, to your inferiors, obedience and submission; to your equals, courtesy and affability; to your superiors, kindness and condescension. Universal benevolence you are always to inculcate; and, by the regularity of your own behaviour, afford the best example for the conduct of others less informed. The ancient landmarks of the order, entrusted to your care, you are carefully to preserve; and never suffer them to be infringed, or countenance a deviation from the established usages and customs of the fraternity.

"Your virtue, honour and reputation are concerned in supporting with dignity the character you now bear. Let no motive, therefore, make you swerve from your duty, violate your vows, or betray your trust; but be true and faithful, and imitate the example of that celebrated artist whom you this evening represent. Thus you will render yourself deserving of the honour which we have conferred, and merit the confidence that we have reposed."

CHAPTER XI.

REMARKS ON THE FOURTH, OR MARK MASTER MASON'S DEGREE.

THIS degree of mafonry was not lefs ufeful in its original inftitution, nor has it proved lefs beneficial to mankind, than thofe which precede it.

By the influence of this degree, each operative mafon, at the erection of the temple of Solomon, was known and diftinguifhed by the Senior Grand Warden.

By its effects, the diforder and confufion that might otherwife have attended fo immenfe an undertaking were completely prevented; and not only the craftfmen themfelves, who were eighty thoufand in number, but every part of their workmanfhip, was difcriminated with the greateft nicety, and the utmoft facility. If defects were found in the work, by the help of this degree the overfeers were enabled without difficulty to afcertain who was the faulty workman : fo that its deficiencies might be remedied, without injuring the credit, or diminifhing the reward, of the induftrious and faithful of the craft.

Charge to be read at Opening the Lodge.

"Wherefore, brethren, lay afide all malice, and guile, and hypocrifies, and envies, and all evil fpeakings.

7

"If fo be ye have tafted that the Lord is gracious, to whom coming as unto a living ftone, difallowed indeed of men, but chofen of God, and precious; ye alfo, as living ftones, be ye built up a fpiritual houfe, an holy priefthood, to offer up facrifices acceptable to God.

"Wherefore, alfo, it is contained in the fcriptures, Behold, I lay in Zion, for a foundation, a tried ftone, a precious corner ftone, a fure foundation; he that believeth fhall not make hafte to pafs it over. Unto you, therefore, which believe, it is an honour; and even to them which be difobedient, the ftone which the builders difallowed, the fame is made the head of the corner.

"Brethren, this is the will of God, that with well doing ye put to filence the ignorance of foolifh men. As free, and not ufing your liberty for a cloak of malicioufnefs, but as the fervants of God. Honour all men, love the brotherhood, fear God."

REMARKS ON THE FOURTH LECTURE.

THE FIRST SECTION

Explains the manner of convocating and opening a mark mafter's lodge. It teaches the ftations and duties of the refpective officers, and recapitulates the myftic ceremony of introducing a candidate.

In this fection is exemplified the regularity and good order that was obferved by the craftfmen on Mount Libanus, and in the plains and quarries of Zeredathah, and it ends with a beautiful display of the manner in which one of the principal events originated, which characterizes this degree.

IN THE SECOND SECTION

The mark master is particularly instructed in the origin and history of this degree, and the indispensable obligations he is under to stretch forth his assisting hand to the relief of an indigent and worthy brother, to a certain and specified extent.

The progress made in architecture, particularly in the reign of Solomon, is remarked; the number of artists employed in building the temple of Jerusalem, and the privileges they enjoyed, are specified; the mode of rewarding merit, and of punishing the guilty, are pointed out; and the marks of distinction which were conferred on our ancient brethren, as the rewards of excellence, are named.

In the course of the lecture, the following texts of scripture are introduced and explained, viz.

Rev. of St. John, ii. 17.—To him that overcometh will I give to eat of the hidden manna, and will give him a *white stone*, and in the stone a *new name* written, which no man knoweth, saving him that receiveth it.

2 *Chron.* ii. 16.—And we will cut wood out of Lebanon, as much as thou shalt need; and we will bring it to thee in floats by sea to Joppa, and thou shalt carry it up to Jerusalem.

Psalm, cxviii. 22.—The stone which the builders refused is become the head stone of the corner.

Matt. xxi. 42.—Did ye never read in the fcriptures, The ftone which the builders rejected is become the head of the corner.

Mark xii. 10.—And have ye not read this fcripture, The ftone which the builders rejected is become the head of the corner.

Luke xx. 17.—What is this, then, that is written, The ftone which the builders rejected is become the head of the corner.

Acts iv. 11.—This is the ftone which was fet at nought of you builders, which is become the head of the corner.

Rev. iii. 13.—He that hath *an ear* to hear, let him hear.

Ezekiel, xliv. 1, 3 & 5.—Then he brought me back the way of the gate of the outward fanctuary, which looketh toward the eaft, and it was fhut. Then faid the Lord unto me, This gate fhall be fhut, it fhall not be opened, and no man fhall enter in by it ; becaufe the Lord, the God of Ifrael, hath entered in by it, therefore it fhall be fhut. It is for the prince ; the prince he fhall fit in it to eat bread before the Lord ; he fhall enter by the way of the porch of that gate, and fhall go out by the way of the fame. And the Lord faid unto me, Son of man, mark well, and behold with thine eyes, and hear with thine ears, all that I fay unto thee concerning all the ordinances of the houfe of the Lord, and all the laws thereof; and mark well the entering in of the houfe, with every going forth of the fanctuary.

The *working tools* of a mark mafter are the *chifel* and *mallet*.

The *chifel* morally demohftrates the advantages of difcipline and education. The mind, like the diamond in its original ftate, is rude and unpolifhed; but as the effect of the chifel on the external coat foon prefents to view the latent beauties of the diamond, fo education difcovers the latent virtues of the mind, and draws them forth to range the large field of matter and fpace, to difplay the fummit of human knowledge, our duty to God and to man.

The *mallet* morally teaches to correct irregularities, and to reduce man to a proper level; fo that, by quiet deportment, he may, in the fchool of difcipline, learn to be content. What the mallet is to the workman, enlightened reafon is to the paffions: it curbs ambition, it depreffes envy, it moderates anger, and it encourages good difpofitions; whence arifes, among good mafons, that comely order,

" Which nothing earthly gives, or can deftroy,
" The foul's calm funshine, and the heart-felt joy."

Charge to be delivered when a Candidate is advanced to the Fourth Degree.

" BROTHER,

" I congratulate you on having been thought worthy of being promoted to this honourable degree of mafonry. Permit me to imprefs it on your mind, that your affiduity fhould ever be commenfurate with your duties, which become more and more extenfive as you advance in mafonry.

7*

"The fituation to which you are now promoted will draw upon you not only the fcrutinizing eyes of the world at large, but thofe alfo of your brethren, on whom this degree of mafonry has not been conferred: all will be juftified in expecting your conduct and behaviour to be fuch as may with fafety be imitated.

"In the honourable character of mark mafter mafon, it is more particularly your duty to endeavour to let your conduct in the lodge and among your brethren be fuch as may ftand the teft of the Grand Overfeer's fquare, that you may not, like the unfinifhed and imperfect work of the negligent and unfaithful of former times, be rejected and thrown afide, as unfit for that fpiritual building, that houfe not made with hands, eternal in the heavens.

"While fuch is your conduct, fhould misfortunes affail you, fhould friends forfake you, fhould envy traduce your good name, and malice perfecute you; yet may you have confidence, that among mark mafter mafons you will find friends who will adminifter relief to your diftreffes, and comfort your afflictions; ever bearing in mind, as a confolation under all the frowns of fortune, and as an encouragement to hope for better profpects, that *the ftone which the builders rejected* (poffeffing merits to them unknown) *became the chief ftone of the corner.*"

Previous to clofing the lodge, the following parable is recited.

MATTHEW xx. 1—16.

"For the kingdom of heaven is like unto a man that is an houfeholder, which went out early in the morning to hire labourers into his vineyard. And when he had agreed with the labourers for a penny a day, he fent them into his vineyard. And he went out about the third hour, and faw others ſtanding idle in the market place, and faid unto them, Go ye alfo into the vineyard, and whatfoever is right I will give you. And they went their way. Again he went about the fixth and ninth hour, and did likewife. And about the eleventh hour he went out and found others ſtanding idle, and faith unto them, Why ſtand ye here all the day idle? They fay unto him, Becaufe no man hath hired us. He faith unto them, Go ye alfo into the vineyard, and whatfoever is right, that ſhall ye receive. So when even was come, the lord of the vineyard faith unto his ſteward, Call the labourers, and give them their hire, beginning from the laſt unto the firſt. And when they came that were hired about the eleventh hour, they received every man a penny. But when the firſt came, they fuppofed that they ſhould have received more, and they likewife received every man a penny. And when they had received it, they murmured againſt the good man of the houfe, faying, Thefe laſt have wrought but one hour, and thou haſt made them equal unto us, which have borne the burthen and heat of the day. But he anfwered one of them, and faid, Friend, I do thee no wrong: didſt thou not agree with me for a penny? Take that thine is, and go thy way; I will give unto this laſt even as unto thee. Is it not lawful for me to do what I will with mine own? Is thine eye evil becaufe I am good? So the laſt ſhall be firſt, and the firſt laſt: for many be called, but few choſen."

The ceremony of cloſing a lodge in this degree, when properly conducted, is peculiarly intereſting. It aſſiſts in ſtrengthening the ſocial affections; it teaches us the duty we owe to our brethren in particular, and the whole family of mankind in general; by aſcribing praiſe to the meritorious, and diſpenſing rewards to the diligent and induſtrious.

SONG, during the Closing Ceremony.

BY BROTHER T. S. WEBB.

MARK MASTERS, all appear
Before the Chief O'erseer;
  In concert move;
Let him your work inspect,
For the Chief Architect,
If there is no defect,
  He will approve.

Those who have pass'd the Square,
For your rewards prepare,
  Join heart and hand;
Each with his mark in view,
March with the just and true;
Wages to you are due,
  At your command.

Hiram, the widow's son,
Sent unto Solomon
  Our great key-stone,
On which appears the name
That raises high the fame
Of all to whom the same
  Is truly known.

Now to the westward move,
Where, full of strength and love,
  Hiram doth stand;
But if impostors are
Mix'd with the worthy there,
Caution them to beware
  Of the right hand.

Now to the praise of those
Who triumphed o'er the foes
  Of masons' arts;
To the praiseworthy three,
Who founded this degree:
May all their virtues be
  Deep in our hearts.

CHAPTER XII.

OBSERVATIONS ON THE DEGREE OF PRESENT OR PAST MASTER.

THIS degree fhould be carefully ftudied, and well underftood, by every mafter of a lodge. It treats of the government of our fociety; the difpofition of our rulers; and illuftrates their requifite qualifications. It includes the ceremony of opening and clofing lodges in the feveral preceding degrees; and alfo the forms of inftallation and confecration, in the grand lodge, as well as private lodges. It comprehends the ceremonies at laying the foundation ftones of public buildings, and alfo at dedications and at funerals, by a variety of particulars explanatory of thofe cermonies.

REMARKS ON THE FIFTH LECTURE.

THE FIRST SECTION.

Of the manner of Conftituting a Lodge of Mafter Mafons.

Any number of mafter mafons, not under feven, defirous of forming a new lodge, muft apply, by petition, to the grand lodge of the state in which they reside, setting forth,

"That they are free and accepted master masons; that they are at present, or have been, members of regular lodges; that, having the prosperity of the fraternity at heart, they are willing to exert their best endeavours to promote and diffuse the genuine principles of masonry; that, for the conveniency of their respective dwellings, and for other good reasons, they are desirous of forming a new lodge, in the town of ...., to be named .... ; that, in consequence of this desire, they pray for letters of dispensation, or a warrant of constitution, to empower them to assemble, as a legal lodge, to discharge the duties of masonry, in a regular and constitutional manner, according to the original forms of the order, and the regulations of the grand lodge. That they have nominated and do recommend A B to be the first master; C D to be the first senior warden, and E F to be the first junior warden, of the said lodge: that, if the prayer of the petition should be granted, they promise a strict conformity to all the constitutional laws and regulations of the grand lodge."

This petition, being signed by at least seven regular masons, and recommended by a lodge or lodges adjacent to the place where the new lodge is to be holden, is delivered to the grand secretary, who lays it before the grand lodge.

If the petition meets the approbation of the grand lodge, they generally order a dispensation to be issued, which is signed by the grand or deputy grand master, and authorizes the petitioners to assemble as a *legal* lodge, for a certain specified term of time.

In some jurisdictions, the grand and deputy grand masters, respectively, are invested with authority to grant dispensations, at pleasure, during the recess of the grand lodge; in others, they are never issued without the special direction of the grand lodge.

Lodges working under dispensations are considered merely as agents of the grand lodge;

their prefiding officers are not entitled to the
rank of paft mafters; their officers are not pri-
vileged with a vote or voice in the grand lodge;
they cannot change their officers without the
fpecial approbation and appointment of the
grand lodge; and in cafe of the ceffation of fuch
lodges, their funds, jewels, and other property,
accumulated by initiations into the feveral degrees, become the property of the grand lodge,
and muft be delivered over to the grand treafurer.

When lodges, that are at firft inftituted by
difpenfation, have paffed a proper term of probation, they make application to the grand lodge
for a charter of conftitution. If this be obtained,
they are then confirmed in the poffeffion of their
property, and poffefs all the rights and privileges
of regularly conftituted lodges, as long as they
conform to the conftitutions of mafonry.

After a charter is granted by the grand lodge,
the grand mafter appoints a day and hour for
conftituting and confecrating the new lodge,
and for inftalling its mafter, wardens, and other
officers.

If the grand mafter, in perfon, attends the
ceremony, the lodge is faid to be conftituted in
ample form; if the deputy grand mafter only,
it is faid to be conftituted in *due form ;* but if
the power of performing the ceremony is vefted
in a fubordinate lodge, it is faid to be conftituted in *form.*

When charters of conftitution are granted for
places where the diftance is fo great as to render

it inconvenient for the grand officers to attend,
the grand master, or his deputy, issues a written
instrument under his hand and private seal, to
some worthy present or past master, with full
power to conjugate, constitute and install the
petitioners.

Ceremony of Constitution and Confecration.

On the day and hour appointed, the grand
master and his officers meet in a convenient
room near to that in which the lodge to be constituted is assembled, and open the grand lodge
in the three degrees of masonry.

The officers of the new lodge are to be examined by the deputy grand master, after which
they return to their lodge.

The new lodge then sends a messenger to the
grand master with the following message, viz.

" Most Worshipful,

" The officers and brethren of .... lodge,
who are now assembled at ...., have instructed
me to inform you, that the most worshipful
grand lodge [or grand master] was pleased to
grant them a letter of dispensation, bearing date
the .... day of ...., in the year ...., au-
thorising them to form and open a lodge of free
and accepted masons, in the town of ....; that
since that period they have regularly assembled,
and conducted the business of masonry according to the best of their abilities ; that their proceedings having received the approbation of the
M. W. grand lodge, they have obtained a charter

of conftitution, and are defirous that their lodge fhould be confecrated, and their officers inftalled, agreeably to the ancient ufages and cuftoms of the craft ; for which purpofe they are now met, and await the pleafure of the moft worfhipful grand mafter."

He then returns to his lodge, who prepare for the reception of the grand lodge. When notice is given that they are prepared, the grand lodge walk in proceffion to their hall. When the grand mafter enters, the grand honours are given by the new lodge ; the officers of which refign their feats to the grand officers, and take their feveral ftations on the left.

The neceffary cautions are then given, and all, excepting mafters and paft mafters of lodges, are requefted to retire until the mafter of the new lodge is placed in the chair of Solomon. He is then bound to the faithful performance of his truft, and invefted with the characteriftics of the chair.

Upon due notice, the grand marfhal reconducts the brethren into the hall, and all take their places, except the members of the new lodge, who form a proceffion on one fide of the hall, to falute their mafter. As they advance, the grand mafter addreffes them, " *Brethren, behold your mafter !*" As they pafs, they make the proper falutation ; and when they have all paffed, he joins them, and takes his appropriate ftation.

8

A grand proceffion is then formed in the following order, viz.

Tyler, with a Drawn Sword;
Two Stewards, with White Rods;
Entered Apprentices;
Fellow Crafts;
Master Masons;
Stewards;
Junior Deacons;
Senior Deacons;
Secretaries;
Treasurers;
Past Wardens;
Junior Wardens;
Senior Wardens;
Past Masters;
Royal Arch Masons;
Knights Templars;
Masters of Lodges.

The New Lodge.

Tyler, with a Drawn Sword;
Stewards, with White Rods;
Entered Apprentices;
Fellow Crafts;
Master Masons;
Deacons;
Secretary and Treasurer;
Two Brethren, carrying the Lodge;*
Junior and Senior Wardens;
The Holy Writings, carried by the Oldest Member not in office;
The Master;
Music.

The Grand Lodge.

Grand Tyler, with a Drawn Sword;
Grand Stewards, with White Rods;
A Brother, carrying a Golden Vessel of Corn;†
Two Brethren, carrying Silver Vessels, one of Wine, the other of Oil;
Grand Secretaries;
Grand Treasurer;
A Burning Taper, borne by a Past Master;
A Past Master, bearing the Holy Writings;
Square and Compass, supported by two Stewards, with Rods;

* *Flooring.*
† *Wheat.*

Two Burning Tapers, borne by two Past Masters;
Clergy and Orator;
The Tuscan and Composite Orders;
The Doric, Ionic and Corinthian Orders;
Past Grand Wardens;
Past Deputy Grand Masters;
Past Grand Masters;
The Globes;
Junior and Senior Grand Wardens;
Right Worshipful Deputy Grand Master;
The Master of the Oldest Lodge, carrying the Book of Constitutions;
The M. W. GRAND MASTER;
The Grand Deacons, on a line seven feet apart, on the right and left
of the Grand Master, with Black Rods;
Grand Sword Bearer, with a Drawn Sword;
Two Stewards, with White Rods.

The whole proceffion moves on to the church or houfe where the fervices are to be performed. When the front of the proceffion arrives at the door, they halt, open to the right and left, and face inward, while the grand mafter, and others in fucceffion, pafs through, and enter the houfe.

A platform is erected in front of the pulpit, and provided with feats for the accommodation of the grand officers.

The bible, fquare and compafs, and book of conftitutions, are placed upon a table, in front of the grand mafter; the *lodge* is placed in the centre, upon the platform, covered with white fatin or linen, and encompaffed by the three tapers, and the veffels of corn, wine and oil.

A piece of mufic is performed, and the public fervices commence with prayer. An oration, or fermon, upon the defign and principles of the inftitution, is then delivered by the grand chaplain, or fome one appointed for that purpofe, which is fucceeded by a piece of mufic.

The grand marfhal then directs the officers and members of the new lodge to form in front.

of the grand master.   The deputy grand master
addresses the grand master, as follows :

" MOST WORSHIPFUL,

" A number of brethren, duly instructed in
the mysteries of masonry, having assembled together, at stated periods, for some time past, by
virtue of a dispensation granted them for that
purpose, do now desire to be *constituted* into a
regular lodge, agreeably to the ancient usages and
customs of the fraternity."

Their secretary then delivers the dispensation
and records to the master elect, who presents
them to the grand master.
The grand master examines the records, and
if they are found correct, proclaims,

" The records appear to be properly entered,
and are approved.   Upon due deliberation, the
grand lodge have granted the brethren of this
new lodge a charter, confirming them in the
rights and privileges of a *regularly constituted
lodge ;* which the grand secretary will now read."

After the charter is read, the grand master
then says,

" We shall now proceed, according to ancient
usage, to constitute these brethren into a regular lodge."

Whereupon the several officers of the new
lodge deliver up their jewels and badges to *their*
master, who presents them, with his own, to
the deputy grand master, and he to the grand
master.

The deputy grand master now presents the master elect of the new lodge to the grand master, saying,

"MOST WORSHIPFUL,

"I present you brother ...., whom the members of the lodge now to be constituted have chosen for their master."

The grand master asks them if they remain satisfied with their choice. (*They bow in token of assent.*)

The master then presents, severally, his wardens, and other officers, naming them and their respective offices. The grand master asks the brethren if they remain satisfied with each and all of them. (*They bow as before.*)

The officers and members of the new lodge then form in the broad aisle, in front of the grand master; and the business of consecration commences with solemn music.

Ceremony of Consecration.

The grand master, attended by the grand officers, and the grand chaplain, form themselves in order, round the lodge, which is then uncovered. All devoutly kneeling, the first clause of the consecration prayer is rehearsed, as follows, viz.

"Great Architect of the Universe! Maker and Ruler of all Worlds! deign, from thy celestial temple, from realms of light and glory, to bless us in all the purposes of our present assembly!

8*

"We humbly invoke thee to give us, at this and at all times, *wisdom* in all our doings, *strength* of mind in all our difficulties, and the *beauty* of harmony in all our communications!

"Permit us, O thou Author of Light and Life, Great Source of Love and Happiness, to erect this lodge, and now solemnly to *consecrate* it to the honour of thy glory!

"*Glory be to God on high.*"

[Response by the Brethren.]

"*As it was in the beginning, is now, and ever shall be! Amen.*"

During the response, the deputy grand master, and the grand wardens, take the vessels of corn, wine and oil, and sprinkle the elements of consecration upon the lodge.

[*The grand chaplain then continues :*]

"Grant, O Lord our God, that those who are now about to be invested with the government of this lodge may be endued with wisdom to instruct their brethren in all their duties. May *brotherly love, relief* and *truth* always prevail among the members of this lodge; and may this bond of union continue to strengthen the lodges throughout the world!

"Bless all our brethren, wherever dispersed; and grant speedy relief to all who are either oppressed or distressed.

"We affectionately commend to thee all the members of thy whole family. May they increase in the knowledge of thee, and in the love of each other.

" Finally : May we finifh all our work here below with thine approbation ; and then have our tranfition from this earthly abode to thy heavenly temple above, there to enjoy light, glory and blifs, ineffable and eternal !

" *Glory be to God on high !*"

[Refponfe by the Brethren.]

" *As it was in the beginning, is now, and ever fhall be !*

" *Amen ! fo mote it be ! Amen !*"

Then fucceeds folemn mufic, while the lodge is covered. The grand chaplain then DEDICATES the lodge in the following terms :

" To the memory of HOLY SAINT JOHN, we dedicate this lodge. May every brother revere his character, and imitate his virtues.

" *Glory be to God on high !*"

[Refponfe.]

" *As it was in the beginning, is now, and ever fhall be, world without end !*

" *Amen ! fo mote it be ! Amen !*"

A piece of mufic is then performed, while the brethren of the new lodge advance in proceffion to falute the grand lodge, with their hands croffed upon their breafts, and bowing as they pafs. They then take their places, and ftand as they were.

The grand mafter then rifes, and conftitutes the new lodge in the form following :

" In the name of the moft worfhipful grand lodge, I now conftitute and form you, my good

brethren, into a lodge of free and accepted mafons.   From henceforth I empower you to act
as a regular lodge, conftituted in conformity to
the rites of our order, and the charges of our
ancient and honourable fraternity; and may
the Supreme Architect of the Univerfe profper,
direct and counfel you in all your doings."

[Refponfe by all the Brethren.]

"*So mote it be.*"

The ceremony of inftallation then fucceeds.

SECOND SECTION.

Ceremony of Inftallation.

The grand mafter* afks his deputy, "Whether
he has examined the mafter nominated in the
warrant, and finds him well fkilled in the noble
fcience and the royal art."   The deputy, an-
fwering in the affirmative,† by the grand mafter's
order, takes the candidate from among his fellows, and prefents him at the pedeftal, faying,

"MOST WORSHIPFUL GRAND MASTER,

"I prefent my worthy brother, A B, to be
inftalled mafter of this new lodge.   I find him to
be of good morals, and of great fkill, true and
trufty ; and as he is a lover of the whole fraternity, wherefover difperfed over the face of the
earth, I doubt not that he will difcharge his
duty with fidelity."

* In this, and other fimilar inftances, where the grand mafter is
specified in acting, may be underftood any mafter who performs the
ceremony.

† A private examination is underftood to precede the installation
of every officer.

The grand mafter then addreffes him:

"BROTHER,

"Previous to your inveftiture, it is neceffary that you fhould fignify your affent to thofe ancient charges and regulations which point out the duty of a mafter of a lodge."

The grand mafter then reads, or orders to be read, a fummary of the ancient charges to the mafter elect, as follows, viz.

"I. You agree to be a good man and true, and ftrictly to obey the moral law.

"II. You agree to be a peaceable fubject, and cheerfully to conform to the laws of the country in which you refide.

"III. You promife not to be concerned in plots and confpiracies againft government, but patiently to fubmit to the decifions of the fupreme legiflature.

"IV. You agree to pay a proper refpect to the civil magiftrate, to work diligently, live creditably, and act honourably by all men.

"V. You agree to hold in veneration the original rulers and patrons of the order of mafonry, and their regular fucceffors, fupreme and fubordinate, according to their ftations; and to fubmit to the awards and refolutions of your brethren when convened, in every cafe confiftent with the conftitutions of the order.

"VI. You agree to avoid private piques and quarrels, and to guard againft intemperance and excefs.

"VII. You agree to be cautious in carriage

and behaviour, courteous to your brethren, and faithful to your lodge.

" VIII. You promife to refpect genuine brethren, and to difcountenance impoftors, and all diffenters from the original plan of mafonry.

" IX. You agree to promote the general good of fociety, to cultivate the focial virtues, and to propagate the knowledge of the art.

" X. You promife to pay homage to the grand mafter for the time being, and to his officers when duly inftalled ; and ftrictly to conform to every edict of the grand lodge, or general affembly of mafons, that is not fubverfive of the principles and ground work of mafonry.

" XI. You admit that it is not in the power of any man, or body of men, to make innovations in the body of mafonry.

" XII. You promife a regular attendance on the committees and communications of the grand lodge, on receiving proper notice, and to pay attention to all the duties of mafonry, on convenient occafions.

" XIII. You admit that no new lodge fhall be formed without permiffion of the grand lodge ; and that no countenance be given to any irregular lodge, or to any perfon clandeftinely initiated therein, being contrary to the ancient charges of the order.

" XIV. You admit that no perfon can be regularly made a mafon in, or admitted a member of, any regular lodge, without previous notice, and due inquiry into his character.

" XV. You agree that no vifitors fhall be received into your lodge without due examination, and producing proper vouchers of their having been initiated in a regular lodge."*

* As the curious reader may wish to know the ancient charges that were used on this occasion, we shall here insert them verbatim as they are contained in a MS in possession of the Lodge of Antiquity in London, written in the reign of James the Second.

". . . . . And furthermore, at diverse assemblies, have been put and ordained diverse crafties by the best advice of magistrates and fellowes.

"Every man that is a mason take good heed to these charges (wee pray) that if any man find himselfe guilty of any of these charges, that he may amend himselfe, or principally for dread of God you that be charged to take good heed that you keepe all these charges well, for it is a great evill for a man to forswear himselfe upon a book.

"The first charge is, That yee shall be true men to God and the holy Church, and to use no errour or heresie by your understanding, and by wise men's teaching.

"Allso, secondly, yee shall be true one to another, (that is to say) every mason of the craft that is mason allowed, yee shall doe to him as yee would be done unto yourselfe.

"Thirdly, And yee shall keepe truely all the counsell that ought to be kept in the way of masonhood, and all the counsell of the lodge or of the chamber. Also, that yee shall be no thiefe nor thiefes to your knowledge free: that ye shall be true to the king, lord or master that yee serve, and truely to see and work for his advantage.

"Fourthly, Yee shall call all masons your fellowes, or your brethren, and no other names.

"Fifthly, Yee shall not take your fellowes wife in villainy, nor deflower his daughter or servant, nor put him to no disworship.

"Sixthly, Yee shall truely pay for your meat or drinke wheresoever ye goe to table or boarde. Allso, yee shall do no villainy there, whereby the craft or science may be slandered.

"These shall be the charges general to every true mason, both masters and fellowes.

"Now will I rehearse other charges single for masons allowed or accepted.

"First, That no mason take on him no lordes worke, nor any other man's, unless he know himselfe well able to perform the worke, so that the craft have no slander.

"Secondly, Allso, that no master take worke but that he take reasonable pay for itt: so that the lord may be truely served, and the master to live honestly, and to pay his fellowes truely. And that no master or fellowe supplant others of their worke; (that is to say) that if he hath taken a worke, or else stand master of any worke, that he shall not put him out, unless he be unable of cunning to make an end of his worke. And no master nor fellowe shall take an apprintice for less than seaven yeares. And that the apprintice be free born, and of limbs whole as a man ought to be, and no bastard. And

Thefe are the regulations of free and accepted mafons.

that no master or fellowe take no allowance to be made mason without the assent of his fellowes, at the least six or seaven.

"Thirdly, That he that be made be able in all degrees; that is, free born, of a good kindred, true, and no bondsman, and that he have his right limbs as a man ought to have.

"Fourthly, That a master take no apprintice without he have occupation to occupy two or three fellowes at the least.

"Fifthly, That no master or fellowe put away any lordes worke to task that ought to be journey worke.

"Sixthly, That every master give pay to his fellowes and servants as they may deserve, soe that he be not defamed with false workeing. And that none slander another behind his backe, to make him loose his good name.

"Seaventhly, That no fellowe in the house or abroad answear another ungodly or reproveable without a cause.

"Eighthly, That every master mason doe reverence his elder; and that a mason be no common plaier at the cards, dice, or hazzard, nor at any other unlawfull plaies, through which the science and craft may be dishonoured or slandered.

"Ninthly, That no fellowe goe into the town by night, except he have a fellowe with him, who may bear him record that he was in an honest place.

"Tenthly, That every master and fellowe shall come to the assemblie, if it be within fifty miles of him, if he have any warning. And if he have trespassed against the craft, to abide the award of masters and fellowes.

"Eleventhly, That every master mason and fellowe that hath trespassed against the craft shall stand to the correction of other masters and fellowes to make him accord; and if they cannot accord, to go to the common law.

"Twelfthly, That a master or fellowe make not a mould stone, square nor rule, to no lowen, nor let no lowen worke within their lodge, nor without, to mould stone.

"Thirteenthly, That every mason receive and cherish strange fellowes when they come over the countrie, and set them on worke if they will worke, as the manner is; (that is to say) if the mason have any mould stone in his place, he shall give him a mould stone, and sett him on worke; and if he have none, the mason shall refresh him with money unto the next lodge.

"Fourteenthly, That every mason shall truely serve his master for his pay.

"Fifteenthly, That every master shall truely make an end of his worke, taske, or journey, whethersoe it be.

"These be all the charges and covenants that ought to be read at the instalment of master, or making of a freemason or freemasons. The Almighty God of Jacob, who ever have you and me in his keeping, bless us now and ever. Amen."

The grand mafter then addreffes the mafter elect in the following manner :

" Do you fubmit to thefe charges, and promife to fupport thefe regulations, as mafters have done in all ages before you ?"

The new mafter having fignified his cordial fubmiffion as before, the grand mafter thus addreffes him :

" Brother A B, in confequence of your cheerful conformity to the charges and regulations of the order, you are now to be inftalled mafter of this new lodge, in full confidence of your care, fkill and capacity, to govern the fame."

The new mafter is then regularly invefted with the infignia of his office, and the furniture and implements of his lodge.

The various implements of the profeffion are emblematical of our conduct in life, and upon this occafion carefully enumerated.

" The *Holy Writings*, that great light in mafonry, will guide you to all truth ; it will direct your paths to the temple of happinefs, and point out to you the whole duty of man.

" The *Square* teaches to regulate our actions by rule and line, and to harmonize our conduct by the principles of morality and virtue.

" The *Compafs* teaches to limit our defires in every ftation, that, rifing to eminence by merit, we may live refpected, and die regretted.

" The *Rule* directs that we fhould punctually obferve our duty ; prefs-forward in the path of virtue, and, neither inclining to the right nor to the left, in all our actions have *eternity* in view.

" The *Line* teaches the criterion of moral rectitude, to avoid diffimulation in converfation and action, and to direct our fteps to the path which leads to *immortality*.

" The *Book of Conftitutions* you are to fearch at all times. Caufe it to be read in your lodge, that none may pretend ignorance of the excellent precepts it enjoins.

" Laftly, you receive in charge the *By Laws* of your lodge, which you are to fee carefully and punctually executed."

The jewels of the officers of the new lodge being then returned to the mafter, he delivers them, refpectively, to the feveral officers of the grand lodge, according to their rank.

The fubordinate officers of the new lodge are then invefted with their jewels, by the grand officers of correfponding rank ; and are by them, feverally in turn, conducted to the grand mafter, who delivers each of them a fhort charge, as follows, viz.

The Senior Warden.

" Brother C D, you are appointed Senior Warden of this new lodge, and are now invefted with the enfign of your office.

" The *Level* demonftrates that we are defcended from the fame ftock, partake of the fame nature, and fhare the fame hope ; and though diftinctions among men are neceffary to preferve fubordination, yet no eminence of ftation fhould make us forget that we are brethren ; for he who is placed on the loweft fpoke of fortune's wheel may be entitled to our regard ; becaufe a time will come, and the wifeft knows not how foon, when all diftinctions, but that of goodnefs, fhall ceafe; and death, the grand leveller of human greatnefs, reduce us to the fame ftate.

"Your regular attendance on our ftated meetings is effentially neceffary; in the abfence of the mafter, you are to govern this lodge; in his prefence, you are to affift him in the government of it: I firmly rely on your knowledge of mafonry, and attachment to the lodge, for the faithful difcharge of the duties of this important truft.—*Look well to the Weft!*"

The Junior Warden.

"Brother E F, you are appointed Junior Warden of this new lodge; and are now invefted with the badge of your office.

"The *Plumb* admonifhes us to walk uprightly in our feveral ftations, to hold the fcale of juftice in equal poife, to obferve the juft medium between intemperance and pleafure, and to make our paffions and prejudices coincide with the line of our duty.

"To you, with fuch affiftance as may be neceffary, is entrufted the examination of vifitors, and the reception of candidates. To you is alfo committed the fuperintendence of the craft during the hours of refrefhment; it is therefore indifpenfably neceffary, that you fhould not only be temperate and difcreet, in the indulgence of your own inclinations, but carefully obferve that none of the craft be fuffered to convert the purpofes of refrefhment into intemperance and excefs.

" Your regular and punctual attendance is particularly requested ; and I have no doubt that you will faithfully execute the duty which you owe to your present appointment.—*Look well to the South !*"

The Treasurer.

" Brother G H, you are appointed Treasurer of this new lodge. It is your duty to receive all moneys from the hands of the secretary, keep just and regular accounts of the same, and pay them out at the worshipful master's will and pleasure, with the consent of the lodge. I trust your regard for the fraternity will prompt you to the faithful discharge of the duties of your office."

The Secretary.

" Brother I K, you are appointed Secretary of this new lodge. It is your duty to observe the worshipful master's will and pleasure, to record the proceedings of the lodge, to receive all moneys, and pay them into the hands of the treasurer.

" Your good inclination to masonry and this lodge, I hope, will induce you to discharge your office with fidelity, and by so doing you will merit the esteem and applause of your brethren."

The Senior and Junior Deacons.

" Brothers L M and N O, you are appointed Deacons of this new lodge. It is your province to attend on the master and wardens, and to act as their proxies in the active duties of the lodge ;

such as in the reception of candidates into the different degrees of masonry; the introduction and accommodation of visitors, and in the immediate practice of our rites. Those columns, as badges of your office, I trust to your care, not doubting your vigilance and attention."

The Stewards.

"Brothers P Q and R S, you are appointed Stewards of this new lodge. The duties of your office are, to assist in the collection of dues and subscriptions, to keep an account of the lodge expenses, to see that the tables are properly furnished at refreshment, and that every brother is suitably provided for; and generally to assist the deacons and other officers in performing their respective duties. Your regular and early attendance will afford the best proof of your zeal and attachment to the lodge."

The Tyler

Is then appointed, and receives the instrument of his office, with a short charge on the occasion.

The grand master then addresses the officers and members of the new lodge as follows.

Charge upon the Installation of the Officers of a Lodge.

"WORSHIPFUL MASTER,

"The grand lodge having committed to your care the superintendance and government of the brethren who are to compose this new lodge, you cannot be insensible of the obligations which

9*

devolve on you, as their head; nor of your refponfibility for the faithful difcharge of the important duties annexed to your appointment.

"The honour, reputation and ufefulnefs of
your lodge will materially depend on the fkill
and affiduity with which you manage its concerns; while the happinefs of its members will
be generally promoted, in proportion to the zeal
and ability with which you propagate the genuine principles of our inftitution.

"For a pattern of imitation, confider the great
luminary of nature, which, rifing in the *Eaft*,
regularly diffufes light and luftre to all within its
circle. In like manner it is your province to
fpread and communicate light and inftruction to
the brethren of your lodge. Forcibly imprefs
upon them the dignity and high importance of
mafonry; and ferioufly admonifh them never
to difgrace it. Charge them to practife, *out* of
the lodge, thofe duties which they have been
taught *in* it; and by amiable, difcreet and virtuous conduct, to convince mankind of the
goodnefs of the inftitution; fo that when any
one is faid to be a member of it, the world may
know that he is one to whom the burthened
heart may pour out its forrows; to whom dif-
trefs may prefer its fuit; whofe hand is guided
by juftice, and his heart expanded by benevolence. In fhort, by a diligent obfervance of the
by-laws of your lodge, the conftitutions of mafonry, and above all the Holy Scriptures, which
are given as a rule and guide to your faith, you
will be enabled to acquit yourfelf with honour
and reputation, and lay up a *crown of rejoicing*,

which shall continue when time shall be no more."

" BROTHER SENIOR AND JUNIOR WARDENS,

" You are too well acquainted with the principles of masonry to warrant any apprehension that you will be found wanting in the discharge of your respective duties. Suffice it to mention, that what you have seen praiseworthy in others you should carefully imitate ; and what in them may have appeared defective you should in yourselves amend. You should be examples of good order and regularity ; for it is only by a due regard to the laws in your own conduct, that you can expect obedience to them from others. You are assiduously to assist the master in the discharge of his trust ; diffusing light, and imparting knowledge, to all whom he shall place under your care. In the absence of the master, you will succeed to higher duties ; your acquirements must therefore be such, as that the craft may never suffer for want of proper instruction. From the spirit which you have hitherto evinced, I entertain no doubt that your future conduct will be such as to merit the applause of your brethren, and the testimony of a good conscience."

" BRETHREN OF .... LODGE,

" Such is the nature of our constitution, that as some must of necessity rule and teach, so others must of course learn to submit and obey. Humility in both is an essential duty. The officers who are appointed to govern your lodge

are fufficiently converfant with the rules of propriety, and the laws of the inftitution, to avoid
exceeding the powers with which they are entrufted; and you are of too generous difpofitions to envy their preferment. I therefore
truft that you will have but one aim, to pleafe
each other, and unite in the grand defign of being happy, and communicating happinefs.

"Finally, my brethren, as this affociation has
been formed and perfected in fo much unanimity and concord, in which we greatly rejoice, fo
may it long continue. May you long enjoy
every fatisfaction and delight which difintereft-
ed friendfhip can afford. May kindnefs and
brotherly affection diftinguifh your conduct as
men and as mafons. Within your peaceful
walls, may your children's children celebrate
with joy and gratitude the tranfactions of this
aufpicious folemnity. And may *the tenets of our
profeffion* be tranfmitted through your lodge,
pure and unimpaired, from generation to generation."

The grand marfhal then proclaims the new
lodge, in the following manner, viz.

"In the name of the moft worfhipful grand
lodge of the ftate of ...., I proclaim this new
lodge, by the name of .... Lodge, duly conftituted."

This proclamation is made thrice, and each
time followed with a flourifh of drums or trumpets.

The grand chaplain then makes the concluding
prayer, which ends the public ceremonies.

The grand proceffion is then formed in the fame order as before, and returns to the hall.

The grand mafter, deputy grand mafter, and grand wardens, being feated, all but mafter mafons are caufed to retire, and the proceffion continues round the hall, and upon paffing the feveral grand officers pays them due homage, by the ufual congratulations and honours, in the different degrees. During the proceffion, (which paffes three times round the lodge) the following fong is fung, which concludes the ceremony of inftallation.

HAIL, MASONRY divine!
Glory of ages shine;
  Long may'st thou reign:
Where'er thy lodges stand,
May they have great command,
And always grace the land,
  Thou Art divine!

Great fabrics still arise,
And grace the azure skies;
  Great are thy schemes;
Thy noble orders are
Matchless beyond compare;
No art with thee can share,
  Thou Art divine!

Hiram, the architect,
Did all the craft direct
  How they should build;
Sol'mon, great Isr'el's king, }
Did mighty blessings bring,   } Chorus,
And left us room to sing,   } Three Times.
  Hail, royal Art!   }

The lodge is then clofed with the ufual folemnities in the different degrees by the grand mafter and his officers.

This is the ufual ceremony obferved by

lar mafons at the conftitution of a new lodge, which the grand mafter may abridge or extend at pleafure; but the material points are on no account to be omitted. The fame ceremony and charges attend every fucceeding inftallation of new officers.

THE THIRD SECTION.

Ceremony obferved at Laying the Foundation Stone of Public Structures.

This ceremony is conducted by the grand mafter and his officers, affifted by the members of the grand lodge, and fuch officers and members of private lodges as can conveniently attend. The chief magiftrate, and other civil officers of the place where the building is to be erected, alfo generally attend on the occafion.

At the time appointed, the grand lodge is convened in fome fuitable place, approved by the grand mafter. A band of martial mufic is provided, and the brethren appear in the infignia of the order, and with white gloves and aprons. The lodge is opened by the grand mafter, and the rules for regulating the proceffion to and from the place where the ceremony is to be performed are read by the grand fecretary. The neceffary cautions are then given from the chair, and the lodge is adjourned; after which the proceffion fets out in the following order:

PROCESSION AT LAYING FOUNDATION STONES.

Two Tylers, with Drawn Swords;
Tyler of the Oldest Lodge, with do.;
Two Stewards of the Oldest Lodge;
Entered Apprentices;
Fellow Crafts;
Master Masons;
Stewards;
Junior Deacons;
Senior Deacons;
Secretaries;
Treasurers;
Past Wardens;
Junior Wardens;
Senior Wardens;
Past Masters;
Royal Arch Masons;
Knights Templars;
Masters of Lodges, in office;
Music;
Grand Tyler, with a Drawn Sword;
Grand Stewards, with White Rods;
A Brother, with a Golden Vessel containing Corn;
Two Brethren, with Silver Vessels, one containing Wine, and
the other Oil;
Principal Architect, with Square, Level and Plumb;
Grand Secretary and Treasurer;
Bible, Square and Compass, carried by a Master of a Lodge, support-
ed by two Stewards;
Grand Chaplain;
The Five Orders;
Past Grand Wardens;
Past Deputy Grand Masters;
Past Grand Masters;
Chief Magistrate of the Place;
Two Large Lights, borne by two Masters of Lodges;
Grand Wardens;
One Large Light, borne by a Master of a Lodge;
Deputy Grand Master;
Master of the Oldest Lodge, bearing the Book of Constitutions, on a
Velvet Cushion;
Grand Deacons, with Black Rods, on a line seven feet apart;
GRAND MASTER;
Grand Sword Bearer, with a Drawn Sword;
Two Stewards, with White Rods.

Marshal.

A triumphal arch is usually erected at the
place where the ceremony is to be performed.

The proceſſion paſſes through the arch, and the brethren repairing to their ſtands, the grand maſter and his officers take their places on a temporary platform, covered with carpet. An ode on maſonry is ſung. The grand marſhal commands ſilence, and the neceſſary preparations are made for laying the ſtone, on which is engraved the year of maſonry, the name and titles of the grand maſter, &c. &c.

The ſtone is raiſed up, by means of an engine erected for that purpoſe, and the grand chaplain or orator repeats a ſhort prayer. The grand treaſurer then, by the grand maſter's command, places under the ſtone various ſorts of coin and medals of the preſent age. Solemn muſic is introduced, and the ſtone let down into its place. The principal architect then preſents the working tools to the grand maſter, who applies the *plumb*, *ſquare* and *level* to the ſtone, in their proper poſitions, and pronounces it to be " WELL FORMED, TRUE AND TRUSTY."

The golden and ſilver veſſels are next brought to the table, and delivered, the former to the deputy grand maſter, and the latter to the grand wardens, who ſucceſſively preſent them to the grand maſter : and he, according to ancient ceremony, pours the corn, the wine and the oil, which they contain, on the ſtone, ſaying,

" May the all-bounteous Author of Nature bleſs the inhabitants of this place with all the neceſſaries, conveniences, and comforts of life ; aſſiſt in the erection and completion of this building ; protect the workmen againſt every accident, and long preſerve this ſtructure from decay ; and grant to us all, in needed supply, the CORN of *nourishment*, the WINE of *refreshment*, and the OIL of *joy !*"

"*Amen ! so mote it be ! Amen !*"

He then strikes the stone thrice with the mallet, and the *public* honours of masonry are given.

The grand master then delivers over to the architect the various implements of architecture, entrusting him with the superintendence and direction of the work ; after which, he re-ascends the platform, and an oration suitable to the occasion is delivered. A voluntary collection is made for the workmen, and the sum collected is placed upon the stone by the grand treasurer. A song in honour of masonry concludes the ceremony ; after which the procession returns to the place whence it set out, and the lodge is closed.

THE FOURTH SECTION.

Ceremony observed at the Dedication of Masons' Halls.

On the day appointed for the celebration of the ceremony of dedication, the grand master and his officers, accompanied by the members of the grand lodge, meet in a convenient room near to the place where the ceremony is to be performed, and the grand lodge is opened in ample form in the first three degrees of masonry. The master of the lodge to which the hall to be dedicated belongs, being present, rises, and addresses the grand master, as follows.

" MOST WORSHIPFUL,

" The brethren of .... Lodge, being animated with a desire of promoting the honour and interest of the craft, have, at great pains and expense, erected a masonic hall, for their convenience and accommodation. They are now desirous that the same should be examined by the M. W. grand lodge; and, if it should meet their approbation, that it should be solemnly dedicated to masonic purposes, agreeably to ancient form."

The grand master then directs the grand secretary to read the order of procession, which is delivered over to the grand marshal; and a general charge, respecting propriety of behaviour, is given by the deputy grand master.

A grand procession is then formed in the order laid down in the first section, page 86. The whole move forward to the hall which is to be dedicated, and upon the arrival of the front of the procession at the door, they halt, open to the right and left, and face inward; while the grand master, and others in succession, pass through, and enter. The music continues while the procession marches three times round the hall.

The lodge is then placed in the centre; and the grand master having taken the chair, under a canopy of state, the grand officers, and the masters and wardens of the lodges, repair to the places previously prepared for their reception; the three lights, and the gold and silver pitchers, with the corn, wine and oil, are placed round the lodge, at the head of which stands the pedeſtal, with the bible open, and the ſquare and compaſs laid thereon, with the conſtitution roll, on a crimſon velvet cuſhion. Matters being thus diſpoſed, an anthem is ſung, and an exordium on maſonry given; after which the architect addreſſes the grand maſter, as follows:

"MOST WORSHIPFUL,

"Having been entruſted with the ſuperintendence and management of the workmen employed in the conſtruction of this edifice; and having, according to the beſt of my ability, accompliſhed the taſk aſſigned me; I now return my thanks for the honour of this appointment, and beg leave to ſurrender up the implements which were committed to my care when the foundation of this fabric was laid; humbly hoping, that the exertions which have been made on this occaſion will be crowned with your approbation, and that of the moſt worſhipful grand lodge."

To which the grand maſter makes the following reply:

"BROTHER ARCHITECT,

"The ſkill and fidelity diſplayed in the execution of the truſt repoſed in you, at the commencement of this undertaking, have ſecured the entire approbation of the grand lodge; and they ſincerely pray, that this edifice may continue a laſting monument of the taſte, ſpirit and liberality of its founders."

An ode in honour of maſonry is ſung, accompanied with inſtrumental muſic.

The deputy grand master then rifes, and fays:

"MOST WORSHIPFUL,

"The hall in which we are now affembled, and the plan upon which it has been conftructed, having met with your approbation, it is the defire of the fraternity that it fhould be now dedicated, according to ancient form and ufage."

Whereupon the grand master requefts all to retire but fuch as are mafter mafons. A proceffion is then formed in the following order, viz.

Grand Sword Bearer;
A Past Master, with a Light;
A Past Master, with Bible, Square and Compass, on a Velvet Cushion;
Two Past Marters, each with a Light;
Grand Secretary and Treasurer, with Emblems;
Grand Junior Warden, with Pitcher of Corn;
Grand Senior Warden, with Pitcher of Wine;
Deputy Grand Master, with Pitcher of Oil;
Grand Master;
Two Stewards, with Rods.

All the other brethren keep their places, and affift in performing an ode, which continues during the proceffion, excepting only at the intervals of dedication. The lodge is uncovered, and the firft proceffion being made round it, the junior grand warden prefents the pitcher of corn to the grand mafter, who pours it out upon the lodge, at the fame time pronouncing,

"In the name of the great Jehovah, to whom be all honour and glory, I do folemnly dedicate this hall to MASONRY."

The grand honours are given.

The fecond proceffion is then made round the lodge, and the grand fenior warden prefents the

pitcher of wine, to the grand mafter, who fprinkles it upon the lodge, at the fame time faying,
"In the name of holy Saint John, I do folemnly dedicate this hall to VIRTUE."

The grand honours are twice repeated.

The third proceffion is then made round the
lodge, and the deputy grand mafter prefents the
pitcher of oil to the grand mafter, who fprinkles
it upon the lodge, faying,

"In the name of the whole fraternity, I do
folemnly dedicate this hall to UNIVERSAL BENE-
VOLENCE."

The grand honours are thrice repeated.

A folemn invocation is made to Heaven, by
the grand chaplain, and an anthem fung; after
which the lodge is covered, and the grand mafter retires to his chair. An oration is then delivered, and the ceremonies conclude with mufic. The grand lodge is then clofed in ample
form, in the feveral degrees.

THE FIFTH SECTION.

*The Ceremony obferved at Funerals, according to
ancient cuftom; with the Service ufed on the occafion.*

No mafon can be interred with the formalities of the order, unlefs it be by his own fpecial
requeft, communicated to the mafter of the lodge
of which he died a member, foreigners and fo-
journers excepted; nor unlefs he has been advanced to the third degree of mafonry; and
from this reftriction there can be no exception.

I.O*

Fellow crafts, or apprentices, are not entitled to funeral obfequies, nor to attend the mafonic procession on fuch occasions.

The mafter of a lodge, having received notice of a mafter mafon's death, and of his requeft to be interred with the ceremonies of the order, fixes the day and hour for the funeral, and iffues his command to fummon the lodge. He may invite as many lodges as he thinks proper, and the members of thofe lodges may accompany their officers in form; but the whole ceremony muft be under the direction of the mafter of the lodge to which the deceafed belonged, and he and his officers muft be duly honoured, and cheerfully obeyed, on the occafion.* But in cafe the deceafed was not a member of either of the attending lodges, the proceffion and cere- mony muft be under the direction of the mafter of the oldeft lodge.

All the brethren who walk in proceffion fhould obferve, as much as poffible, an uniformity in their drefs. Decent mourning, with white ftock- ings, gloves and aprons, is moft fuitable.

The Funeral Service.

The brethren being affembled at the lodge room, (or fome other convenient place) the pre- fiding mafter opens the lodge, in the third de- gree, with the ufual forms; and having ftated the purpofe of the meeting, the fervice begins.

---

* Except when the grand or deputy grand mafter is prefent, and exercifes his authority.

Master. " What man is he that liveth, and shall not see death ? Shall he deliver his soul from the hand of the grave ?"

Response. " Man walketh in a vain shadow; he heapeth up riches, and cannot tell who shall gather them."

Master. " When he dieth, he shall carry nothing away; his glory shall not descend after him."

Response. " Naked he came into the world, and naked he must return."

Master. " The Lord gave, and the Lord hath taken away; blessed be the name of the Lord !"

The grand honours are then given, and certain forms used, which cannot be here explained.

The master then, taking the *sacred roll* in his hand, says,

" Let us die the death of the righteous, and let our last end be like his !"

The brethren answer,

" God is our God forever and ever; he will be our guide even unto death !"

The master then records the name and age of the deceased upon the roll, and says,

" Almighty Father ! into thy hands we commend the soul of our loving brother."

The brethren answer three times (giving the grand honours each time)

" The will of God is accomplished ! so be it."

The master then deposits the roll in the archives, and repeats the following prayer :

" Most glorious God ! author of all good, and giver of all mercy ! pour down thy blessings upon us, and strengthen our solemn engagements with the ties of fincere affection! May the prefent inftance of mortality remind us of our approaching fate, and draw our attention toward thee, the only refuge in time of need! that when the awful moment fhall arrive, that we are about to quit this tranfitory fcene, the enlivening profpect of thy mercy may difpel the gloom of death; and after our departure hence in peace and in thy favour, we may be received into thine everlafting kingdom, to enjoy, in union with the fouls of our departed friends, the juft reward of a pious and virtuous life. *Amen.*"

A proceffion is then formed, which moves to the houfe of the deceafed, and from thence to the place of interment. The different lodges rank according to feniority, excepting that the lodge of which the deceafed was a member walks neareft the corpfe. Each lodge forms one divifion, and the following order is obferved:

ORDER OF PROCESSION AT A FUNERAL.

Tyler, with a Drawn Sword;
Stewards, with White Rods;
Musicians (if they are masons, otherwise they follow the tyler);
Master Masons;
Senior and Junior Deacons;
Secretary and Treasurer;
Senior and Junior Wardens;
Past Masters;
The Holy Writings, on a cushion covered with black cloth, carried by the Oldest Member of the Lodge;
The Master;
Clergy;

with the insignia placed thereon,
and two THE BODY, swords crossed;
Pall Bearers; Pall Bearers.

The brethren are not to defert their ranks, or change places, but keep in their different departments. When the proceffion arrives at the church yard, the members of the lodge form a circle round the grave, and the clergyman and officers of the acting lodge taking their ftation at the head of the grave, and the mourners at the foot, the fervice is refumed, and the following exhortation given :

" Here we view a ftriking inftance of the uncertainty of life, and the vanity of all human purfuits. The laft offices paid to the dead are only ufeful as lectures to the living ; from them we are to derive inftruction, and confider every folemnity of this kind as a fummons to prepare for our approaching diffolution.

" Notwithftanding the various mementoes of mortality with which we daily meet ; notwithftanding death has eftablifhed his empire over all the works of nature ; yet through fome unaccountable infatuation we forget that we are born to die : we go on from one defign to another, add hope to hope, and lay out plans for the employment of many years, till we are fuddenly alarmed with the approach of death, when we leaft expect him, and at an hour which we probably conclude to be the meridian of our exiftence.

" What are all the externals of majefty, the pride of wealth, or charms of beauty, when nature has paid her juft debt ? Fix your eyes on the laft fcene, and view life ftript of her ornaments, and expofed in her natural meannefs ; you will then be convinced of the futility of thofe empty delufions. In the grave, all fallacies are detected, all ranks are levelled, and all diftinctions are done away.

"While we drop the fympathetic tear over the grave of our deceafed friend, let charity incline us to throw a veil over his foibles, whatever they may have been, and not withhold from his memory the praife that his virtues may have claimed. Suffer the apologies of human nature to plead in his behalf. Perfection on earth has never been attained; the wifeft as well as the beft of men have erred.

"Let the prefent example excite our moft ferious thoughts, and ftrengthen our refolutions of amendment. As life is uncertain, and all earthly purfuits are vain, let us no longer poftpone the important concern of preparing for eternity; but embrace the happy moment, while time and opportunity offer, to provide againft the great change, when all the pleafures of this world fhall ceafe to delight, and the reflections of a virtuous life yield the only comfort and confolation. Thus our expectations will not be fruftrated, nor we hurried unprepared into the prefence of an all-wife and powerful Judge, to whom the fecrets of all hearts are known.

"Let us, while in this ftate of exiftence, fupport with propriety the character of our profeffion, advert to the nature of our folemn ties, and purfue with affiduity the facred tenets of our order: Then, with becoming reverence, let us fupplicate the divine grace to enfure the favour of that eternal Being, whofe goodnefs and power know no bound; that when the awful moment arrives, be it soon or late, we may be enabled to prosecute our journey, without dread or apprehension, to that far distant country whence no traveller returns."

The following invocations are then made by the Master:

Master. "May we be true and faithful; and may we live and die in love!"

Answer. "So mote it be."

Master. "May we profess what is good, and always act agreeably to our profession!"

Answer. "So mote it be."

Master. "May the Lord bless us, and prosper us; and may all our good intentions be crowned with success!"

Answer. "So mote it be."

Master. "Glory be to God on high! on earth peace! good will towards men!"

Answer. "So mote it be, now, from henceforth, and for evermore."

The brethren then move in procession round the place of interment, and severally drop a sprig of evergreen into the grave, accompanied with the usual honours.

The master then concludes the ceremony at the grave, in the following words:

"From time immemorial it has been the custom among the fraternity of free and accepted masons, at the request of a brother, to accompany his corpse to the place of interment, and there to deposit his remains with the usual formalities.

"In conformity to this usage, and at the special request of our deceased brother, whose memory we revere, and whofe lofs we now deplore, we have affembled in the character of mafons, to refign his body to the earth whence it came, and to offer up to his memory, before the world, the laft tribute of our affection; thereby demonftrating the fincerity of our paft efteem, and our fteady attachment to the principles of the order.

"The great Creator having been pleafed, out of his mercy, to remove our brother from the cares and troubles of a tranfitory exiftence, to a ftate of eternal duration, and thereby to weaken the chain, by which we are united, man to man; may we, who furvive him, anticipate our approaching fate, and be more ftrongly cemented in the ties of union and friendfhip; that, during the fhort fpace allotted to our prefent exiftence, we may wifely and ufefully employ our time; and, in the reciprocal intercourfe of kind and friendly acts, mutually promote the welfare and happinefs of each other.

"Unto the grave we refign the body of our deceafed friend, there to remain until the general refurrection; in favourable expectation that his immortal foul may then partake of joys which have been prepared for the righteous from the beginning of the world. And may Almighty God, of his infinite goodnefs, at the grand tribunal of unbiaffed juftice, extend his mercy towards him, and all of us, and crown our hope with everlafting blifs in the expanded realms of a boundlefs eternity! This we beg, for the honour of his name; to whom be glory, now and forever. *Amen.*"

Thus the service ends, and the procession returns in form to the place whence it set out, where the necessary duties are complied with, and the business of masonry is renewed. The insignia and ornaments of the deceased, if an officer of a lodge, are returned to the master with the usual ceremonies, after which the charges for regulating the conduct of the brethren are rehearsed, and the lodge is closed in the third degree.

NOTES.

If a past or present grand master should join the procession of a private lodge, or deputy grand master, or a grand warden, a proper attention is to be paid to them. They take place after the master of the lodge. Two deacons with black rods are appointed by the master to attend a grand warden; and when the grand master is present, or deputy grand master, the book of constitutions is borne before him, a sword bearer follows him, and the deacons, with black rods, are placed on his right and left, at an angular distance of seven feet.

Marshals are to walk or ride, on the left of the procession.

On entering public buildings, the bible, square and compass, book of constitutions, &c. are placed before the grand master. The grand marshal and grand deacons keep near him.

CHAPTER XIII.

REMARKS ON THE SIXTH, OR MOST EXCELLENT MASTER'S DEGREE.

None but the meritorious and praiseworthy; none but those who through diligence and industry have advanced far towards perfection; none but those who have been seated in the

Oriental Chair, by the unanimous fuffrages of their brethren, can be admitted to this degree of mafonry.

In its original eftablifhment, when the temple of Jerufalem was finifhed, and the fraternity celebrated the cape-ftone with great joy, it is demonftrable that none but thofe, who had proved themfelves to be complete mafters of their profeffion, were admitted to this honour; and indeed the duties incumbent on every mafon, who is accepted and acknowledged as a moft excellent mafter, are fuch as render it indifpenfable that he fhould have a perfect knowledge of all the preceding degrees.

One of the following paffages of fcripture is rehearfed at opening, accompanied by folemn ceremonies:

Psalm xxiv.

" The earth is the Lord's, and the fulnefs thereof; the world, and they that dwell therein. For he hath founded it upon the feas, and eftablifhed it upon the floods. Who fhall afcend into the hill of the Lord? or who fhall ftand in his holy place? He that hath clean hands, and a pure heart; who hath not lifted up his foul unto vanity, nor fworn deceitfully. He fhall receive the bleffing from the Lord, and righteoufnefs from the God of his falvation. This is the generation of them that feek him, that feek thy face, O Jacob. Selah. Lift up your heads, O ye gates, and be ye lift up, ye everlafting doors, and the King of Glory fhall come in. Who is this King of Glory? The Lord, ftrong and mighty; the Lord, mighty in battle. Lift up your heads, O ye gates, even lift them up, ye everlasting doors, and the King of Glory shall come in. Who is this King of Glory? The Lord of Hosts, he is the King of Glory. Selah."

PSALM cxxii.

" I was glad when they said unto me, Let us go into the house of the Lord. Our feet shall stand within thy gates, O Jerusalem. Jerusalem is builded as a city that is compact together: whither the tribes go up, the tribes of the Lord, unto the testimony of Israel, to give thanks unto the name of the Lord. For there are set thrones of judgment, the thrones of the house of David.

" Pray for the peace of Jerusalem; they shall prosper that love thee. Peace be within thy walls, and prosperity within thy palaces. For my brethren and companions' sakes, I will now say, Peace be within thee. Because of the house of the Lord our God, I will seek thy good."

The following passages of scripture are also introduced, accompanied with solemn ceremonies.

2 CHRON. vi.

[Then said Solomon, The Lord hath said that he would dwell in the thick darkness. But I have built an house of habitation for thee, and a place for thy dwelling forever.

And the king turned his face, and blessed the whole congregation of Israel, (and all the congregation of Israel stood:) And he said, Blessed be the Lord God of Israel, who hath with his hands fulfilled that which he spake with his mouth to my father David, saying, Since the day that I brought forth my people out of the land of Egypt, I chose no city among all the tribes of Israel to build an house in, that my name might be there; neither chose I any man to be a ruler over my people Israel; but I have chosen Jerusalem, that my name might be there; and have chosen David to be over my people Israel.

Now it was in the heart of David, my father, to build an house for the name of the Lord God of Israel. But the Lord said to David my father, Forasmuch as it was in thine heart to build an house for my name, thou didst well in that it was in thine heart: notwithstanding, thou shalt not build the house; but thy son, which shall come forth out of thy loins, he shall build the house for my name. The Lord, therefore, hath performed his word that he hath spoken; for I am risen up in the room of David my father, and am set on the throne of Israel, as the Lord promised, and have built the house for the name of the Lord God of Israel: and in it have I put the ark, wherein is the covenant of the Lord, that he made with the children of Israel.

And he stood before the altar of the Lord, in the presence of all the congregation of Israel, and spread forth his hands: For Solomon had made a brazen scaffold of five cubits long, and five cubits broad, and three cubits high, and had set it in the midst of the court; and upon it he stood, and kneeled down upon his knees before all the congregation of Israel, and spread forth his hands toward heaven, and said,

O Lord God of Israel, there is no god like thee in the heaven, nor in the earth; which keepest covenant and shewest mercy unto thy servants that walk before thee with all their hearts; thou which hast kept with thy servant David my father that which thou hast promised him; and spakest with thy mouth, and hast fulfilled it with thine hand, as it is this day. Now, therefore, O Lord God of Israel, keep with thy servant David my father, that which thou hast promised him, saying, There shall not fail thee a man in my sight to sit upon the throne of Israel; yet so that thy children take heed to their way to walk in my law, as thou hast walked before me. Now then, O Lord God of Israel, let thy word be verified, which thou hast spoken unto thy servant David. (But will God in very deed dwell with men on the earth? Behold, heaven, and the heaven of heavens, cannot contain thee; how much less this house which I have builded!) Have respect, therefore, to the prayer of thy servant, and to his supplication, O Lord my God, to hearken unto the cry and the prayer which thy servant prayeth before thee: that thine eyes may be open upon this house day and night, upon the place whereof thou hast said that thou wouldest put thy name there; to hearken unto the prayer which thy servant prayeth towards this place.

Hearken, therefore, unto the supplications of thy servant, and of thy people Israel, which they shall make towards this place: hear thou from thy dwelling place, even from heaven; and, when thou hearest, forgive.]

[If a man sin against his neighbour, and an oath be laid upon him to make him swear, and the oath come before thine altar in this house. Then hear thou from heaven, and do and judge thy servants, by requiting the wicked, by recompensing his way upon his own head; and by justifying the righteous, by giving him according to his righteousness.

And if thy people Israel be put to the worse before the enemy, because they have sinned against thee, and shall return and confess thy name, and pray and make supplication before thee in this house: Then hear thou from the heavens, and forgive the sin of thy people Israel, and bring them again unto the land which thou gavest to them and to their fathers.

When the heaven is shut up, and there is no rain, because they have sinned against thee ; yet if they pray towards this place, and confess thy name, and turn from their sin when thou dost afflict them: Then hear thou from heaven, and forgive the sin of thy servants, and of thy people Israel, when thou hast taught them the good way wherein they should walk ; and send rain upon thy land, which thou hast given unto thy people for an inheritance.

If there be dearth in the land, if there be pestilence, if there be blasting or mildew, locusts or caterpillars ; if their enemies besiege them in the cities of their land ; whatsoever sore or whatsoever sickness there be · Then what prayer or what supplication soever shall be made of any man, or of all thy people Israel, when every one shall know his own sore, and his own grief, and shall spread forth his hands in this house: Then hear thou from heaven thy dwelling place, and forgive, and render unto every man according unto all his ways, whose heart thou knowest ; (for thou only knowest the hearts of the children of men:) that they may fear thee, to walk in thy ways so long as they live, in the land which thou gavest unto our fathers.

Moreover, concerning the stranger, which is not of thy people Israel, but is come from a far country for thy great name's sake, and thy mighty hand and thy stretched-out arm ; if they come and pray in this house: Then hear thou from the heavens, even from thy dwelling place, and do according to all that the stranger calleth to thee for ; that all people of the earth may know thy name, and fear thee, as doth thy people Israel ; and may know that this house, which I have built, is called by thy name.

If thy people go out to war against their enemies, by the way that thou shalt send them, and they pray unto thee toward this city which thou hast chosen, and the house which I have built for thy name: Then hear thou from the heavens their prayer and their supplication, and maintain their cause.

If they sin against thee (for there is no man which sinneth not) and thou be angry with them, and deliver them over before their enemies, and they carry them away captives unto a land far off or near ; yet if they bethink themselves in the land whither they are carried captive, and turn and pray unto thee in the land of their captivity, saying, We have sinned, we have done amiss, and have dealt wickedly ; if they return to thee with all their heart, and with all their soul, in the land of their captivity, whither they have carried them captives, and pray toward their land which thou gavest unto their fathers, and toward the city which thou hast chosen, and toward the house which I have built for thy name: Then hear thou from the heavens, even from thy dwelling place, their prayer and their supplication,

I I*

and maintain their cause, and forgive thy people which have sinned against thee..

Now, my God, let, I beseech thee, thine eyes be open, and let thine ears be attent unto the prayer that is made in this place.

Now, therefore, arise, O Lord God, into thy resting-place, thou and the ark of thy strength : let thy priests, O Lord God, be clothed with salvation, and let thy saints rejoice in goodness.

O Lord God, turn not away the face of thine anointed : remember the mercies of David thy servant.]

2 Chron. vii. 1—4.

[Now, when Solomon had made an end of praying, the fire came down from heaven, and consumed the burnt offering and the sacrifices ; and the glory of the Lord filled the house.   And the priests could not enter into the house of the Lord, because the glory of the Lord had filled the Lord's house.

And when all the children of Israel saw how the fire came down, and the glory of the Lord upon the house, they bowed themselves with their faces to the ground, upon the pavement, and worshipped, and praised the Lord, saying, For he is good ; for his mercy endureth forever.]

Charge to be delivered to a Brother, who is accepted and acknowledged as a Most Excellent Master.

" Brother,

" Your admittance to this degree of masonry is a proof of the good opinion the brethren of this lodge entertain of your masonic abilities. Let this consideration induce you to be careful of forfeiting, by misconduct and inattention to our rules, that esteem which has raised you to the rank you now possess.

" It is one of your great duties, as a most excellent master, to dispense light and truth to the uninformed mason ; and I need not remind you of the impossibility of complying with this obligation without possessing an accurate acquaintance with the lectures of each degree.

" If you are not already completely conversant in all the degrees heretofore conferred on you, remember, that an indulgence, prompted by a belief that you will apply yourself with double diligence to make yourself so, has induced the brethren to accept you.

"Let it therefore be your unremitting study to acquire such a degree of knowledge and information as shall enable you to difcharge with propriety the various duties incumbent on you, and to preferve unfullied the title now conferred upon you of a Moft Excellent Mafter."

CHAPTER XIV.

OBSERVATIONS ON THE SEVENTH, OR DEGREE OF ROYAL ARCH MASON.

THIS degree is indefcribably more auguft, fublime, and important, than all which precede it ; and is the fummit and perfection of ancient mafonry. It impreffes on our minds a belief of the being and exiftence of a Supreme Deity, without beginning of days or end of years ; and reminds us of the reverence due to his holy name.

This degree brings to light many effentials of the craft, which were for the fpace of four hundred and feventy years buried in darknefs ; and without a knowledge of which the mafonic character cannot be complete.

The following paffage of fcripture is read at opening :

2 THESSALONIANS, iii. 6—17.

"Now we command you, brethren, that ye withdraw yourfelves from every brother that walketh diforderly, and not after the tradition which ye received of us. For yourfelves know how ye ought to follow us, for we behaved ourfelves not diforderly among you. Neither did we eat any man's bread for nought, but wrought with labour and travail day and night, that we might not be chargeable to any of you. Not becaufe we have not power, but to make ourfelves an enfample unto you to follow us. For even when we were with you, this we commanded you, that if any would not work, neither fhould he eat: For we hear that there are fome who walk among you diforderly, working not at all, but are bufy-bodies. Now them that are fuch, we command and exhort, that with quietnefs they work, and eat their own bread. But ye, brethren, be not weary in well doing. And if any man obey not our word, note that man, and have no company with him, that he may be afhamed. Yet count him not as an enemy, but admonifh him as a brother. Now the Lord of peace himfelf give you peace always. The falutation of Paul, with mine own hand, which is the token: fo I write."

OBSERVATIONS ON THE SEVENTH LECTURE.

The lecture of this degree is divided into two fections, and fhould be well underftood by every royal arch mafon. Upon an accurate acquaintance with it, will depend his usefulness at our assemblies; and without it, he will be unqualified to perform the duties of the various stations in which his services may be required by the chapter.

THE FIRST SECTION

Opens to our view a large field for contemplation and study. It furnishes us with many interesting particulars relative to the state of the fraternity, during and since the reign of King Solomon; and illustrates the causes and consequences of some very important events which occurred during his reign.

This section explains the mode of government in this class of masons; it designates the appellation, number and situation of the several officers, and points out the purposes and duties of their respective stations.

THE SECOND SECTION

Contains much valuable historical information, and proves, beyond the power of contradiction, and in the most striking colours, that prosperity and happiness are ever the ultimate consequences of virtue and justice, while disgrace and ruin invariably follow the practices of vice and immorality.

A proper arrangement of the following charges, &c. is essentially necessary to be observed in every chapter; and their application should be familiar to every royal arch mason.

Isaiah xlii. 16. "I will bring the blind by a way that they knew not; I will lead them in paths that they have not known; I will make darkness light before them, and crooked things straight: These things will I do unto them, and will not forsake them."

Prayer rehearsed during the Ceremony of Exaltation to the Degree of Royal Arch Mason.

"Supreme Architect of Universal Nature, who, by thine almighty word, didst speak into being the stupendous Arch of Heaven, and for the instruction and pleasure of thy rational creatures didst adorn us with greater and lesser lights; thereby magnifying thy power, and endearing thy goodness unto the sons of men: we humbly adore and worship thine unspeakable perfection. We bless thee that when man had fallen from his innocence and his happiness, thou didst still leave unto him the powers of reasoning, and capacity of improvement and of pleasure. We thank thee that amidst the pains and calamities of our present state, so many means of refreshment and satisfaction are reserved unto us, while travelling the *rugged path of life.* Especially would we at this time render thee our thanksgiving and praise for the institution, as members of which we are at this time assembled, and for all the pleasures we have derived from it. We thank thee that the few here assembled before thee have been favoured with new inducements, and laid under new and ftronger obligations, to virtue and holinefs. May thefe obligations, O bleffed Father, have their full effect upon us. Teach us, we pray thee, the true reverence of thy great, mighty, and terrible name. Infpire us with a firm and unfhaken refolution in our virtuous purfuits. Give us grace diligently to fearch thy word in the Book of Nature, and in the holy fcriptures, wherein the duties of our high vocation are inculcated with divine authority. May the folemnity of the ceremonies of our inftitution be duly impreffed on our minds, and have a lafting and happy effect upon our lives. O thou, who didft aforetime appear unto thy fervant Mofes *in a flame of fire out of the midft of a bufh*, enkindle, we befeech thee, in each of our hearts, a flame of devotion to thee, of love to each other, and of charity to all mankind. May all thy *miracles and mighty works* fill us with the dread, and thy goodnefs imprefs us with the love, of thy holy name. May *holinefs to the Lord* be engraven on all our thoughts, words and actions. May the incenfe of piety afcend continually unto thee from the *altar* of our hearts, and burn, day and night, as a facrifice of a fweet fmelling favour, well pleafing unto thee. And fince fin has deftroyed within us the *firft temple* of purity and innocence, may thy heavenly grace guide and affift us in rebuilding a *fecond temple* of reformation, and may the glory of this latter houfe be greater than the glory of the former. *Amen.*"

Exodus iii. 1—6. "Now Mofes kept the flock of Jethro his father-in-law, the prieft of Midian; and he led the flock to the back fide of the defert, and came to the mountain of God, even to Horeb. And the angel of the Lord appeared unto him in a flame of fire out of the midft of a bufh: and he looked, and behold, the bufh burned with fire, and the bufh was not confumed. And Mofes faid, I will now turn afide, and fee this great fight, why the bufh is not burned. And when the Lord faw that he turned afide to fee, God called unto him out of the midft of the bufh, and faid, Mofes, Mofes! And he faid, Here am I. And he faid, Draw not nigh hither; put off thy fhoes from off thy feet, for the place whereon thou ftandeft is holy ground. Moreover he faid, I am the God of thy father, the God of Abraham, the God of Ifaac, and the God of Jacob. And Mofes hid his face, for he was afraid to look upon God."

2 Chron. xxxvi. 11—20. "Zedekiah was one and twenty years old when he began to reign, and reigned eleven years in Jerufalem. And he did that which was evil in the fight of the Lord his God, and humbled not himfelf before Jeremiah the prophet, fpeaking from the mouth of the Lord. And he alfo rebelled againft King Nebuchadnezzar, and ftiffened his neck, and hardened his heart, from turning unto the Lord God of Ifrael.

"Moreover all the chief of the priefts and the people tranfgreffed very much, after all the abominations of the heathen, and polluted the houfe of the Lord, which he had hallowed in Jerufalem.

And the Lord God of their fathers fent to them by his meffengers; becaufe he had compaffion on his people, and on his dwelling place. But they mocked the meffengers of God, and defpifed his words, and mifufed his prophets, until the wrath of the Lord arofe againft his people, till there was no remedy. Therefore he brought upon them the king of the Chaldees, who flew their young men with the fword, in the houfe of their fanctuary, and had no compaffion upon young man or maiden, old man, or him that ftooped for age: he gave them all into his hand. And all the veffels of the houfe of God, great and fmall, and the treafures of the houfe of the Lord, and the treafures of the king, and of his princes; all thefe he brought to Babylon. And they burnt the houfe of God, and brake down the wall of Jerufalem, and burnt all the palaces thereof with fire, and deftroyed all the goodly veffels thereof. And them that had efcaped from the fword, carried he away to Babylon; where they were fervants to him and his fons, until the reign of the kingdom of Perfia."

Ezra i. 1—3. "Now in the firft year of Cyrus, king of Perfia, the Lord ftirred up the fpirit of Cyrus, king of Perfia, that he made a proclamation throughout all his kingdom, and put it alfo in writing, faying, Thus faith Cyrus, king of Perfia, The Lord God of Heaven hath given me all the kingdoms of the earth, and he hath charged me to build him an houfe at Jerufalem, which is in Judah. Who is there among you of all his people? his God be with him, and let him

I 2

go up to Jerufalem which is in Judah, and build the houfe of the Lord God of Ifrael, which is in Jerufalem."

Exodus iii. 13, 14. " And Mofes faid unto God, Behold, when I come unto the children of Ifrael, and fhall fay unto them, The God of your fathers hath fent me unto you; and they fhall fay to me, What is his name? what fhall I fay unto them?

" And God faid unto Mofes, I AM THAT I AM: And thus fhalt thou fay unto the children of Ifrael, I AM hath fent me unto you."

Pfalm cxli. " Lord, I cry unto thee: make hafte unto me: give ear unto my voice. Let my prayer be fet forth before thee as incenfe, and the lifting up of my hands as the evening facrifice. Set a watch, O Lord, before my mouth: keep the door of my lips. Incline not my heart to any evil thing, to practife wicked work with men that work iniquity. Let the righteous fmite me, it fhall be a kindnefs; and let him reprove me, it fhall be an excellent oil. Mine eyes are unto thee, O God the Lord: in thee is my truft; leave not my foul deftitute. Keep me from the fnares which they have laid for me, and the gins of the workers of iniquity, Let the wicked fall into their own nets, while that I withal efcape."

Pfalm cxlii. " I cried unto the Lord with my voice; with my voice unto the Lord did I make my fupplication. I poured out my complaint before him: I fhowed before him my trouble. When my fpirit was overwhelmed within me, then thou kneweft my path: in the way wherein

I walked have they privily laid a fnare for me. I looked on my right hand, and beheld, but there was no man that would know me : refuge failed me : no man cared for my foul. I cried unto thee, O Lord : I faid, Thou art my refuge, and my portion in the land of the living. Attend unto my cry ; for I am brought very low : deliver me from my perfecutors ; for they are ftronger than I. Bring my foul out of darknefs, that I may praife thy name."

Pfalm cxliii. "Hear my prayer, O Lord; give ear to my fupplications : in thy faithfulnefs anfwer me, and in thy righteoufnefs. And enter not into judgment with thy fervant : for in thy fight fhall no man living be juftified. For the enemy hath perfecuted my foul ; he hath fmitten my life down to the ground : he hath made me to dwell in darknefs. Therefore is my fpirit overwhelmed within me : my heart within me is defolate. Hear me fpeedily, O Lord; my fpirit faileth ; hide not thy face from me, left I be like unto them that go down into the pit. Caufe me to hear thy loving kindnefs in the morning ; for in thee do I truft : caufe me to know the way wherein I fhould walk ; for I lift up my foul unto thee. Teach me to do thy will ; for thou art my God : bring my foul out of trouble, and of thy mercy cut off mine enemies, for I am thy fervant."

Exodus iv. 1—10. "And Mofes anfwered and faid, But behold, they will not believe me, nor hearken unto my voice : for they will fay, The Lord hath not appeared unto thee. And the Lord faid unto him, What is that in thine hand ?

And he said, A rod. And he said, Caft it on the ground ; and he caft it on the ground, and it became a ferpent ; and Mofes fled from before it. And the Lord faid unto Mofes, Put forth thine hand, and take it by the tail. And he put forth his hand, and caught it, and it became a rod in his hand. That they may believe that the Lord God of your fathers, the God of Abraham, the God of Ifaac, and the God of Jacob, hath appeared unto thee.

"And the Lord faid furthermore unto him, Put now thine hand into thy bofom : and he put his hand into his bofom ; and when he took it out, behold, his hand was leprous as fnow. And he faid, Put thine hand into thy bofom again : and he put his hand into his bofom again, and plucked it out of his bofom, and, behold, it was turned again as his other flefh. And it fhall come to pafs, if they will not believe thee, neither hearken to the voice of the firft fign, that they will believe the voice of the latter fign.

"And it fhall come to pafs, if they will not believe alfo thefe two figns, neither hearken unto thy voice, that thou fhalt take of the water of the river, and pour it upon the dry land : and the water which thou takeft out of the river, fhall become blood upon the dry land."

Haggai ii. 1—9, 23. "In the feventh month, in the one and twentieth day of the month, came the word of the Lord by the prophet Haggai, faying, Speak now to Zerubbabel the fon of Shealtiel, governor of Judah, and to Jofhua the fon of Jofedech, the high prieft, and to the refidue of the people, faying, Who is left among

you that faw this houfe in her firft glory? and
how do you fee it now? is it not in your eyes
in comparifon of it as nothing? Yet now be
ftrong, O Zerubbabel, and be ftrong, O Jofhua,
fon of Jofedech the high prieft, and be ftrong all
ye people of the land, and work; for I am with
you, according to the word which I covenanted
with you when ye came out of Egypt, fo my
fpirit remaineth among you: fear ye not. For
thus faith the Lord of Hofts, Yet once, it is a
little while, and I will fhake the heavens, and the
earth, and the fea, and the dry land: and I will
fhake all nations, and the defire of all nations
fhall come, and I will fill this houfe with glory.
The filver is mine, and the gold is mine. The
glory of this latter houfe fhall be greater than of
the former, and in this place will I give peace.
"In that day will I take thee, O Zerubbabel,
my fervant, the fon of Shealtiel, faith the Lord,
and will make thee as a fignet: for I have chofen
thee."

Zechariah iv. 6—10. "This is the word of
the Lord unto Zerubbabel, faying, Not by might
nor power, but by my fpirit. Who art thou, O
great mountain? before Zerubbabel thou fhalt
become a plain, and he fhall bring forth the head
ftone thereof with fhouting, crying Grace, grace,
unto it. Moreover the word of the Lord came
unto me, faying, The hands of Zerubbabel have
laid the foundation of this houfe, his hands fhall
alfo finifh it; and thou fhalt know that the Lord
of Hofts hath fent me unto you. For who hath
defpifed the day of fmall things? for they fhall

12*

rejoice, and fhall fee the plummet in the hands of Zerubbabel with thofe feven."

John i. 1—5. "In the beginning was the Word, and the Word was with God, and the Word was God. The fame was in the beginning with God. All things were made by him; and without him was not any thing made that was made. In him was life, and the life was the light of men. And the light fhineth in darknefs, and the darknefs comprehendeth it not."

Deuter. xxxi. 24—26. "And it came to pafs, when Mofes had made an end of writing the words of this law in a book, until they were finifhed, that Mofes commanded the Levites which bare the ark of the covenant of the Lord, faying, Take this book of the law, and put it in the fide of the ark of the covenant of the Lord your God, that it may be there for a witnefs againft thee."

Exodus xxv. 21. "And thou fhalt put the mercy feat above, upon the ark; and in the ark thou fhalt put the teftimony that I fhall give thee."

Exodus xvi. 32—34. "And Mofes faid, This is the thing which the Lord commandeth: Fill an omer of the manna, to be kept for your generations; that they may fee the bread wherewith I have fed you in the wildernefs, when I brought you forth from the land of Egypt. And Mofes faid unto Aaron, Take a pot, and put an omer full of manna therein, and lay it up before the Lord, to be kept for your generations. As the Lord commanded Mofes, fo Aaron laid it up before the teftimony to be kept."

Numbers xvii. 10. "And the Lord said unto Mofes, Bring Aaron's rod again before the teftimony, to be kept for a token."

Hebrews ix. 2—5. "For there was a tabernacle made, the firft, wherein was the candleftick, and the table, and the fhewbread; which is called The Sanctuary. And after the vails, the tabernacle, which is called The Holieft of all; which had the golden cenfer, and the ark of the covenant overlaid round about with gold, wherein was alfo the golden pot that had manna, and Aaron's rod that budded, and the tables of the covenant; and over it the cherubims of glory, fhadowing the mercy feat; of which we cannot now fpeak particularly."

Amos ix. 11. "In that day will I raife up the tabernacle of David that is fallen, and clofe up the breaches thereof, and I will raife up his ruins; and I will build it as in the days of old."

Exodus vi. 2, 3. "And God fpake unto Mofes, and faid unto him, I am the Lord; and I appeared unto Abraham, unto Ifaac, and unto Jacob, by the name of God Almighty, but by my name JEHOVAH was I not known to them."

The following particulars, relative to King Solomon's Temple, may with propriety be here introduced, and cannot be uninterefting to a royal arch mafon.

This famous fabric was fituated on Mount Moriah, near the place where Abraham was about to offer up his fon Ifaac, and where David met and appeafed the deftroying angel. It was begun in the fourth year of the reign of Solomon; the third after the death of David;

four hundred and eighty years after the passage
of the Red Sea, and on the second day of the
month Zif, being the second month of the sacred year, which answers to the 21st of April,
in the year of the world 2992, and was carried
on with such prodigious speed, that it was finished, in all its parts, in little more than seven
years.

By the masonic art, and the wise regulations
of Solomon, every part of the building, whether
of stone, brick, timber or metal, was wrought
and prepared before they were brought to Jerusalem; so that the only tools made use of in
erecting the fabric were wooden instruments
prepared for that purpose. The noise of the axe,
the hammer, and every other tool of metal, was
confined to the forests of Lebanon, where the
timber was procured, and to Mount Libanus,
and the plains and quarries of Zeredathah, where
the stones were raised, squared, marked and
numbered; that nothing might be heard among
the masons at Jerusalem but harmony and peace.

In the year of the world 3029, King Solomon
died, and was succeeded by his son Rehoboam,
who, immediately after the death of his father,
went down to Shechem, where the chiefs of the
people were met together to proclaim him king.

When Jeroboam, the son of Nebat, who was
in Egypt, whither he had fled from the presence
of Solomon, and whose ambition had long aspir-
ed to the throne, heard of the death of the king,
he hastened to return from Egypt, to put himself
at the head of the discontented tribes, and lead
them on to rebellion. He accordingly assembled

them together, and came to king Rehoboam,
and spake to him after this manner :
" Thy father made our yoke grievous ; now,
therefore, eafe thou fomewhat the grievous fer-
vitude of thy father, and his heavy yoke that he
put upon us, and we will ferve thee. And he
faid unto them, Come again unto me after three
days. And the people departed. And king
Rehoboam took counfel with the old men that
had ftood before Solomon his father while he
yet lived, faying, What counfel give ye me, to
return anfwer to this people ? And they fpake
unto him, faying, If thou be kind to this people, and pleafe them, and fpeak good words to
them, they will be thy fervants forever. But
he forfook the counfel which the old men gave
him, and took counfel with the young men that
were brought up with him, that ftood before
him. And he faid unto them, what advice give
ye, that we may return anfwer to this people,
which have fpoken to me, faying, Eafe fomewhat the yoke that thy father did put upon us ?
And the young men that were brought up with
him fpake unto him, faying, Thus fhalt thou
anfwer the people that fpake unto thee, faying,
Thy father made our yoke heavy, but make
thou it fomewhat lighter for us ; thus fhalt
thou fay unto them, My little finger fhall be
thicker than my father's loins. For, whereas
my father put a heavy yoke upon you, I will
put more to your yoke : my father chaftifed
you with whips, but I will chaftife you with
fcorpions. So Jeroboam and all the people
came to Rehoboam on the third day, as the

king bade, faying, Come again to me on the third day. And the king anfwered them roughly; and king Rehoboam forfook the counfel of the old men, and anfwered them after the advice of the young men, faying, My father made your yoke heavy, but I will add thereto: my father chaftifed you with whips, but I will chaftife you with fcorpions. And when all Ifrael faw that the king would not hearken unto them, the people anfwered the king, faying, What portion have we in David? and we have none inheritance in the fon of Jeffe; every man to your tents, O Ifrael; and now, David, fee to thine own houfe. So all Ifrael went to their tents."

See 2 Chron. chap x.

But as for the children of Ifrael that dwelt in the cities of Judah and Benjamin, Rehoboam reigned over them.

In this manner were the tribes of Ifrael divided, and under two diftinct governments, for 254 years, when the ten revolted tribes, having become weak and degenerated, by following the wickednefs and idolatry of the kings who governed them, fell a prey to Salmanezer, king of Affyria, who in the reign of Hofhea, king of Ifrael, befieged the city of Samaria, laid their country wafte, and utterly extirpated their government. Such was the wretched fate of a people who difdained fubjection to the laws of the houfe of David, and whofe impiety and effeminacy ended in their deftruction.

After a feries of changes and events, of which an account may be found in the hiftory of the Temple, Nebuchadnezzar, king of Babylon, with his forces, took poffeffion of Jerufalem, and having made captive Jehoiachim the king of Judah, elevated his uncle Zedekiah to the throne, after binding him by a folemn oath neither to make innovations in the government, nor to take part with the Egyptians in their wars againft Babylon. At the end of eight years, Zedekiah violated his oath to Nebuchadnezzar, by forming a treaty offenfive and defenfive with the Egyptians; thinking that jointly they could fubdue the king of Babylon. Nebuchadnezzar immediately marched, and ravaged Zedekiah's country, feized his caftle and fortrefs, and proceeded to the fiege of Jerufalem. Pharaoh, learning how Zedekiah was preffed, advanced to his relief, with a view of raifing the fiege. Nebuchadnezzar, having intimation thereof, would not wait his approach, but proceeded to give him battle, and in one conteft drove him out of Syria. This circumftance fufpended the fiege.

In the ninth year of Zedekiah's reign, the king of Babylon again befieged Jerufalem, with a large army, and for a year and a half exerted all his ftrength to conquer it; but the city did not yield, though enfeebled by famine and peftilence.

In the eleventh year, the fiege went on vigoroufly; the Babylonians completed their works, having raifed towers all round the city, fo as to drive the invaded party from its walls. The place, though a prey to plague and famine, was obftinately defended during the fpace of a year and a half. But at length want of provifions and forces compelled its furrender, and it was

accordingly delivered, at midnight, to the officers of Nebuchadnezzar.

Zedekiah, feeing the troops enter the temple,
abfconded by a narrow pafs to the defert, with
his officers and friends ; but advice of his efcape
being given to the Babylonians, they purfued
them early in the morning, and furrounded them
near Jerico, where they were bound and carried
before the king, who ordered his wives and children to be put to death in his fight, and then
ordered Zedekiah's eyes to be put out, and himfelf conducted in chains to Babylon.

After this victory, Nebuchadnezzar difpatch-
ed his principal officer, Nebuzaradan, to Jerufalem, to ranfack and burn both palace and temple, to raze the city to the ground, and conduct
the captive inhabitants to Babylon ; this order
he accordingly executed. Among the captives
were the following perfons of eminence : Serai-
ah, the high prieft ; Zephaniah, next in rank ;
the fecretary to the king ; three principal keepers of the temple ; feven of the king's chofen
friends, and other perfons of diftinction.

In the feventieth year of the captivity of the
Jews, and the firft of the reign of Cyrus, king
of Perfia, he iffued his famous edict, purporting
that the God adored by the Ifraelites was the
eternal being through whofe bounty he enjoyed
the regal dignity, and that he had found himfelf
honourably mentioned by the prophets of ancient date as the perfon who fhould caufe Jerufalem to be rebuilt, and reftore the Hebrews to
their former ftate of grandeur and independen-
cy ; he therefore gave orders for the releafe of

the captives, with his permiffion to return to their own native country, to rebuild the city; and the houfe of the Lord.

The principal people of the tribes of Judah and Benjamin, with the priefts and Levites, immediately departed for Jerufalem, and commenced the undertaking; but many of the Jews determined to remain in Babylon, rather than relinquifh the poffeffions they had obtained in that city.

Charge to a newly exalted Companion.

"WORTHY COMPANION,

"By the confent and affiftance of the members of this chapter, you are now exalted to the fublime and honourable degree of a royal arch mafon. Having attained this degree, you have arrived at the fummit and perfection of ancient mafonry; and are confequently entitled to a full explanation of the myfteries of the order.

"The rites and myfteries developed in this degree have been handed down through a chofen few, unchanged by time, and uncontrouled by prejudice: and we expect and truft they will be regarded by you with the fame veneration, and tranfmitted with the fame fcrupulous purity to your fucceffors.

"No one can reflect on the ceremonies of gaining admiffion into this place, without being

13

forcibly struck with the important lessons which they teach.

"Here we are necessarily led to contemplate with gratitude and admiration the sacred source from whence all earthly comforts flow; here we find additional inducements to continue steadfast and immoveable in the discharge of our respective duties; and here we are bound, by the most solemn ties, to promote each other's welfare, and correct each other's failings, by advice, admonition, and reproof.

"As it is our most earnest desire, and a duty we owe to our companions of this order, that the admission of every candidate into this chapter should be attended by the approbation of the most scrutinizing eye, we hope always to possess the satisfaction of finding none among us, but such as will promote to the utmost of their power the great end of our institution. By paying due attention to this determination, we expect you will never recommend any candidate to this chapter, whose abilities and knowledge of the foregoing degrees you cannot freely vouch for, and whom you do not firmly and confidently believe will fully conform to the principles of our order, and fulfil the obligations of a royal arch mason. While such are our members, we may expect to be united in one object, without lukewarmness, inattention or neglect; and that zeal, fidelity and affection will be the distinguishing characteristics of our society, and that satisfaction, harmony and peace be enjoyed at our meetings, which no other society can afford."

Closing.

The chapter is closed with solemn ceremonies; and the following prayer is rehearsed, by the most excellent high priest:

" By the *Wisdom* of the Supreme High Priest may we be directed, by his *Strength* may we be enabled, and by the *Beauty* of virtue may we be incited, to perform the obligations here enjoined on us, to keep inviolably the mysteries here unfolded to us, and invariably to practise all those duties *out* of the chapter, which are inculcated in it."

Response. *So mote it be. Amen.*

⸻○⸺

After these observations, little more can be wanted to encourage the zealous mason to persevere in his researches. Whoever has traced the art in regular progression from the commencement of the first to the conclusion of the seventh degree, according to the plan here laid down, will have amassed an ample store of useful learning; and must reflect with pleasure on the good effects of his past diligence and attention; while, by applying the whole to the general advantage of society, he will observe method in the proper distribution of what he has acquired, and secure to himself the veneration of masons, and the approbation of all good men.

CHAPTER XV.

OBSERVATIONS ON THE ORDER OF HIGH PRIEST.

THIS order appertains to the office of High Prieſt of a Royal Arch Chapter, and no one can be legally entitled to receive it until he has been elected to ſuſtain that office in ſome regular chapter of Royal Arch Maſons.

The following paſſages of ſcripture are made uſe of during the ceremonies appertaining to this order, viz.

Gen. xiv. 12—24. "And they took Lot, Abram's brother's ſon, (who dwelt in Sodom) and his goods, and departed. And there came one, that had eſcaped, and told Abram the Hebrew; for he dwelt in the plain of Mamre the Amorite, brother of Eſhcol, and brother of Aner: and theſe were confederate with Abram. And when Abram heard that his brother was taken captive, he armed his trained ſervants, born in his own houſe, three hundred and eighteen, and purſued them unto Dan. And he divided himſelf againſt them, he and his ſervants, by night, and ſmote them, and purſued them unto Hobah, which is on the left hand of Damaſcus. And he brought back all the goods, and alſo brought again his brother Lot, and his goods, and the women alſo, and the people. And the king of Sodom went out to meet him (after his return from the ſlaughter of Chedorlaomer, and of the kings that were with him) at the valley of Shevch, which is the king's dale. And Melchifedec, king of Salem, brought forth bread and wine: and he was the prieft of the Moft High God. And he bleffed him, and faid, Bleffed be Abram of the Moft High God, poffeffor of heaven and earth: and bleffed be the Moft High God, which hath delivered thine enemies into thy hand. And he gave him tithes of all. And the king of Sodom faid unto Abram, Give me the perfons, and take the goods to thyfelf. And Abram faid to the king of Sodom, I have lifted up mine hand unto the Lord, the Moft High God, the poffeffor of heaven and earth, that I will not take from a thread even to a fhoe-latchet, and that I will not take any thing that is thine, left thou fhouldeft fay, I have made Abram rich : Save only that which the young men have eaten, and the portion of the men which went with me, Aner, Efhcol and Mamre; let them take their portion."

Numb. vi. 22—26. "And the Lord fpake unto Mofes, faying, Speak unto Aaron, and unto his fons, faying, On this wife ye fhall blefs the children of Ifrael, faying unto them, The Lord blefs thee, and keep thee; the Lord make his face fhine upon thee, and be gracious unto thee ; the Lord lift up his countenance upon thee, and give thee peace."

Heb. vii. 1—6. "For this Melchifedec, king of Salem, prieft of the Moft High God, (who met Abraham returning from the flaughter of the kings, and bleffed him ; to whom alfo Abraham gave a tenth part of all ;) abideth a prieft continually. Now confider how great this man

13*

was, unto whom even the patriarch Abraham gave the tenth of the spoils. And verily they that are of the sons of Levi, who receive the office of the priesthood, have a commandment to take tithes of the people according to the law, that is, of their brethren, though they come out of the loins of Abraham."

"For he testifieth, Thou art a priest forever, after the order of Melchisedec.

"And inasmuch as not without an oath he was made priest."

"For those priests (*under the Levitical law*) were made without an oath; but this with an oath, by him that said unto him, The Lord sware and will not repent, Thou art a priest forever, after the order of Melchisedec."

FREEMASON'S MONITOR.

PART FIRST.

BOOK II.

CHAPTER I.

Of the Government of Royal Arch Chapters.

THE firft three degrees of mafonry are holden under the authority of *Grand Lodges*, compofed of the mafter and wardens of all the lodges within a certain diftrict, together with the proper grand officers; the organization of which will be noticed in another part of this work.

In like manner chapters of royal arch mafons, with power to confer the preparatory degrees of mark mafter, paft mafter, and moft excellent mafter, are holden under the authority of grand chapters, compofed of the three principal officers of all the royal arch chapters within a certain diftrict, together with the proper grand officers.

Until the year 1797, no grand chapter of royal arch mafons was organized in America. Previoufly to this period, a competent number of companions of that degree, poffeffed of fufficient abilities, under the fanction of a mafter's warrant, proceeded to exercife the rights and privileges of royal arch chapters, whenever they thought it expedient and proper; although in most cases the approbation of a neighbouring chapter was deemed useful if not essential.

This unrestrained mode of proceeding was subject to many inconveniences; unsuitable characters might be admitted; irregularities in the mode of working introduced; the purposes of the society perverted; and thus the order degraded, by falling into the hands of those who might be regardless of the reputation of the institution. If differences should arise between two chapters, who was to decide upon them? If unworthy characters, who for want of due caution had gained admission, should attempt to open new chapters, for their own emolument, or for the purposes of conviviality or intemperance, who was to restrain them? If the established regulations and ancient landmarks should be violated or broken down, where was there power sufficient to remedy the evil?

Sensible of the existence of these and many other inconveniences, to which the order were subjected, the chapters of royal arch masons, in various parts of the United States, have, within a few years past, taken the proper and necessary measures for forming and establishing grand royal arch chapters, for their better government and regulation.

On the 24th of October, 1797, a convention of delegates, from several chapters in the northern states, assembled at Masons Hall, in Boston; being appointed (as expressed in their credentials) "to meet with any or every chapter of royal arch masons, within the states of New-

Hampshire, Massachusetts, Rhode-Island, Connecticut, Vermont, and New-York; or with any committee or committees, duly appointed and authorized by any or all of said chapters, and to deliberate upon the propriety and expediency of forming and establishing a grand chapter of royal arch masons, for the government and regulation of the several chapters within the said states."

M. E. THOMAS SMITH WEBB was chosen Chairman.

Comp. WILLIAM WOART, Scribe.

The convention, having taken the matter into consideration, came to a determination to forward to each of the chapters within the six states, before mentioned, a circular letter, expressive of their opinions on the subject, which letter was in the words following, viz.

(CIRCULAR.)

BOSTON, OCT. 24, 1797.

"COMPANIONS,

"FROM time immemorial, we find that Grand Lodges of Free and Accepted Masons have been established wherever masonry has flourished; for the purpose of granting warrants for instituting private Lodges, as well as for establishing certain general rules and regulations for the government of the same.

"It is an opinion generally received, and we think well authenticated, that no grand lodge of master masons can claim or exercise authority over any convention or chapter of *Royal Arch Masons*; nor can any chapter, although of standing immemorial, exercise the authority of a grand chapter: We therefore think it highly expedient for the regular government of all chapters within the said states, who exercise the rights and privileges of *Royal Arch Masons*, and to prevent irregularities in the propagation and use of those rights and privileges, that there should be a *Grand Chapter of Royal Arch Masons* established within the said states: And whereas this convention has received official information from our companions at Philadelphia, that the several chapters within their vicinity have recently assembled, and established a *Grand Chapter of Royal Arch Masons* for their government; in conformity to their example, we think it our duty to recommend to the several chapters within the said states of New-Hampshire, Massachusetts, Rhode-Island, Connecticut, Vermont and New-York, to unite and form a *Grand Chapter* for the said states.

"The local situation of the states before mentioned, the easy and frequent intercourse between their several principal towns and cities, as well as the similarity of habits, manners and customs, as citizens and as masons, which prevail throughout the said states, induce us to believe that a union of all the chapters therein in one *Grand Chapter* will have the most useful, lasting and happy effects in the uniform distribution and propagation of the sublime degrees of Masonry. They therefore take the liberty of recommending to the consideration of your Most Excellent Chapter, the propriety of appointing one or more delegate or delegates, to represent your chapter, at a meeting of the several chapters before mentioned, to be holden at the city of Hartford, in the state of Connecticut, on the fourth Wednesday of January next ensuing; investing them with full power and authority, in conjunction with the other delegates, to form and open a *Grand Chapter* of *Royal Arch Masons*, and to establish a Constitution for the government and regulation of all the chapters that now are, or may hereafter be, erected within the said states."

In consequence of this address, the several chapters within the states therein enumerated (with the exception of two or three chapters only) appointed delegates, who assembled at Hartford, on the fourth Wednesday in January, 1798, and after several days deliberation upon the subject they formed and adopted a constitution for the government of the royal arch chapters, and lodges of mark masters, past masters, and most excellent masters, throughout the said states; and having elected and installed their grand officers, the grand chapter became completely organized.

CHAPTER II.

Powers vested in the General Grand Officers.

AGREEABLY to the General Grand Royal Arch Conſtitution, Grand Royal Arch Chapters were eſtabliſhed in the ſeveral Northern States, where there were royal arch chapters exiſting ; and in every inſtance the private chapters have united with, and acknowledged the authority of, the ſaid grand chapters.

The long deſired and neceſſary authority for correcting abuſes, and regulating the concerns, of royal arch maſonry, in the northern ſtates, being thus happily eſtabliſhed, the ſublime degrees ſoon became flouriſhing and reſpectable. Royal arch maſons in the ſouthern ſtates (where there were no grand chapters) obſerved with pleaſure and ſatisfaction the eſtabliſhment of grand chapters in the northern ſtates, under the authority of a general conſtitution, and became deſirous of uniting with them, under the ſame authority. Applications were accordingly made for the privilege of opening new chapters in the ſouthern ſtates ; but there being no proviſion made in the conſtitution 'for extending its authority beyond the limits firſt contemplated, the ſtate grand chapters took the ſubject into conſideration, and paſſed a concurrent decree, veſting power and authority in the three firſt general grand officers, or any two of them, conjointly, to grant and iſſue letters of diſpenſation for the inſtitution of lodges of mark maſters, paſt maſ-

ters, moſt excellent maſters, and chapters of royal arch maſons, within any ſtate in which there
was not a grand chapter eſtabliſhed.   By virtue
of this authority, on the firſt day of December,
1804, the general grand officers granted a letter
of diſpenſation for forming and holding a chapter of royal arch maſons in the city of Savannah,
in the ſtate of Georgia, by the name of GEORGIA
CHAPTER ; and on the firſt day of March, 1805,
they granted a letter of diſpenſation for forming
and opening a new royal arch chapter in the
town of Beaufort, in the ſtate of South Carolina, by the name of UNITY CHAPTER.

At the ſucceeding meeting of the general grand
royal arch chapter, the powers before mentioned were confirmed and made permanent in the
general grand officers, by the ninth ſection of
the firſt article of the general conſtitution ; and
the proceedings of the general grand officers
under the decree before mentioned were approved and confirmed.

CHAPTER III.

THE GENERAL GRAND CHAPTER.

On the ninth day of January, 1799, the grand
chapter of the northern ſtates met, by adjournment, at Providence, in the ſtate of Rhode-
Iſland, and reviſed their conſtitution.

The ſecond ſection of the firſt article of the
conſtitution, as reviſed, directed that the general

grand chapter fhould convene feptennially, for the choice of officers, and other bufinefs. A meeting was accordingly holden at the city of Middletown, (Conn.) commencing on the 9th day of January, A. D. 1806.

Prefent,

Reprefentatives from the refpective grand chapters of the ftates of Rhode-Ifland, Connecticut, New-York and Vermont.

The general grand chapter refolved itfelf into a committee of the whole upon the general grand royal arch conftitution, when fundry alterations and amendments were propofed and confidered, and afterwards ratified and confirmed, by the general grand chapter.

Among other amendments of the conftitution was the following, viz. The ftyle or title to be " The General Grand Royal Arch Chapter of the United States." The jurifdiction was declared to extend throughout the United States, and to any ftate or territory wherein no grand chapter was regularly eftablifhed.

A communication was prefented from Rutland, in the ftate of Vermont, informing this general grand chapter of the formation of a grand royal arch chapter in the faid ftate, and fubjoining a copy of their regulations, and alfo a certificate of the appointment of a proxy for the grand high prieft of the faid grand chapter.

A communication was alfo received from the fecretary of the grand chapter of the ftate of New-York, containing the report of a committee appointed by the faid grand chapter upon the subject of the formation of a grand chapter in the state of Vermont.

The two communications before mentioned having been read and confidered, it was refolved, That this general grand chapter admit, and they do hereby admit, the faid grand chapter of Vermont, into a union with us, under the general grand royal arch conftitution.

A communication was received from the general grand king, and the general grand fcribe, ftating, that by virtue of authority derived from a fpecial decree of feveral of the ftate grand chapters, they had conjointly iffued a warrant for inftituting a chapter of royal arch mafons in the town of *Beaufort*, in the ftate of South Carolina, by the name of " *Unity Chapter* ;" and alfo another warrant for inftituting a chapter of royal arch mafons, in the city of *Savannah*, in the ftate of Georgia, by the name of " *Georgia Chapter*."

Whereupon it was refolved, That this general grand chapter do approve of the proceedings of the general grand king, and the general grand fcribe, relative to the formation of *Unity Chapter*, in *Beaufort*, and *Georgia Chapter*, in *Savannah* ; and that their refpective warrants be confirmed, and made permanent, by either of the aforenamed general grand officers.

A committee was appointed, confifting of the general grand king, and the general grand fecretary, to tranfcribe, and procure to be printed, a fuitable number of copies of the conftitution, and tranfmit them to the feveral ftates.

The general grand chapter proceeded to a choice of officers, agreeably to the conftitution, when the companions, whose names follow, were elected to the offices annexed to their respective names, viz.

M. E. *Benjamin Hurd*, jun. Esq. of Charlestown, (Mass.) *General Grand High Priest.*

M. E. *Thomas S. Webb*, Esq. of Boston, (Mass.) *General Grand King.*

M. E. *Ezra Ames*, of Albany, (N. Y.) *General Grand Scribe.*

E. *Otis Ammidon*, of Providence, (R. I.) *General Grand Secretary.*

E. *James Harrison*, of Boston, (Mass.) *General Grand Treasurer.*

E. and Rev. *Jonathan Nye*, of New Fane, (Vermont) *General Grand Chaplain.*

E. *Joseph Huntingdon*, of Norwich, (Conn.) *General Grand Marshal.*

Agreeably to the powers vested in the general grand officers by the ninth section of the first article of the constitution, the general grand high priest and general grand king issued a charter for the establishment of a royal arch chapter in the town of Hanover, in the state of New-Hampshire, by the name of *St. Andrew's Chapter*, dated the twenty sixth day of January, A. D. 1807. They also issued a charter for the establishment of a royal arch chapter in the town of Hopkinton, in the state of New-Hampshire, by the name of *Trinity Chapter*, dated the sixteenth day of February, A. D. 1807.

Resolved, That the next septennial meeting of the general grand chapter be holden in the city of New-York, on the second Thursday in September, A. D. 1812.

The cafualties of war having prevented the feptennial meeting which was to have been holden on the fecond Thurfday in September, 1812, the prefiding officers, after the return of peace, agreeably to the powers vefted in them by the 3d Sect. 1ft Art. of the Conftitution, caufed notice to be iffued for convening a fpecial meeting of the General Grand Chapter, in the city of New-York, on Thurfday, the 6th of June, A. D. 1816.

PROCEEDINGS

OF THE

General Grand Royal Arch Chapter.

PURSUANT to special notice, the General Grand Royal Arch Chapter of the United States assembled at New-York, in the State of New-York, on Thursday, June 6, 5816.

General Grand Officers present, to wit :

M. E. THOMAS S. WEBB, Esq. General Grand King.
M. E. EZRA AMES, Esq. G. G. Scribe.
E. and Rev. JONATHAN NYE, G. G. Chaplain.

The General G. Secretary being absent, the M. E. G. G. King was pleased to appoint M. E. JOHN ABBOT, Esq. G. G. Secretary pro tem.

The following Companions appeared, and presented credentials as officers and proxies of officers of the several State Grand Chapters, to wit :

From Massachusetts.

M. E. JOHN ABBOT, Esq. G. H. Priest.
M. E. HENRY FOWLE, G. King.

From Rhode-Island.

M. E. WILLIAM WILKINSON, Esq. D. G. H. Priest.
E. SETH PECK, Esq. Grand Scribe.
E. CALEB EARLE, Esq. as proxy of JOHN CARLILE, G. H. Priest.
E. PETER GRINNELL, Esq. as proxy of JOHN DAVIS, G. King.

From New-York.

M. E. EZRA AMES, Esq. G. H. Priest.
M. E. JOEL HART, Esq. D. G. H. Priest.
E. JOSEPH ENOS, G. K.
E. JOHN BRUSH, G. S.

From Connecticut.

E. JOHN H. LYNDE, Esq. G. King.

From Vermont.

M. E. CHARLES K. WILLIAMS, Esq. G. H. Priest. He also appeared as proxy of
E. JOSIAH DUNHAM, D. G. H. Priest.
E. JEDUTHUN LOOMIS, G. K.
E. ELIJAH BUCK, G. S.

From South Carolina.

M. E. THOMAS S. WEBB, Esq. as proxy of
M. E. WILLIAM YOUNG, G. H. Priest,
E. FOSTER BURNET, as proxy of BENJAMIN PHILLIPS, G. Scribe.

From Maryland.

The following Companions appeared as delegates from the Grand Chapter of the State of Maryland, *to wit:*

M. E. PHILIP P. ECKEL, Esq. G. H. Priest.
E. BENJAMIN EDES, Esq. G. Secretary.

The foregoing credentials being presented to the G. G. Secretary pro tem. the M. E. G. G. King was thereupon pleased to appoint M. E. G. G. Scribe, and M. E. G. G. Chaplain, as a committee to examine the said credentials, who, after examination of the same, reported, that the foregoing Companions, from the States of Massachusetts, Rhode-Island, New-York, Connecticut, Vermont and South Carolina, are duly qualified to sit and act in the said G. G. R. A. Chapter; and that the said Companions from the said State of Maryland are duly qualified as delegates.

Voted to adjourn to 4 o'clock in the afternoon.

Attest.   JOHN ABBOT, G. G. Sec. pro tem.

June 6, 5816, 4, P. M. Met according to adjournment. The M. E. G. G. King having been pleased to appoint Companion JOSEPH JACOBS, G. G. Tyler; and the G. Grand Royal Arch Chapter having in due form been opened, the minutes of the forenoon being read, voted to accept the same.

The M. E. G. G. King directed the G. G. R. A. Constitution to be read, which was done by the G. G. Secretary pro tem. accordingly.

Certain letters and documents from the G. G. H. Priest, King and Scribe, respectively, relative to the G. G. Chapter's not meeting in September, A. L. 5812, being read, voted to commit the same to

14*

Companions JONATHAN NYE, HENRY FOWLE and CHARLES K. WILLIAMS, who afterwards reported as follows:

"That the situation of the country was such at that time as to render it highly inconvenient for the G. G. Chapter then to convene; and the meeting having been prevented by a casualty such as is contemplated by the 8th section of the first article of the G. G. R. A. Constitution, your Committee are unanimously of opinion, that the present meeting is holden in pursuance of the said Constitution, and is legally competent to do and transact any business which may come before them."   J. NYE, per order.

Which report being read, voted to accept the same.

On motion, voted that a committee of one Companion from each State represented, be raised to report what alterations or explanations, if any, are necessary to be made in the Constitution of the G. G. Chapter. Companions JOHN ABBOT, WILLIAM WILKINSON, JOHN BRUSH, JOHN H. LYNDE, CHARLES K. WILLIAMS, and FOSTER BURNET, were appointed such committee.

Voted to adjourn for half an hour.

Attest.   JOHN ABBOT, G. G. Sec. pro tem.

Met according to adjournment.

On motion, voted to raise a committee of three to confer with the delegates from Maryland relative to their forming a masonic union with the grand chapters of the several states, now acknowledging and under the jurisdiction of the general grand royal arch chapter of the United States.

Companions JOEL HART, HENRY FOWLE, and EZRA AMES, were appointed such committee.

Voted to choose a committee of three to audit the accounts of the G. G. Secretary and Treasurer.

Companions JONATHAN NYE, PETER GRINNELL, and JOSEPH ENOS, were appointed such committee.

Voted to choose a committee of three relative to the granting of sundry charters for royal arch chapters, by the G. G. King, and G. G. Scribe.

Companions HENRY FOWLE, JONATHAN NYE, and JOSEPH ENOS, were appointed such committee.

Voted to proceed to the election of general grand officers to-morrow, June 7th, at 12 o'clock, M.

Voted to choose a committee of one to make arrangements preparatory to a discourse to be delivered to-morrow by Rev. Companion NYE.

Companion JOEL HART was appointed such committee.

Voted to adjourn till to-morrow, June 7th, to meet at this place, 10 o'clock, A. M.

Attest.   JOHN ABBOT, G. G. Sec. pro tem.

June 7, 5816. Met according to adjournment; and the minutes of June 6 being read, voted to accept the same.

The committee to whom was referred the general grand royal arch constitution for revision, made the following report: that article 1, section 1, be in the following words, instead of said article in the general grand royal arch constitution, as the same therein is written, to wit:

SECT. 1. There shall be a general grand chapter of royal arch masons for the United States of America, which shall be holden, as is hereinafter directed, and shall consist of a general grand high priest, deputy general grand high priest, general grand king, general grand scribe, secretary, treasurer, chaplain and marshal; and likewise of the several grand and deputy grand high priests, kings and scribes, for the time being, of the several state grand chapters, under the jurisdiction of this general grand chapter; and of the past general grand high priests, deputy general grand high priests, kings and scribes, of the said general grand chapter; and the aforesaid officers, or their proxies, shall be the only members and voters in said general grand chapter. And no person shall be constituted a proxy, unless he be a present or past officer of this or a state grand chapter.

Whereupon it was resolved to substitute the above section, as reported by the committee, in place of the first section of the first article of the general grand royal arch constitution.

On motion, the following resolution was passed unanimously by the general grand chapter, to wit:

Resolved, that the G. G. R. A. Constitution be so far amended as that the deputy general grand high priest shall have and possess powers and prerogatives, equal and similar to those possessed by, and vested in the general grand high priest, king and scribe of the general grand chapter, by the said constitution.

The committee appointed to confer with the delegates of the grand chapter of Maryland and District of Columbia on the subject of a masonic union, made the following report, to wit:

The undersigned, having been appointed a committee for the purpose of conferring with M. E. Companions PHILIP P. ECKEL and BENJAMIN EDES, delegates from the grand royal arch chapter of the state of Maryland, beg leave to report that they have had an interview with the above named companions, from whom they received the following proposition, to wit:

The grand chapter for the state of Maryland and district of Columbia are willing to support the Constitution of this general grand chapter. It will not grant any warrants out of its district, and will discountenance all chapters formed contrary to the general grand constitution; but requests that it shall not be forced to alter its mode of working, if any difference should exist, at present, and to be received on an equality with the other grand chapters.

Under a consideration of all the above circumstances, your committee recommend that the said grand chapter of the state of Maryland be admitted to an union with this general grand chapter.

EZRA AMES,
JOEL HART,
HENRY FOWLE.

New-York, June 7, 5816.

The undersigned delegates from the grand chapter of the state of Maryland and district of Columbia agree to the above report.

P. P. ECKEL, G. H. P.
BENJAMIN EDES.

Which report being read, voted to accept the same; and thereupon voted to receive the said grand chapter of the state of Maryland and district of Columbia under the jurisdiction of the general grand chapter; and said grand chapter of the state of Maryland and district of Columbia is accordingly admitted under said jurisdiction, subject to the constitution and regulations of the said general grand chapter.

The committee to whom was referred the granting of charters for opening royal arch chapters by the general grand king, and general grand scribe, made the following report:

That the general grand king has granted warrants or charters for the following chapters, to wit:

St. Andrew's Chapter, Hanover, N. H. 27th January, 5807.
Trinity Chapter, Hopkinton, N. H. 16th February, 5807.
Phoenix Chapter, Fayetteville, North-Carolina, 1st Sept. 5815.
Washington Chapter, Portsmouth, New-Hampshire, Nov. 5815.
Union Chapter, Louisville, Georgia, 16th Dec. 5815.
Cheshire Chapter, Keene, New-Hampshire, 4th May, 5816.
Concord Chapter, Wilmington, North-Carolina, 5815.

That the general grand scribe has granted warrants or charters for the following chapters, to wit:

Washington Chapter, Newark, New-Jersey, 26th May, 5813.
Washington Chapter, Chilicothe, Ohio, 20th Sept. 5815.
Cincinnati Mark Lodge, No. 1, Hanover, New-Jersey, April, 5811.
Union Mark Lodge, No. 2, Orange, New-Jersey, July, 5812.

And your committee are of opinion that the above warrants or charters have been issued agreeably to the constitution of the general grand chapter, and ought to be confirmed by the same. All which is respectfully submitted by

HENRY FOWLE,
JOSEPH ENOS,
JONATHAN NYE.

Which being read, voted to accept the same, and that said warrants or chapters be, and they are hereby, confirmed accordingly.

The time for election of general grand officers having arrived, voted that the general grand king, scribe, and secretary, be a committee to receive, sort and count the votes, which being done, the following companions were declared to be duly elected to the offices respectively affixed to their names, to wit:

M. E. and Hon. DE WITT CLINTON, Esq. of New-York, State of New-York, GENERAL GRAND HIGH PRIEST.

M. E. THOMAS SMITH WEBB, Esq. of Boston, Massachusetts, DEPUTY GENERAL GRAND HIGH PRIEST.

M. E. JOHN H. LYNDE, Esq. of New-Haven, Connecticut, GENERAL GRAND KING.

M. E. PHILIP P. ECKEL, Esq. of Baltimore, Maryland, GENERAL GRAND SCRIBE.

M. E. JOHN ABBOT, Esq. of Westford, Massachusetts, *General Grand Secretary.*

M. E. PETER GRINNELL, Esq. of Providence, Rhode-Island, *General Grand Treasurer.*

M. E. and Rev. JONATHAN NYE, of Newfane, Vermont, *General Grand Chaplain.*

M. E. JOHN HARRIS, Esq. of Hopkinton, New-Hampshire, *General Grand Marshal.*

Voted and chose Companions JOEL HART, JOHN BRUSH, and JONATHAN NYE, a committee to wait on the M. E. and Hon. DE WITT CLINTON, Esq. and notify him of his election to the office of general grand high priest.

Voted to adjourn to half past three o'clock in the afternoon, then to meet at this place.

Attest. JOHN ABBOT, G. G. Sec. pro tem.

Met according to adjournment.

An elegant and ingenious discourse having been delivered before the general grand chapter, by M. E. and Rev. Companion NYE, according to appointment, voted and chose M. E. THOMAS S. WEBB, EZRA AMES, and JOHN ABBOT, a committee to return companion NYE the thanks of this general grand chapter, and respectfully request him to furnish the general grand secretary with a copy of said discourse to be placed on the files of the said general grand chapter.

The committee, appointed to wait on the M. E. and Hon. DE WITT CLINTON, reported his acceptance of the office of general grand high priest, and that he would attend the general grand chapter to-morrow at eleven o'clock, A. M. for the purpose of installation.

Voted to adjourn till to-morrow, June 8, 1816, to meet at this place at 10 o'clock, A. M. Attest. JOHN ABBOT, G. G. Sec. pro tem.

June 8, 1816. Met according to adjournment, and the minutes of yesterday, June 7, being read, voted to accept the same.

On motion, voted that the next meeting of the general grand chapter be holden in the city of New-York, state of New-York, unless the first four, or a majority of the first four general grand officers shall designate some other place, and cause timely notice thereof to be given to all companions interested.

The general grand officers appeared, and were duly installed into their respective offices.

The following resolution was passed by the general grand chapter, to wit:

"Resolved, That for every companion heretofore exalted in any chapter holden by dispensation or warrant from either of the general grand officers, such chapter shall pay the sum of one dollar into the general grand treasury; and that for every companion that may be hereafter exalted in any chapter holden as aforesaid, the sum of two dollars shall be paid in like manner. And that the general grand secretary notify the said chapters hereof, and request them to settle their dues accordingly.

The foregoing minutes, of June 8, being read, voted to accept the same.

The general grand chapter was then closed in due form, to meet on the second Thursday in September, A. D. 1819.

Attest. JOHN ABBOT, G. G. Sec.

THE GENERAL GRAND ROYAL ARCH

CONSTITUTION,

FOR THE

UNITED STATES OF AMERICA.

ARTICLE I.

OF THE GENERAL GRAND CHAPTER.

SECT. 1. There shall be a General Grand Chapter of Royal Arch Masons for the United States of America, which shall be holden as is hereinafter directed, and shall consist of a General Grand High Priest, Deputy General Grand High Priest, General Grand King, General Grand Scribe, Secretary, Treasurer, Chaplain, and Marshal; and likewise of the several Grand and Deputy Grand High Priests, Kings and Scribes, for the time being, of the several state grand chapters, under the jurisdiction of this general grand chapter; and of the Past General Grand High Priests, Deputy General Grand High Priests, Kings and Scribes of the said general grand chapter; and the aforesaid officers, or their proxies, shall be the only members and voters in said general grand chapter. And no person shall be constituted a proxy, unless he be a present or past officer of this or a state grand chapter.

SECT. 2. The general grand chapter shall meet septennially, on the second Thursday in September, for the choice of officers, and other business: dating from the second Thursday in September, A. D. 1805, at such place as may, from time to time, be appointed.

SECT. 3. A special meeting of the general grand chapter shall be called whenever the General Grand High Priest, Deputy General Grand High Priest, General Grand King, and General Grand Scribe, or any two of them, may deem it necessary; and also whenever it may be required by a majority of the grand chapters of the states aforesaid, provided such requisition be made known in writing, by the said grand chapters respectively, to the General Grand High Priest, Deputy General Grand High Priest, King or Scribe. And it shall be the duty of the said general officers, and they are each of them severally authorised, empowered and directed, upon receiving official notice of such requisition from a majority of the grand chapters aforesaid, to appoint a time and place of meeting, and notify each of the state grand chapters thereof accordingly.

SECT. 4. It shall be incumbent on the General Grand High Priest, Deputy General Grand High Priest, General Grand King, and General Grand Scribe, severally, to improve and perfect themselves in the sublime arts and work of Mark Masters, Past Masters, Most Excellent Masters, and Royal Arch Masons; to make themselves masters of the several masonic lectures and ancient charges; to consult with each other, and with the Grand and Deputy Grand High Priests, Kings and Scribes of the several States aforesaid, for the purpose of adopting measures suitable and proper for diffusing a knowledge of the said lectures and charges, and an uniform mode of *working*, in the several chapters and lodges throughout this jurisdiction; and the better to effect this laudable purpose, the aforesaid general grand officers are severally hereby authorised, and empowered, to visit and preside in any and every chapter of Royal Arch Masons, and lodge of Most Excellent, Past, or Mark Master Masons, throughout the said States, and to give such instructions and directions as the good of the fraternity may require; always adhering to the ancient landmarks of the order.

SECT. 5. In all cases of the absence of any officer from any body of masons, instituted or holden by virtue of this constitution, the officer next in rank shall succeed his superior; unless through courtesy said officer should decline in favour of a past superior officer present. And in case of the absence of all the officers from any legal meeting of either of the bodies aforesaid, the members present, according to seniority and abilities, shall fill the several offices.

SECT. 6. In every chapter or lodge of Masons, instituted or holden by virtue of this constitution, all questions (except upon the admission of members or candidates) shall be determined by a majority of votes; the presiding officer for the time being, being entitled to vote, if a member; and in case the votes should at any time be equally divided, the presiding officer as aforesaid, shall give the casting vote.

SECT 7. The general grand royal arch chapter shall be competent (on concurrence of two thirds of its members present) at any time hereafter, to revise, amend and alter this constitution.

SECT. 8. In case any casualty should at any time hereafter prevent the septennial election of officers, the several general grand officers shall sustain their respective offices until successors are duly elected and qualified.

SECT. 9. The General Grand High Priest, Deputy General Grand High Priest, General Grand King, and General Grand Scribe, shall severally have power and authority to institute new Royal Arch Chapters, and Lodges of the subordinate degrees, in any State in which there is not a grand chapter regularly established. But no new chapter shall be instituted in any State wherein there is a chapter or chapters under the authority of this constitution, without a recommendation from the chapter nearest the residence of the petitioners. The fees for instituting a new Royal Arch Chapter, with the subordinate degrees, shall be ninety dollars; and for a new Mark Master's Lodge, twenty dollars; exclusive of such compensation to the Grand Secretary, as the Grand Officers aforesaid may deem reasonable.

ARTICLE II.

OF THE STATE GRAND ROYAL ARCH CHAPTERS.

SECT. 1. The State Grand Chapters shall severally consist of a Grand High Priest, Deputy Grand High Priest, Grand King, Grand Scribe, Grand Secretary, Grand Treasurer, Grand Chaplain, and Grand Marshal, and likewise of the High Priests, Kings and Scribes, for the time being, of the several chapters over which they shall respectively preside, and of the Past Grand and Deputy Grand High Priests, Kings and Scribes of the said grand chapters; and the said enumerated officers (or their proxies) shall be the only members and voters in the said grand chapters respectively.

SECT. 2. The state grand chapters shall severally be holden at least once in every year, at such times and places as they shall respectively direct; and the grand or deputy grand high priests respectively, for the time being, may at any time, call a special meeting, to be holden at such place as they shall severally think proper to appoint.

SECT. 3. The officers of the state grand chapters shall be chosen annually, by ballot, at such time and place as the said grand chapters shall respectively direct.

SECT. 4. The several state grand chapters (subject to the provisions of this constitution) shall have the sole government and superintendence of the several royal arch chapters, and lodges of most excellent, past, and mark master masons, within their respective jurisdictions; to assign their limits, and settle controversies that may happen between them; and shall have power, under their respective seals, and the sign manual of their respective grand or deputy grand high priests, kings and scribes, (or their legal proxies) attested by their respective secretaries, to constitute new chapters of royal arch masons, and lodges of most excellent, past, and mark master masons, within their respective jurisdictions.

SECT. 5. The grand and deputy grand high priests, severally, shall have the power and authority, whenever they shall deem it expedient, (during the recess of the grand chapter of which they are officers) to grant letters of dispensation, under their respective hands, and private seals, to a competent number of petitioners (possessing the qualifications required by the 9th section of the 2d article) empowering them to open a chapter of royal arch masons, and lodge of most excellent, past, and mark master masons, for a certain specified term of time; provided, that the said term of time shall not extend beyond the next meeting of the grand chapter of the state in which such dispensation shall be granted; and provided further, that the same fees as are required by this constitution for warrants, shall be first deposited in the hands of the grand treasurer. And in all cases of such dispensations, the grand or deputy grand high priests, respectively, who may grant the same, shall make report thereof, at the next stated meeting of the grand chapters of their respective jurisdictions, when the said grand chapters, respectively, may either continue or recall the said dispensations, or may grant the petitioners a warrant of constitution. And in case such warrant shall be granted, the fees first deposited shall be credited in payment for the same; but if a warrant should not be granted, nor the dispensation continued, the said fees shall be refunded to the petitioners, excepting only such part thereof as shall have been actually expended by means of their application.

SECT. 6. The several state grand chapters shall possess authority, upon the institution of new royal arch chapters, or lodges of mark masters, within their respective jurisdictions, to require the payment of such fees as they may deem expedient and proper; which said fees shall be advanced and paid into the treasury before a warrant or charter shall be issued.

SECT. 7. No warrant shall be granted for instituting lodges of most excellent or past masters, independent of a chapter of royal arch masons.

SECT. 8. The grand chapters, severally, shall have power to require from the several chapters and lodges under their respective jurisdictions, such reasonable proportion of sums, received by them for the exaltation or advancement of candidates, and such certain annual sums from their respective members, as by their ordinances or regulations shall hereafter be appointed; all which said sums or dues shall be made good, and paid annually, by the said chapters and lodges respectively, into the grand treasury of the grand chapter under which they hold their authority, on or before the first day of the respective annual meetings of the said grand chapters.

SECT. 9. No warrant for the institution of a new chapter of royal arch masons shall be granted, except upon the petition of nine regular royal arch masons; which petition shall be accompanied by a certificate from the chapter nearest to the place where the new chapter is intended to be opened, vouching for the moral characters, and masonic abilities, of the petitioners, and recommending to the grand chapter, under whose authority they act, to grant their prayer. And no warrant for the institution of a lodge of mark master masons shall be granted, except upon the petition of (at least) five regular mark master masons, accompanied by vouchers from the nearest lodge of that degree, similar to those required upon the institution of a chapter.

SECT. 10. The grand secretaries of the state grand chapters shall severally make an annual communication to each other, and also to the general grand secretary, containing a list of grand officers, and all such other matters as may be deemed necessary for the mutual information of the said grand chapters. And the said grand secretaries shall also regularly transmit to the general grand secretary a copy of ill their by-laws and regulations.

SECT. 11. Whenever there shall have been three, or more, royal arch chapters instituted in any state, by virtue of authority derived from this constitution, a grand chapter may be formed in such state, (with the approbation of one or more of the general grand officers) by the high priests, kings and scribes of the said chapters, who shall be

15

authorized to elect the grand officers. Provided always, 'that no new state grand chapter shall be formed until after the expiration of one year from the establishment of the junior chapter in such state.

SECT. 12. The several grand and deputy grand high priests, kings and scribes, for the time being, of the several state grand chapters, are bound to the performance of the same duties, and are invested with the same powers and prerogatives, throughout their respective jurisdictions, as are prescribed to the general grand officers, in the 4th section, 1st article, of this constitution.

SECT 13. The jurisdiction of the several state grand chapters, shall not extend beyond the limits of the state in which they shall respectively be holden.

ARTICLE III.
OF THE SUBORDINATE CHAPTERS AND LODGES.

SECT. 1. All legally constituted assemblies of royal arch masons are called CHAPTERS; as regular bodies of mark masters, past masters and most excellent masters, are called LODGES. Every chapter ought to assemble for work at least once in every three months; and must consist of an high priest, king, scribe, captain of the host, principal sojourner, royal arch captain, three grand masters, secretary, treasurer, and as many members as may be found convenient for working to advantage.

SECT. 2. Every chapter of royal arch masons, and lodge of mark master masons, throughout this jurisdiction, shall have a warrant of constitution, from the grand chapter of the state in which they may respectively be holden, or a warrant from one of the general grand officers. And no chapter or lodge shall be deemed legal without such warrant; and masonic communication (either publick or private) is hereby interdicted and forbidden, between any chapter or lodge under this jurisdiction, or any member of either of them, and any chapter, lodge or assembly, that may be so illegally formed, opened or holden, without such warrant, or any or either of their members, or any person exalted or advanced in such illegal chapter or lodge. But nothing in this section shall be construed to affect any chapter or lodge which was established before the adoption of the grand royal arch constitution, at Hartford, (on the 27th day of January, A. D. 1798.)

SECT. 3. Whenever a warrant is issued for instituting a chapter of royal arch masons, with a power in said warrant to open and hold a lodge of most excellent, past and mark master masons, the high priest, king and scribe, for the time being, of such chapter, shall be the master and wardens in said lodges, according to seniority.

SECT. 4. All applications for the exaltation or advancement of candidates, in any chapter or lodge, under this jurisdiction, shall lie over, at least one meeting, for the consideration of the members.

SECT. 5. No mason shall be a member of two separate and distinct bodies, of the same denomination, at one and the same time.

SECT. 6. No chapter shall be removed, without the knowledge of the high priest, nor any motion made for that purpose in his absence; but if the high priest be present, and a motion is made and seconded for removing the chapter to some more convenient place (within the limits prescribed in their warrant) the high priest shall forthwith cause notifications to be issued to all the members, informing them of the motion for removal, and of the time and place when the question is to be determined; which notice shall be issued at least ten days previous to the appointed meeting. But if the high priest (after motion duly made and seconded as aforesaid) should refuse or neglect to cause the notices to be issued as aforesaid, the officer next in rank, who may be present at the next regular meeting following, (upon motion made and seconded for that purpose) may in like manner issue the said notices.

SECT. 7. All mark master masons' lodges shall be regulated, in cases of removal, by the same rules as are prescribed in the foregoing section for the removal of Chapters.

SECT. 8. The high priest, and other officers, of every chapter, and the officers of every lodge of mark master masons, shall be chosen annually, by ballot.

SECT. 9. The high priest of every chapter has it in special charge as appertaining to his office, duty, and dignity, to see that the by-laws of his chapter, as well as the general grand royal arch constitution, and the general regulations of the grand chapter, be duly observed; that all the other officers of his chapter perform the duties of their respective offices faithfully, and are examples of diligence and industry to their companions; that true and exact records be kept of all the proceedings of the chapter, by the secretary; that the treasurer keep and render exact and just accounts of all the monies belonging to the chapter; that regular returns be made by the secretary, annually, to the grand chapter of all admissions of candidates or members; and that the annual dues to the grand chapter be regularly and punctually paid. He has the special care and charge of the warrant of his chapter. He has the right and authority of calling his chapter at pleasure, upon any emergency or occurrence which in his judgment may require their meeting, and he is to fill the chair when present. It is likewise his duty, together with his king and scribe, to attend the meetings of the grand chapter (when duly summoned by the grand secretary) either in person, or by proxy.

SECT. 10. For the preservation of secrecy and good harmony, and in order that due decorum may be observed while the chapter is engaged in business, a worthy royal arch mason is to be appointed from time to time for tyling the chapter. His duty is fixed by custom, and known in all regular chapters. He may be elected annually, but is to continue in office only during good behaviour, and is to be paid for his services.

SECT. 11. All lodges of mark master masons are bound to observe the two preceding articles, as far as they can be applied to the government of a lodge.

SECT. 12. No chapter shall confer the degrees of mark master mason, past master, most excellent master, and royal arch mason, upon any brother, for a less sum than twenty dollars. And no lodge of mark master masons shall advance a brother to that degree for a less sum than four dollars.

SECT. 13. When either of the officers or members of the general grand chapter, or of any of the state grand chapters, cannot personally attend their respective meetings, they shall severally have the authority to constitute a proxy, which proxy shall have the same right to a seat and vote as his constituent.

ARTICLE IV.

OF CONSTITUTING NEW CHAPTERS.

SECT. 1. When a warrant of constitution is granted, by either of the general grand officers, or either of the state grand chapters, for constituting a new chapter of royal arch masons, the grand officers, respectively, shall appoint a day and hour for constituting the same, and installing the new officers. On the day and hour appointed, the grand or deputy grand high priest,* with his officers, meet in a convenient room, near to the place where the new chapter is to be constituted. The officers of the new chapter are to be examined, by the deputy grand high priest, or some companion appointed for that purpose; after they are approved, they are to return to the hall, and prepare for the reception of the grand chapter. When notice is given, by the grand marshal, that they are prepared, the grand chapter walks, in procession to the hall, when the officers appointed for the new chapter resign their seats to the grand officers, and take their several stations on the left; the necessary cautions are then given from the chair, and the ceremony commences by performing an anthem or ode, adapted to the occasion. The officers and members of the new chapter then form in front of the grand high priest.

The deputy grand high priest then informs the grand high priest, that " A number of companions duly instructed in the sublime mysteries, being desirous of promoting the honour of the art, have applied to the grand chapter for a warrant to constitute a new chapter of royal arch masons, which having obtained, they are now assembled for the purpose of being constituted, and having their officers installed in due and ancient form."

The grand high priest then directs the grand secretary to read the warrant, which being done, he asks the members of the new chapter if they still approve of the officers nominated therein; this being signified accordingly, the grand high priest rises and says,

" By virtue of the high powers in me vested, I do form you, my worthy companions, into a regular chapter of royal arch masons; from henceforth you are authorized and empowered to open and hold a lodge of mark masters, past masters, and most excellent masters, and a chapter of royal arch masons; and to do and perform all such things as thereunto may appertain; conforming in all your doings to the general grand royal arch constitution, and the general regulations of the state grand chapter; and may the God of your fathers be with you, guide and direct you in all your doings."   *Grand Honours.*

* Or the presiding officer for the time being.

The furniture, jewels, implements, utensils, &c. belonging to the chapter (having previously been placed in due form, covered, in the centre) are then uncovered, and the new chapter is dedicated, in antient manner and form, as is well described in the most excellent master's degree. The deputy grand high priest then presents the first officer of the new chapter to the grand high priest, saying,

"*Most excellent grand high priest,*

"I present you my worthy companion .... nominated in the warrant, to be installed high priest of this new chapter; I find him to be skilful in the royal art, and attentive to the moral precepts of our forefathers, and have therefore no doubt but he will discharge the duties of his office with fidelity."

The grand high priest then addresses him as follows:

"*Most excellent companion,*

"I feel much satisfaction in performing my duty on the present occasion, by installing you into the office of high priest of this new chapter. It is an office highly honourable to all those who diligently perform the important duties annexed to it; your reputed masonic knowledge, however, precludes the necessity of a particular enumeration of those duties; I shall therefore only observe, that by a frequent recurrence to the constitution, and general regulations, and a constant practice of the several sublime lectures and charges, you will be best able to fulfil them; and I am confident, that the companions who are chosen to preside with you, will give strength to your endeavours, and support your exertions. I shall now propose certain questions to you, relative to the duties of your office, and to which I must request your unequivocal answer.

"1. Do you solemnly promise that you will redouble your endeavours to correct the vices, purify the morals, and promote the happiness of those of your brethren who have attained this sublime degree.

"2. That you will never suffer your chapter to be opened unless there be present nine regular royal arch masons.

"3. That you will never suffer either more or less than three brethren to be exalted in your chapter at one and the same time.

"4. That you will not exalt any one to this degree, who has not shewn a charitable and humane disposition; or who has not made a considerable proficiency in the foregoing degrees.

"5. That you will promote the general good of our order, and on all proper occasions be ready to give and receive instructions, and particularly from the general and state grand officers.

"6. That to the utmost of your power you will preserve the solemnities of our ceremonies, and behave, in open chapter, with the most profound respect and reverence, as an example to your companions.

"7. That you will not acknowledge or have intercourse with any
15*

chapter that does not work under a constitutional warrant or dispensation.

"8. That you will not admit any visitor into your chapter who has not been exalted in a chapter legally constituted, without his being first formally healed.

"9. That you will observe and support such by-laws as may be made by your chapter, in conformity to the general grand royal arch constitution, and the general regulations of the grand chapter.

"10. That you will pay due respect and obedience to the instructions of the general and state grand officers, particularly relating to the several lectures and charges, and will resign the chair to them, severally, when they may visit your chapter.

"11. That you will support and observe the general grand royal arch constitution, and the general regulations of the grand royal arch chapter under whose authority you act.

"Do you submit to all these things, and do you promise to observe and practise them faithfully?"

These questions being answered in the affirmative, the companions all kneel in due form, and the grand high priest, or grand chaplain, repeats the following, or some other suitable prayer.

"Most holy and glorious Lord, God, the great high priest of heaven and earth!

"We approach thee with reverence, and implore thy blessing on the companion appointed to preside over this new assembly, and now prostrate before thee; fill his heart with thy fear, that his tongue and actions may pronounce thy glory. Make him steadfast in thy service; grant him firmness of mind; animate his heart, and strengthen his endeavours; may he teach thy judgments and thy laws; and may the incense he shall put before thee, upon thine altar, prove an acceptable sacrifice unto thee. Bless him, O Lord, and bless the work of his hands. Accept us in mercy; hear thou from heaven thy dwelling place, and forgive our transgressions.

"Glory be to God the Father; as it was in the beginning," &c. Response, "So mote it be."

All the companions, except high priests and past high priests, are then desired to withdraw, while the new high priest is solemnly bound to the performance of his duties; and after the performance of other necessary ceremonies, not proper to be written, they are permitted to return.

The grand high priest then addresses the new high priest, as follows:

"*Most excellent companion,*

"In consequence of your cheerful acquiescence with the charges and regulations just recited, I now declare you duly installed and anointed high priest of this new chapter; not doubting your determination to support the reputation and honour of our sublime order. I now cheerfully deliver unto you the warrant under which you are to work; and I doubt not you will govern with such good order and regularity, as will convince your companions that their partiality has not been improperly placed."

The grand high priest then clothes and invests the new high priest with the various implements and insignia of the order, with suitable charges to each of them.

The grand high priest then installs the several subordinate officers in turn ; and points out to them the duties appertaining to their respective offices ; after which he pronounces a suitable address to the new chapter, and closes the ceremony, with the following benediction :

" The Lord be with you all ; let brotherly love continue ; be not forgetful to entertain strangers. Now the God of peace, our supreme High Priest, make you perfect to do his will.

" Glory be to God on high, and on earth peace and good will to men. As it was in the beginning, is now, and ever shall be," &c.

SECT. 2. At the institution of all lodges of mark master masons, under this jurisdiction, the same ceremonies as are prescribed in the foregoing section, are to be observed, as far as they will apply to that degree.

SECT. 3. Whenever it shall be inconvenient for the general grand officers, or the grand or deputy grand high priests, respectively, to attend in person, to constitute a new chapter or lodge, and install the officers, they shall severally have power and authority to appoint some worthy high priest, or past high priest, to perform the necessary ceremonies.

SECT.-4. The officers of every chapter and lodge under this jurisdiction, before they enter upon the exercise of their respective offices, and also the members of all such chapters and lodges, and every candidate upon his admission into the same, shall take the following obligation, viz. " I, A. B. do promise and swear, that I will support and maintain the general grand royal arch constitution."

I HEREBY certify, that the foregoing is a true copy of the general grand royal arch constitution for the United States of America, as altered, amended and ratified, at a meeting of the general grand chapter, begun and holden at New-York, in the state of New-York, on the 6th day of June, A. D. 1816.

WITNESS,

JOHN ABBOT, G. G. Secretary.

CHAPTER IV.

Grand Royal Arch Chapter of Maffachufetts.

PURSUANT to the general conftitution, the grand chapter of this ftate was organized on the twelfth of June, 1798. Its annual meetings are holden alternately at Boston and Newburyport, in the month of September.

The chapters under its jurisdiction are as follows :—

St. *Andrew's Chapter*, No. 1, Boston, meets at the hall in Market Square, the Wednesday preceding the full of the moon, monthly.

King Cyrus' Chapter, No. 2, at Newburyport.

St. John's Chapter, No. 3, at Groton.

Mount Vernon Chapter, No. 4, at Portland.

King Solomon's Chapter, No. 5, at Charlton.

Washington Chapter, No. 6, at Salem.

King Hiram's Chapter, No. 7, at Greenwich.

Adoniram Chapter, No. 8, at Attleborough.

CHAPTER V.

Grand Royal Arch Chapter of Rhode-Island.

THE grand chapter of this state was organized agreeably to the constitution, on the Tuesday following the second Monday in March, 1798.

This grand chapter meets quarterly at Masons' Hall in Providence, on the third Tuesdays of March, June, September and December.

SUBORDINATE CHAPTERS.

Providence Chapter, No. 1, Providence.

Newport Chapter, No. 2, Newport.

Temple Chapter, No. 3, Warren.

The Providence Chapter meets at St. John's Hall, on the Thursday succeeding the full moon, monthly.

CHAPTER VI.

Grand Royal Arch Chapter of Connecticut.

AGREEABLY to the general constitution, the grand chapter of this state was organized at Hartford, on the feventeenth day of May, 1798, when the feveral grand officers were duly elected and inftalled into their refpective offices.

SUBORDINATE CHAPTERS.

Hiram Chapter, Newton.
Solomon Chapter, Derby.
Washington Chapter, Middletown.

Franklin Chapter, New Haven.
VanderbrookChapter,Colchester.
Franklin Chapter, Norwich.
Union Chapter, New-London.

CHAPTER VII.

Grand Royal Arch Chapter of New-York.

AGREEABLY to the conftitution of the general grand chapter, the high priefts, kings and fcribes of the royal arch chapters in the ftate of New-York, affembled at the city of Albany, on the fecond Tuefday in March, A. L. 5798, and organized the grand chapter of the faid ftate, which meets annually on the firft Tuefday in February, at the city of Albany.

SUBORDINATE CHAPTERS.

The old Chapter, No. 1, N. York.
Washington do. No. 2, do.
Hibernian do. No. 3, do.
Montgomery do. No. 4, Stillwater.
Temple do. No. 5, Albany.
Hudson do. No. 6, Hudson.
Horeb do. No. 7, Whitestown.
Jerusalem do. No. 8, New-York.

De la Fayette do. No. 9, Grenville.
Federal do. No. 10, Cambridge.
Cyrus do. No. 11, Schenectady.
Green Mo. do No.12, Rutland,Vt.
New-Lebanon do. No. 13, New-Lebanon.
St. Andrew's do. No. 14, Stamford, Del. C.

SUBORDINATE MARK LODGES.

Hudson M. M's L. No. 3, Hudson.
Orange do. No. 4, Waterford.
Otsego do. No. 5, Cooperstown.
Hosick do. No. 6, Hosick.
Phoenix do. No. 7, New-York.

Rural do. No. 8, Cambridge.
New Canaan do. No. 9, New Canaan.
Montgomery do. No. 10, Broadalbin.

Montgomery do. No. 11, Stillwater.

Bennington do. No. 13; Bennington, Vt.

Fort Edward do. No. 14, Fort
Edward.

Hiram do. No. 15, Lansinburgh.

Aurora do. No. 16, Poultney, Vt.

Asylum do. No. 18, Coeymans.

Campbell's do. Duanesburgh.

Fortitude do. No. 19, Brooklyn.

Patriot do. No. 20, Pittstown.

CHAPTER VIII.

Grand Royal Arch Chapter of South Carolina.

THE officers of the several chapters which had
been instituted in this state, by virtue of authority derived from the constitution, convened in
the city of Charleston, and having obtained the
consent and approbation of the general grand
king, proceeded to organize a grand chapter for
the state of South Carolina. This grand chapter
appointed proxies to attend the ensuing meeting
of the general grand chapter, by whom their
proceedings were ratified and confirmed, and
the said grand chapter was declared to be in union
with the general grand chapter, agreeably to the
general grand royal arch constitution.

CHAPTER IX.

Grand Royal Arch Chapter of Ohio.

ON the 21st day of October, A. D. 1816, the
several royal arch chapters holden in the state of
Ohio, assembled by their officers, in the town of
Worthington, viz.

AMERICAN UNION Chapter, holden at *Marietta*, which originated prior to the 27th January, 1798.

CINCINNATI Chapter, which also originated prior to the 27th Jan. 1798.

HOREB Chapter, holden at *Worthington*, under the general grand royal arch constitution.

WASHINGTON Chapter, holden at *Chilicothe*, under the general grand royal arch constitution.

Upon motion made and seconded, it was resolved, unanimously, that it is proper and expedient, to establish a grand royal arch chapter in the state of Ohio, in connection with, and in subordination to, the general grand royal arch chapter of the United States; conformably to the 11th sect. 1st art. and the 2d sect. 3d art. of the general grand royal arch constitution.

The convention having received information that M. E. Thomas Smith Webb, Deputy General Grand High Priest, was in the vicinity, appointed a committee to wait on him, to inform him of their proceedings, and to solicit his approbation, as required by the 11th sect. 1st art. of the constitution; the committee were directed to invite him to attend at some convenient time, and install the grand officers into their respective offices.

A meeting was accordingly appointed to be holden at Worthington on the 29th Oct. A. D. 1816, on which occasion a public procession was made, which proceeded to the Academy, where an oration was delivered by the Rev. James Kilbourn, grand orator, and the installation ceremonies were performed, by the deputy general grand high priest, in ample form.

SUBORDINATE CHAPTERS.

No. 1, American Union, at Marietta.
No. 2, Cincinnati, at Cincinnati.
No. 3, Horeb, at Worthington.
No. 4, Washington, at Chilicothe.

CHAPTER X.

Convention of Royal Arch Mafons in Kentucky.

A CONVENTION of royal arch mafons, refiding in different parts of the ftate of Kentucky, was holden at Lexington on the 14th day of October, A. D. 1816, when the following proceedings took place, viz.

" Whereas it has been deemed important by the Royal Arch Mafons refiding in the ftate of Kentucky, that they fhould work in a regular and conftitutional manner; that the benefits arifing thereby may be permanent and uniform : and whereas doubts have arifen as to the power of any grand lodge to eftablifh chapters of royal arch mafons : it has therefore been deemed expedient to appoint committees from Lexington, Frankfort, and Shelbyville, at and near which places moft of the R. A. Companions in this ftate refide; to meet at Lexington, on the 14th day of October, A. D. 1816, to take the fubject into confideration.

" The faid committees, having affembled, and produced their credentials, appointed John Willett, M. D. chairman, and Anderfon Miller, Efq. Secretary.

"The object of the meeting having been taken into confideration, it was unanimoufly

"Refolved, as the opinion of this general committee, that for the regular eftablifhment of a chapter of royal arch mafons it is neceffary to procure authority from fome regularly confti-tuted grand royal arch chapter, having power to grant the fame.

"Refolved, that as there is a general grand royal arch chapter for the United States of America, properly conftituted, and propofed to grant charters for the eftablifhment of lodges of mark mafters, paft mafters, moft excellent maf-ters, and chapters of royal arch mafons, our au-thority and power ought to emanate from them.

"Refolved, that it appears by the general grand royal arch conftitution, that either of the firft four general grand officers has authority to grant warrants for inftituting lodges and chap-ters as aforefaid: and whereas the M. E. Thomas Smith Webb, deputy general grand high prieft of the general grand chapter, is now in this place, therefore

"Refolved, that petitions be immediately pre-pared and prefented to the faid M. E. deputy general grand high prieft, for warrants to eftab-lifh chapters of royal arch mafons in the feveral towns of Lexington, Frankfort, and Shelbyville; which faid refolutions and preambles were unani-moufly adopted."

Application having been made to the deputy general grand high prieft in conftitutional form, for authority to eftablifh a royal arch chapter in Lexington, by the name of Lexington Chapter;

16

another in Frankfort, by the name of Frankfort Chapter; and another in Shelbyville, by the name of Shelbyville Chapter; he issued charters for the same accordingly, on the 15th day of October, A. D. 1816.

On the day following, the deputy general grand high priest attended at the masonic hall, in Lexington, and installed the officers of the several chapters before mentioned into their respective offices in ample form.

CHAPTER XI.

Grand Royal Arch Chapter of Vermont.

THE grand royal arch chapter of Vermont was organized A. L. 5806, and admitted into the union under the general grand royal arch constitution. Meeting for the election of the several grand officers on the first Wednesday in June annually.

SUBORDINATE CHAPTERS.

Green Mountain Chapter, No. 1, Rutland.
Jerusalem   do.   No. 2, Vergennes.
Champlain   do.   No. 3, St. Albans.
Temple   do.   No. 4, Bennington.
King Solomon   do.   No. 5, Montpelier.
Windsor   do.   No. 6, Windsor.
....   do.   No. 7, Bradford.

King Solomon's Chapter, N. Y. meets on the third Wednesday of January, March, May, July, September, October and November.

Hiram Union Mark Lodge, Pawlet.
Union Mark Lodge, Middlebury.
Morning Star Mark Lodge, Poultney.

CHAPTER XII.

CEREMONIES and CHARGES,

ON THE

Installation of the Officers of a Royal Arch Chapter.

1. THE grand officers will meet at a convenient place, and open.

2. The fubordinate chapter will meet in the *outer courts* of their hall, and form an *avenue* for the reception of the grand officers.

3. When formed they will difpatch a committee to the place where the grand officers are affembled, to inform the grand marfhal that the chapter is prepared to receive them; the grand marfhal will announce the fame to the grand officers, and introduce the committee.

4. The grand officers will move in proceffion, conducted by the committee, to the hall of the chapter; when the grand high prieft enters, the chapter will give the *grand honours.*

5. When the grand officers have paffed through the avenue, the chapter will form rank entire, and face to the front; the officers of the chapter then file off, and form a front rank two paces in advance of their members.

6. The grand fecretary will then call over the names of the officers elect, and the grand high prieft will afk whether they accept their refpective offices. If they anfwer in the affirmative,

he then afks the members whether they remain
fatisfied with their choice. If they anfwer in
the affirmative, he directs their officers to approach the facred volume, and become qualified
for inftallation, according to ancient ufage and
cuftom.

7. The grand marfhal will then form the
whole in proceffion, in fingle files, and in cafe
the ceremonies are to be performed in public,
they march to the church, or if they are to be
performed in private they will march through
the veils into the *inner apartment*, where they
will furround the *altar*, which is to be previoufly furnifhed and prepared, in ample form, for
the occafion.

8. All prefent will then kneel, and the following prayer will be recited.

PRAYER.

"Almighty and Supreme Governor and Ruler
of heaven and earth! who is there in heaven
but thee, and who upon the earth can ftand in
competition with thee? Thy omnifcient mind
brings all things in review, paft, prefent, and to
come; thine omnipotent arm directs the movements of the vaft creation; thine omniprefent
eye pervades the fecret recefs of every heart;
thy boundlefs beneficence fupplies us with every
comfort and enjoyment; and thine unfpeaka-
ble perfections and glory furpafs the underftand-
ings of the children of men! Our Father, who
art in heaven, we invoke thy benediction upon
the purpofes of our prefent affembly; let this
chapter be eftablifhed to thine honour; let its

officers be endowed with wifdom to difcern, and fidelity to purfue, its trueft interefts; let its members be ever mindful of the duty they owe to their God, the obedience they owe to their fuperiors, the love they owe to their equals, and the good will they owe to all mankind. Let this chapter be confecrated to thy glory, and its members ever exemplify their love to God by their beneficence to man.

"Glory be to God on high!"

Refponfe, "Amen! So mote it be."

9. The whole then repair to their appropriate ftations.*

10. An anthem or ode is to be performed.

11. An oration or addrefs is to be delivered.

12. An ode or piece of mufic.

[13. The deputy grand high prieft then rifes, and informs the grand high prieft, that "a number of companions, duly inftructed in the fublime myfteries, being defirous of promoting the honour and propagating the principles of the art, have applied to the grand chapter for a warrant to conftitute a new chapter of royal arch mafons, which having obtained, they are now affembled for the purpofe of being conftituted, and having their officers inftalled in due and ancient form."]

[14. The grand marfhal will then form the officers and members of the new chapter in front of the grand officers; after which, the grand

* Note.---Those paragraphs, which are enclosed within brackets, apply exclusively to cases when new chapters are constituted, and their officers installed for the first time: the rest apply equally to such cases, as well as to annual installations.

high prieſt directs the grand ſecretary to read the warrant.]

[15. The grand high prieſt then riſes and ſays, " By virtue of the high powers in me veſted, I do form you, my reſpected companions, into a regular chapter of royal arch maſons ; from henceforth you are authorized and empowered to open and hold a lodge of mark maſters, paſt maſters, and moſt excellent maſters, and a chapter of royal arch maſons ; and to do and perform all ſuch things as thereunto may appertain ; conforming in all your doings to the general grand royal arch conſtitution, and the general regulations of the ſtate grand chapter ; and may the God of your fathers be with you, guide and direct you in all your doings."]

[16. The public grand honours will then be given by the officers and members of the new chapter, while paſſing in review in front of the grand officers.]

17. The furniture, clothing, jewels, implements, utenſils, &c. belonging to the chapter, (having been previouſly placed in the centre, in front of the grand officers, covered) are now uncovered, [and the new chapter is dedicated in ancient manner and form, as is well deſcribed in the moſt excellent maſter's degree.]

18. The deputy grand high prieſt will then preſent the firſt officer of the new chapter to the grand high prieſt, ſaying,

" *Moſt excellent grand high prieſt,*

" I preſent you my worthy companion .... nominated in the warrant to be inſtalled high prieſt of this new chapter ; I find him to be ſkilful in the royal art, and attentive to the moral precepts of our forefathers, and have therefore no doubt but he will diſcharge the duties of his office with fidelity."

The grand high prieſt then addreſſes him as follows :

"*Most excellent companion,*

"I feel much satisfaction in performing my duty on the present occasion, by installing you into the office of high priest of this new chapter. It is an office highly honourable to all those who diligently perform the important duties annexed to it; your reputed masonic knowledge, however, precludes the necessity of a particular enumeration of those duties; I shall therefore only observe, that by a frequent recurrence to the constitution, and general regulations, and a constant practice of the several sublime lectures and charges, you will be best able to fulfil them; and I am confident, that the companions who are chosen to preside with you, will give strength to your endeavours, and support your exertions. I shall now propose certain questions to you, relative to the duties of your office, and to which I must request your unequivocal answer.

"1. Do you solemnly promise that you will redouble your endeavours to correct the vices, amend the morals, and promote the happiness of those of your brethren who have attained this sublime degree.

"2. That you will never suffer your chapter to be opened unless there be present nine regular royal arch masons.

"3. That you will never suffer either more or less than three brethren to be exalted in your chapter at one and the same time.

"4. That you will not exalt any one to this degree, who has not shewn a charitable and humane disposition; or who has not made a considerable proficiency in the foregoing degrees.

"5. That you will promote the general good of our order, and on all proper occasions be ready to give and receive instructions, and particularly from the general and state grand officers.

"6. That to the utmost of your power you will preserve the solemnities of our ceremonies, and behave, in open chapter, with the most profound respect and reverence, as an example to your companions.

"7. That you will not acknowledge or have intercourse with any chapter that does not work under a constitutional warrant or dispensation.

"8. That you will not admit any visitor into your chapter who has not been exalted in a chapter legally constituted, without his being first formally healed.

"9. That you will observe and support such by-laws as may be made by your chapter, in conformity to the general grand royal arch constitution, and the general regulations of the grand chapter.

"10. That you will pay due respect and obedience to the instructions of the general and state grand officers, particularly relating to the several lectures and charges, and will resign the chair to them, severally, when they may visit your chapter.

"11. That you will support and observe the general grand royal arch constitution, and the general regulations of the grand royal arch chapter under whose authority you act.

" Do you submit to all these things, and do you promise to observe and practise them faithfully ?"

Thefe queftions being anfwered in the affirmative, the companions all kneel in due form, and the grand high prieft, or grand chaplain, repeats the following, or fome other fuitable prayer.

" Most holy and glorious Lord, God, the great high priest of heaven and earth! We approach thee with reverence, and implore thy blessing on the companion appointed to preside over this new assembly, and now prostrate before thee; fill his heart with thy fear, that his tongue and actions may pronounce thy glory. Make him steadfast in thy service; grant him firmness of mind; animate his heart, and strengthen his endeavours; may he teach thy judgments and thy laws; and may the incense he shall put before thee, upon thine altar, prove an acceptable sacrifice unto thee. Bless him, O Lord, and bless the work of his hands. Accept us in mercy; hear thou from heaven thy dwelling place, and forgive our transgressions.

" Glory be to God the Father; as it was in the beginning," &c.
Response, " So mote it be."

19. The grand high prieft will then caufe the high prieft eleɖ to be invefted with his clothing, badges, &c. after which he will addrefs him as follows, viz.

" COMPANION,

" In confequence of your cheerful acquiefcence with the charges which you have heard recited, you are now qualified for inftallation as the high prieft of this royal arch chapter; and it is incumbent upon me, upon this occafion, to point out fome of the particulars appertaining to your office, duty and dignity.

" All legally conftituted bodies of royal arch mafons are called chapters, as regular bodies of mafons of all other degrees are called lodges. Every chapter ought to affemble for work at leaft once in every three months; and muft confift of a high prieft, king, fcribe, captain of the hoft, principal fojourner, royal arch captain, three mafters of the veils, fecretary, treafurer, and as many members as may be found convenient for working to advantage.

" The officers of the chapter officiate in the lodges holden for conferring the preparatory degrees, according to rank, as follows :

" The high prieft, as mafter.

" The king, as fenior warden.

— " The fcribe, as junior warden.

" The captain of the hoft, as marfhal or mafter of ceremonies.

" The principal fojourner, as junior deacon.

" The royal arch captain, as fenior deacon.

" The mafter of the firft veil, as junior overfeer.

" The mafter of the fecond veil, as fenior overfeer.

" The mafter of the third veil, as mafter overfeer.

" The fecretary, treafurer, and tyler, as officers of correfponding rank.

" The high prieft of every chapter has it in fpecial charge to fee that the by-laws of his chapter, as well as the grand royal arch conftitution, and the regulations of the grand chapter are duly obferved ; that all the officers of his chapter perform the duties of their refpective offices faithfully, and are examples of diligence and induftry to their companions ; that true and accurate records of all the proceedings of the chapter are kept by the fecretary ; that the treafurer keeps and renders exact and juft accounts of all the moneys and other property belonging to the chapter; that the regular returns be made annually to the grand chapter; and that the annual dues to the grand chapter be regularly and punctually paid. He has the right and the authority of calling his chapter together at pleasure, upon any emergency or occurrence, which in his judgment may require their meeting. It is his privilege and duty, together with his king and scribe, to attend the meetings of the grand chapter, either in person or by proxy; and the well being of the institution requires that this duty should on no occasion be omitted.

"Let the *Mitre*, with which you are invested, remind you of the dignity of the office you sustain, and its inscription impress upon your mind a sense of your dependence upon God; that perfection is not given unto man upon the earth, and that perfect holiness belongeth alone unto the Lord.

"The *Breastplate*, with which you are decorated, in imitation of that upon which were engraven the names of the twelve tribes, and worn by the high priest of Israel, is to teach you that you are always to bear in mind your responsibility to the laws and ordinances of the institution, and that the honour and interests of your chapter and its members should be always *near your heart*.

"The *various colours* of the *Robes* you wear are emblematical of every grace and virtue, which can adorn and beautify the human mind; each of which will be briefly illustrated in the course of the charges to be delivered to your subordinate officers.

"You will now take charge of your officers, ſtanding upon their right, and preſent them ſeverally in ſucceſſion to the deputy grand high prieſt, by whom they will be preſented to me for inſtallation."

20. The high prieſt of the chapter will then preſent his ſecond officer to the deputy grand high prieſt, who will preſent him to the grand high prieſt, in the words of the conſtitution. The grand high prieſt will aſk him whether he has attended to the ancient charges and regulations before recited to his ſuperior officer; if he anſwers in the affirmative, he is aſked whether he fully and freely aſſents to the ſame; if he anſwers in the affirmative, the grand high prieſt directs his deputy to inveſt him with his clothing, &c. and then addreſſes him as follows, viz.

Charge to the Second Officer, or King.

"COMPANION,

"The important ſtation to which you are elected in this chapter requires from you exemplary conduct; its duties demand your moſt aſſiduous attention; you are to ſecond and ſupport your chief in all the requirements of his office; and, ſhould caſualties at any time prevent his attendance, you are to ſucceed him in the performance of his duties.

"Your badge (the *level, ſurmounted by a crown*) ſhould remind you, that although you are the repreſentative of a king, and exalted by office above your companions, yet that you remain upon a level with them, as reſpects your duty to God, to your neighbour, and to yourself; that you are equally bound with them to be obedient to the laws and ordinances of the inftitution, to be charitable, humane and juft, and to feek every occafion of doing good.

" Your office teaches a ftriking leffon of humility. The inftitutions of political fociety teach us to confider the king as the chief of created beings, and that the firft duty of his fubjects is to obey *his* mandates; but the inftitutions of our fublime degrees, by placing the king in a fituation fubordinate to the high prieft, teach us that our duty to God is paramount to all other duties, and fhould ever claim the priority of our obedience to man ; and that however ftrongly we may be bound to obey the laws of civil fociety, yet that thofe laws, to be juft, fhould never intermeddle with matters of confcience, nor dictate articles of faith.

" The *fcarlet robe*, an emblem of imperial dignity, fhould remind you of the paternal concern you fhould ever feel for the welfare of your chapter, and the *ardent zeal* with which you fhould endeavour to promote its profperity.

" In prefenting to you the *crown*, which is an emblem of royalty, I would remind you, that to reign fovereign in the hearts and affections of men muft be far more grateful to a generous and benevolent mind, than to rule over their lives and fortunes; and that to enable you to enjoy this preeminence with honour and fatiffaction, you muft fubjec tyour own paffions and prejudices to the dominion of reafon and charity.

" You are entitled to the fecond feat in the

council of your companions. Let the bright
example of your illuftrious predeceffor in the
grand council at Jerufalem, ftimulate you to the
faithful difcharge of your duties; and when the
King of kings fhall fummon you into his immediate prefence, from his hand may you receive
a *crown* of *glory* which fhall never fade away."

21. The king will then retire to the line of
officers, and the fcribe will be prefented in the
manner before mentioned. After his inveftiture, the grand high prieft will address him as
follows, viz.

Charge to the Third Officer, or Scribe.

" COMPANION,

" The office of fcribe, to which you are elected, is very important and refpectable; in the
abfence of your fuperior officers, you are bound
to fucceed them, and to perform their duties.
The purpofes of the inftitution ought never to
fuffer for want of intelligence in its proper officers; you will therefore perceive the neceffity
there is of your poffeffing fuch qualifications as
will enable you to accomplifh thofe duties which
are incumbent upon you in your appropriate
ftation, as well as thofe which may occafionally
devolve on you, by the abfence of your fuperiors.

The *Purple Robe*, with which you are invefted, is an emblem of *union*, and is calculated to
remind you that the harmony and unanimity of
the chapter fhould be your conftant aim; and
to this end you are ftudioufly to avoid all occa-

17

fions of giving offence, or countenancing any thing that may create divifions or diffenfions. You are, by all the means in your power, to endeavour to eftablifh a permanent union and good underftanding among all orders and degrees of mafonry; and, as the glorious fun at its meridian height difpels the mifts and clouds which obfcure the horizon, fo may your exertions tend to diffipate the gloom of jealoufy and difcord whenever they may appear.

" Your badge, (a *Plumb-rule, furmounted by the Turban*) is an emblem of rectitude and vigilance; and while you ftand as a watchman upon the tower, to guard your companions against the approach of thofe enemies of human felicity, *intemperance* and *excefs*, let this faithful monitor ever remind you to walk uprightly in your ftation; admonifhing and animating your companions to fidelity and induftry, while at labour, and to temperance and moderation while at refrefhment. And when the great Watchman of Ifrael, whofe eye never flumbers nor fleeps, fhall relieve you from your poft on earth, may he permit you in heaven to participate in that food and refrefhment which is

"Such as the faints in glory love,
"And such as angels eat."

22. The fcribe will then retire to the line of officers, and the next officer be prefented as before.

Charge to the Fourth Officer, or Captain of the Hoft.

" COMPANION,

" The office with which you are entrufted is of high importance, and demands your moft zealous confideration. The prefervation of the moft effential traits of our ancient cuftoms, ufages, and landmarks, are within your province; and it is indifpenfably neceffary that the part affigned to you, in the immediate practice of our rites and ceremonies, fhould be perfectly underftood, and correctly adminiftered.

"He that brings the blind by a way that they know not, and leads them in paths that they have not known, fhould always be well qualified to make darknefs light before them, and crooked things ftraight.

"Your office correfponds with that of marfhal, or mafter of ceremonies; you are to fuperintend all proceffions of your chapter when moving as a diftinct body, either in public or private; and as the world can only judge of our private difcipline by our public deportment, you will be careful that the utmoft order and decorum be obferved on all fuch occafions.

"I inveft you with the badge of your office, and prefume that you will give to your duties all that ftudy and attention which their importance demands."

23. He will then retire to the line of officers, and the next officer will be prefented.

Charge to the Fifth Officer, or Principal Sojourner.

"COMPANION,

"The office confided to you, though fubordinate in degree, is equal in importance to any in the chapter, that of your chief alone excepted. Your office correfponds with that of *junior dea-*

son in the preparatory degrees.   Among the duties required of you, the preparation and introduction of candidates are not the leaft.   As in our intercourfe with the world experience teaches that *firft impreffions* are often the *moft* durable, and the moft difficult to eradicate, fo it is of great importance in all cafes that thofe impreffions fhould be correct and juft ;   hence it is effential that the officer who fuftains the ftation affigned to you fhould poffefs a thorough knowledge of his various duties ; and that he fhould execute them with a promptitude and propriety of deportment that fhall give them their proper effect.

"Your *Robe of office* is an emblem of humility ; and teaches that, in the profecution of a laudable undertaking, we fhould never decline taking any part that may be affigned us, although it may be the moft difficult or dangerous.

" The *rofe coloured* teffelated border, adorning the robe, is an emblem of ardour and perfeverance, and fignifies, that when we have engaged in a virtuous courfe, notwithftanding all the impediments, hardfhips and trials we may be deftined to encounter, we fhould endure them all with fortitude, and ardently perfevere unto the end ; refting affured of receiving, at the termination of our labours, a noble and glorious reward.

" The *white banner*, entrufted to your care, is emblematical of that purity of life, and rectitude of conduct, which fhould diftinguifh every one that paffes the white veil of the fanctuary.

"Your past exertions will be considered as a pledge of your future assiduity, in the faithful discharge of your duties."

24. He will then retire to the line of officers, and the next officer is presented.

Charge to the Sixth Officer, or Royal Arch Captain.

" COMPANION,

"The well known duties of your station require but little elucidation. Your office in the preparatory degrees corresponds with that of *senior deacon.* It is your particular province, conjointly with the captain of the host, to attend the examination of all visiters, and to take care that none are permitted to enter the chapter but such as have *travelled the rugged path* of trial, and evinced their title to our favour and friendship. You will be ever attentive to the commands of your chief, and always near at hand to execute them.

"I give it to you strongly in charge, never to suffer any one to *pass your post* without the *signet* of truth.

"I present you the badge of your office, in expectation of your performing your duties with intelligence, assiduity, and propriety."

25. He then retires, and the Three Masters of the Veils are presented together.

Charge to the Master of the Third Veil.

" COMPANION,

"I present you with the *Scarlet Banner*, which

17*

is the enfign of your office, and with a fword to protect and defend the fame. The rich and beautiful colour of your banner is emblematical of fervency and fidelity ; it is the appropriate colour of the royal arch degree ; it admonifhes us that we fhould be fervent in the exercife of our devotions to God, and faithful in our endeavours to promote the happinefs of man."

Charge to the Mafter of the Second Veil.

" COMPANION,

" I inveft you with the *Purple Banner*, which is the enfign of your office, and arm you with a fword to enable you to mantain its honour. The colour of your banner is produced by a combination of two diftinct colours, namely Blue and Scarlet ; the former of which is the characteriftic colour of the *fymbolic,* or *firft three degrees* of mafonry, and the latter that of the *royal arch degree.* It is an emblem of union, and is the characteriftic colour of the *intermediate degrees.* It admonifhes us to cultivate and improve that fpirit of union and harmony, between the brethren of the *fymbolic* degrees, and the companions of the fublime degrees, which fhould ever diftinguifh the members of a fociety founded upon the principles of everlafting truth and univerfal philanthropy."

Charge to the Mafter of the Firft Veil.

" COMPANION,

" I inveft you with the *Blue Banner*, which is the enfign of your office, and a fword for its de-

fence and protection. The colour of your banner is one of the most *durable* and *beautiful* in
nature. It is the appropriate colour adopted
and worn by our ancient brethren of the three
symbolic degrees, and is the peculiar characteristic of an inftitution which has ftood the teft of
ages, and which is as much diftinguifhed by the
durability of its materials, or principles, as by
the beauty of its fuperftructure. It is an emblem of *univerfal benevolence*, and inftructs us
that in the mind of a mafon this virtue fhould
be as expanfive as the blue arch of heaven itfelf."

*Charge to the three Mafters of the Veils, as
Overfeers.*

" COMPANIONS,

" Thofe who are placed as overfeers of any
work fhould be well qualified to judge of its
beauties and deformities, its excellencies and defects; they fhould be capable of eftimating the
former, and amending the latter. This confideration fhould induce you to cultivate and improve all thofe qualifications with which you
are already endowed, as well as to perfevere in
your endeavours to acquire thofe in which you
may be in any wife deficient. Let the various
colours of the banners committed to your charge,
admonifh you to the exercife of the feveral virtues of which they are emblematic; and you
are to enjoin the practice of thofe virtues upon
all thofe who fhall prefent themfelves, or the
work of their hands, for your infpection.
" Let no work receive your approbation but
fuch as is calculated to adorn and ftrengthen

the mafonic edifice. Be induftrious; and faithful in practifing and diffeminating a knowledge of the *true and perfect work* which alone can ftand the teft of the Grand Overfeer's fquare in the great day of trial and retribution ; "then, although every rod fhould become a *ferpent*, and every ferpent an enemy to this inftitution, yet fhall their utmoft exertions to deftroy its reputation, or fap its foundation, become as impotent as the leprous hand, or as *water fpilled upon the ground*, which cannot be gathered up again."

26. They then retire, and the Secretary is prefented.

Charge to the Secretary.

" COMPANION,

" I with pleafure inveft you with your badge as Secretary of this chapter. The qualities which fhould recommend a fecretary, are, *promptitude* in iffuing the notifications and orders of his fuperior officers ; *punctuality* in attending the meetings of the chapter; *correctnefs* in recording their proceedings ; *judgment* in difcriminating between what is proper and what is improper to be committed to writing ; *regularity* in making his annual returns to the grand chapter ; *integrity* in accounting for all monies that may pafs through his hands, and *fidelity* in paying the fame over into the hands of the treafurer. The poffeffion of thefe good qualities, I prefume, has defignated you as a fuitable candidate for this important office, and I cannot entertain a doubt that you will difcharge its duties beneficially to the chapter, and honourably to yourfelf. And when you fhall have completed the *record* of your tranfactions here below, and finifhed the term of your probation, may you be admitted into the celeftial grand chapter of faints and angels, and find your name *recorded* in *the book of life eternal.*"

27. He then retires, and the Treafurer is pre-fented.

Charge to the Treafurer.

" COMPANION,

" You are elected treafurer of this chapter, and I have the pleafure of invefting you with the badge of your office. The qualities which fhould recommend a treafurer are *accuracy* and *fidelity;* accuracy, in keeping a fair and minute account of all receipts and difburfements; fidel-ity, in carefully preferving all the property and funds of the chapter that may be placed in his hands, and rendering a juft account of the fame, whenever he is called upon for that purpofe. I prefume that your refpect for the inftitution, your attachment to the interefts of your chap-ter, and your regard for a good name, which is better than precious ointment, will prompt you to the faithful difcharge of the duties of your office."

28. He then retires, and the Stewards are pre-fented.

Charge to the Stewards.

" COMPANIONS,

" You being elected ſtewards of this chapter, I with pleaſure inveſt you with the badges of your office. It is your province to ſee that every neceſſary preparation is made for the convenience and accommodation of the chapter, previous to the time appointed for meeting. You are to ſee that the clothing, implements and furniture of each degree reſpectively, are properly diſpoſed, and in ſuitable array for uſe, whenever they may be required, and that they are ſecured, and proper care taken of them, when the buſineſs of the chapter is over. You are to ſee that neceſſary refreſhments are provided, and that all your companions, and particularly viſiters, are ſuitably accommodated and ſupplied. You are to be frugal and prudent in your diſburſements, and to be careful that no extravagance or waſte is committed in your department ; and when you have faithfully fulfilled your ſtewardſhip here below, may you receive from heaven the happy greeting of " well done, good and faithful ſervants."

29. They then retire, and the Tyler is preſented.

Charge to the Tyler.

" COMPANION,

" You are appointed tyler of this chapter, and I inveſt you with this implement of your office. As the ſword is placed in the hands of the tyler, to enable him effectually to guard againſt the approach of cowans and evefdroppers, and fuffer none to pafs or repafs but fuch as are duly qualified, fo it fhould morally ferve as a conftant admonition to us to fet a guard at the entrance of our thoughts ; to place a watch at the door of our lips ; to poft a centinel at the avenue of our actions, thereby excluding every unqualified and unworthy thought, word and deed, and preferving confciences void of offence towards God and towards man.

"As the firft application from vifiters for admiffion into the chapter is generally made to the tyler at the door, your ftation will often prefent you to the obfervation of ftrangers ; it is therefore effentially neceffary that he who fuftains the office with which you are entrufted fhould be a man of good morals, fteady habits, ftrict difcipline, temperate, affable, and difcreet. I truft that a juft regard for the honour and reputation of the inftitution will ever induce you to perform with fidelity the truft repofed in you : and when the door of this earthly tabernacle fhall be clofed, may you find an abundant entrance through the gates into the temple and city of our God."

30. He will retire, and then follows an

Addrefs to the High Prieft.

"M. E. COMPANION,

"Having been honoured with the free fuffrages of the members of this chapter, you are elected to the moft important office which is within their power to beftow. This expreffion of their efteem and refpect fhould draw from you correfponding fenfations, and your demeanour fhould be fuch as to repay the honour they have fo confpicuoufly conferred upon you, by an honourable and faithful difcharge of the duties of your office.

" The ftation you are called to fill is important, not only as it refpects the correct practice of our rites and ceremonies, and the internal economy of the chapter over which you prefide, but the public reputation of the inftitution will be generally found to rife or fall according to the fkill, fidelity and difcretion, with which its concerns are managed, and in proportion as the characters and conduct of its principal officers are eftimable or cenfurable.

" You have accepted a truft, to which is attached a weight of refponfibility that will require all your efforts to difcharge honourably to yourfelf and fatisfactorily to the chapter. You are to fee that your officers are capable and faithful in the exercifes of their offices; fhould they lack ability, you are expected to fupply their defects; you are to watch carefully the progrefs of their performances, and to fee that the long eftablifhed cuftoms of the inftitution fuffer no derangement in their hands.

" You are to have a careful eye over the general conduct of your chapter; fee that due order and fubordination is obferved on all occafions; that the members are properly inftructed; that a due folemnity be obferved in the practice of our rites; that no improper levity be permitted at *any time*, but more efpecially at the *intro-*

duction of strangers among the workmen.   In fine, you are to be an example to your officers and members, which they need not hesitate to follow; thus securing to yourself the favour of heaven, and the applauses of your brethren and companions."

Address to the Officers generally.

" COMPANIONS IN OFFICE,

"Precepts and example should ever advance with an equal pace.   Those moral duties, which you are required to teach unto others, you should never neglect to practise yourselves.

"Do you desire that the demeanour of your equals and inferiors towards you should be marked with deference and respect? be sure that you omit no opportunity of furnishing them with examples in your own conduct towards your superiors.   Do you desire to obtain instruction from those who are more wise or better informed than yourselves? be sure that you are always ready to impart of your knowledge to those within your sphere, who stand in need of, and are entitled to receive it.   Do you desire distinction among your companions? be sure that your claims to preferment are founded upon superior attainments; let no ambitious passion be suffered to induce you to envy or supplant a companion, who may be considered as better qualified for promotion than yourselves; but rather let a laudable emulation induce you to strive to excel each other in improvement and discipline; ever remembering that he, who *faithfully per-*

18

forms his duty, even in a fubordinate or private ftation, is as juftly entitled to efteem and refpect, as he, who is invefted with fupreme authority."

Addrefs to the Chapter at large.

" COMPANIONS,

" The exercife and management of the fublime degrees of mafonry in your chapter hitherto, are fo highly appreciated, and the good reputation of the chapter fo well eftablifhed, that I muft prefume thefe confiderations alone, were there not others of greater magnitude, would be fufficient to induce you to preferve and perpetuate this valuable and honourable character. But when to thefe is added the pleafure which every philanthropic heart muft feel in doing good, in promoting good order, in diffufing light and knowledge, in cultivating mafonic and chriftian charity, which are the great objects of this fublime inftitution, I cannot doubt that your future conduct, and that of your fucceffors, will be calculated ftill to increafe the luftre of your juftly efteemed reputation.

" May your chapter become *beautiful* as the *temple, peaceful* as the *ark,* and *facred* as its *moft holy place.* May your oblations of piety and praife be *grateful* as the *incenfe ;* your love *warm* as its *flame,* and your charity *diffufive* as its *fragrance.* May your hearts be *pure* as the *altar,* and your conduct *acceptable* as the *offering.*

" May the exercifes of your charity be as conftant as the returning wants of the diftreffed widow and the helplefs orphan. May the approbation of heaven be your encouragement, and the teſtimony of a good confcience your fupport ; may you be endowed with every good and perfect gift, while travelling the thorny path of life, and finally admitted within the veil of heaven to the full enjoyment of life eternal."

"So mote it be."

31. The officers and members of the chapter will then paſs in review in front of the grand officers, and pay them the cuſtomary ſalutations as they paſs.

32. The grand marſhal will then make proclamation as follows, viz. " In the name of the moſt excellent grand high prieſt, I do proclaim this chapter, by the name of .... to be regularly conſtituted, and its officers duly inſtalled."

33. The officers of the chapter will then take their ſtations upon the left of the grand officers refpectively.

34. The ceremonies conclude with an ode or appropriate piece of mufic.

35. When the grand officers retire, the chapter will form an avenue for them to paſs through, and ſalute them with the grand honours. They will be attended as far as the door of their apartment by the committee who introduced them.

36. The two bodies then ſeparately cloſe their refpective chapters.

FREEMASON'S MONITOR.

PART FIRST.

BOOK III.

CHAPTER I.

Obfervations on the Orders of Knighthood.

As feveral orders of knighthood are conferred, both in Europe and America, reputedly under the fanction of, or in connection with, mafonic affemblies, it may be expected that fome notice will be taken of them in this work.

It may be neceffary to premife, that the orders of knighthood compofe no part of the fyftem of freemafonry: they are, in comparifon to it, focieties of but yefterday; and all of them fall fhort of the excellence, harmony, univerfality and utility of that noble inftitution.

The defign of this part of the work will be to collect together fuch obfervations from fcripture and hiftory, as are deemed applicable to the feveral orders; and as in America they are only conferred as honorary degrees, it is poffible that this may be the means of producing a uniformity in their application and ufe.

CHAPTER II.

Of the Order of Knights of the Red Cross.

The incidents upon which this order is founded occurred in the reign of Darius, king of Persia. It is more immediately connected with symbolic masonry than any other order of knighthood. Their meetings are called *councils ;* their sashes are decorated with a *sword* and *trowel,* and trimmed with red and green.

The following passages of scripture are considered by knights of this order as applicable to their institution, and are occasionally rehearsed in their councils.

Ezra iii. 8, 11. " Now in the second year of their coming unto the house of God at Jerusalem, in the second month, began Zerubbabel the son of Shealtiel, and Jeshua the son of Jozadak, and the remnant of their brethren the priests and the Levites, and all they that were come out of the captivity unto Jerusalem ; and appointed the Levites, from twenty years old and upward, to set forward the work of the house of the Lord. Then stood Jeshua, with his sons and his brethren, Kadmiel and his sons, the sons of Judah, together, to set forward the workmen in the house of God ; the sons of Henadad, with their sons and their brethren the Levites. And when the builders laid the foundation of the temple of the Lord, they set the priests in their apparel with trumpets, and the Levites the sons of Asaph with cymbals, to praise the Lord, after the ordinance of David king of Israel. And

18*

they fang together by courfe, in praifing and
giving thanks unto the Lord; becaufe he is
good, for his mercy endureth forever toward Ifrael.   And all the people fhouted with a great
fhout when they praifed the Lord, becaufe the
foundation of the houfe of the Lord was laid.''

Ezra iv.   " Now when the adverfaries of Judah and Benjamin heard that the children of the
captivity builded the temple unto the Lord God
of Ifrael, then they came to Zerubbabel, and to
the chief of the fathers, and faid unto them, Let
us build with you; for we feek your God as ye
do; and we do facrifice unto him, fince the days
of Efarhaddon king of Affur, which brought us
up hither.   But Zerubbabel and Jefhua, and the
reft of the chief of the fathers of Ifrael, faid unto
them, ye have nothing to do with us to build an
houfe unto our God; but we ourfelves together
will build unto the Lord God of Ifrael, as king
Cyrus, the king of Perfia, hath commanded us.
Then the people of the land weakened the hands
of the people of Judah, and troubled them in
building; and hired counfellors againft them, to
fruftrate their purpofe, all the days of Cyrus
king of Perfia, even until the reign of Darius
king of Perfia.   And in the reign of Ahafuerus,
in the beginning of his reign, wrote they unto
him an accufation againft the inhabitants of Judah and Jerufalem.   And in the days of Artaxerxes wrote Bifhlam, Mithredath, Tabeel, and
the reft of their companions, unto Artaxerxes
king of Perfia; and the writing of the letter
was written in the Syrian tongue, and interpret-
ed in the Syrian tongue; Rehum the Chancellor, and Shimfhai the fcribe, wrote a letter

againſt Jeruſalem to Artaxerxes the king, in this ſort : This is the copy of the letter that they ſent unto him, even unto Artaxerxes the king :— Thy ſervants, the men on this ſide the river, and at ſuch a time. Be it known unto the king, that the Jews, which came up from thee to us, are come unto Jeruſalem, building the rebellious and the bad city, and have ſet up the walls thereof, and joined the foundations. Be it known now unto the king, that if this city be builded, and the walls ſet up again, then will they not pay toll, tribute and cuſtom, and ſo thou ſhalt endamage the revenue of the kings. Now becauſe we have maintenance from the king's palace, and it was not meet for us to ſee the king's diſhonour ; therefore have we ſent and certified the king : that ſearch may be made in the book of the records of thy fathers : ſo ſhalt thou find in the book of the records, and know, that this city is a rebellious city, and hurtful unto kings and provinces, and that they have moved ſedition within the ſame of old time : for which cauſe was this city deſtroyed. We certify the king, that if this city be builded again, and the walls thereof ſet up, by this means thou ſhalt have no portion on this ſide the river. Then ſent the king an anſwer unto Rehum the chancellor, and to Shimſhai the ſcribe, and to the reſt of their companions that dwell in Samaria, and unto the reſt beyond the river, Peace, and at ſuch a time. The letter which ye ſent unto us hath been plainly read before me. And I commanded, and ſearch hath been made, and it is found that this city of old

time hath made infurrection againft kings, and
that rebellion and fedition have been made therein. There have been mighty kings alfo over
Jerufalem, which have ruled over all countries
beyond the river ; and toll, tribute and cuftom
was paid unto them. Give ye now commandment to caufe thefe men to ceafe, and that this
city be not builded, until another commandment fhall be given from me. Take heed now
that ye fail not to do this : why fhould damage
grow to the hurt of the kings ? Now, when the
copy of king Artaxerxes' letter was read before
Rehum, and Shimfhai the fcribe, and their companions, they went up in hafte to Jerufalem,
unto the Jews, and made them to ceafe by force
and power. Then ceafed the work of the houfe
of God, which is at Jerufalem. So it ceafed unto the fecond year of the reign of Darius, king
of Perfia.

Darius the king having afcended the throne
of Perfia, the children of the captivity were infpired with new hopes of protection and fupport in completing their noble and glorious undertaking, which had been fo often and fo long
impeded by their adverfaries on the other fide of
the river.

The ancient hiftorians inform us, that Darius,
whilft he was yet a private man, made a vow to
God, that if ever he came to the throne he
would reftore all the holy veffels that were at
Babylon, and fend them back again to Jerufalem. Zerubbabel, one of the moft excellent and
faithful of the rulers of the Jews, having been
formerly diftinguifhed by the favourable notice

and friendſhip of the king whilſt in private life, offered himſelf to encounter the hazardous enterprife of traverſing the Perſian dominions, and feeking admiſſion to the royal preſence, in order that he might ſeize the firſt favourable moment to remind the king of the vow which he had made, and to impreſs upon his mind the almighty force and importance of TRUTH. From the known piety of the king no doubt was entertained of obtaining his conſent that their enemies might be removed far from thence, and that they might be no longer impeded in the glorious undertaking in which they were engaged.

The council of rulers accepted, with great joy, this noble ſacrifice on the part of Zerubbabel, and inveſted him with the neceſſary paſſports and commendations to enable him to paſs through their own dominions in ſafety. Having paſſed the barriers, and entered the Perſian dominions, he was taken captive, clothed in the habiliments of a ſlave, and put in chains ; but not difcouraged by this misfortune, he declared himſelf a prince of the power of Judah, and demanded an audience of the ſovereign. He was told that he could only appear in the preſence of the ſovereign as a captive and ſlave ; to which he confented, being impreſſed with a belief, that if by any means he could gain acceſs to the king he ſhould ſucceed in the object of his journey.

Zerubbabel, having thus gained admiſſion to the royal preſence, was recognized by the king, as the friend and companion of his youth, and was interrogated as to his motives in attempt-

ing to pafs the barriers of his dominions; to
which Zerubbabel replied, that he was induced
to feek the face of the king by the tears and
complaints of his brethren and companions in
Jerufalem, who were impeded by their adverfaries on the other fide of the river in the noble
and glorious undertaking of rebuilding the houfe
of the Lord, in which they had been permitted
to engage by their, late fovereign mafter Cyrus
the king; that this great work having been
made to ceafe by force and power, he had come
to implore the fovereign that he might be reftored to his confidence, and admitted amongft
the fervants of his houfehold.   The king anfwered, that he had often reflected with peculiar
pleafure upon their former intimacy; that he
had heard, with great fatisfaction, of his fame
as a wife and accomplifhed ruler among the _Ar-_
chitects of his country; that having a profound
veneration for an inftitution which was reputed
to practife myfteries which were calculated to
promote the glory of the nation, and the happinefs of the people, he would inftantly reftore
him to favour, upon condition that he would
reveal thofe myfteries which fo eminently diftinguifhed the architects of the Jews from thofe
of all other nations.

Zerubbabel replied, that their inftitutions inculcated the doctrine, that TRUTH is a divine
attribute, and the foundation of every virtue;
that to be good men and _true_ was the firft leffon
they were taught; that his engagements were
inviolable; that if he could obtain the royal
favour only by the facrifice of his integrity,

he fhould humbly beg leave to renounce the
protection of the fovereign, and cheerfully fubmit to an honourable exile, or a glorious death.

The king, ftruck with admiration at the firmnefs and difcretion of Zerubbabel, declared that
his virtue and integrity were truly commendable; that his fidelity to his engagements were
worthy of imitation, and from that moment
he was reftored to his confidence.

Darius, in the firft year of his reign, gave
a fplendid and magnificent entertainment to
the princes and nobility; and after they had
retired, finding himfelf unable to fleep, he fell
into difcourfe with his three favourite officers,
to whom he propofed certain queftions, tell-
ing them, at the fame time, that he who
fhould give him the moft reafonable and fatis-
factory anfwer, fhould be clothed in purple,
drink in a golden cup, wear a filken tiara, and
a golden chain about his neck.

He then propofed this queftion: Which is
greateft, the ftrength of *wine*, of the *king*, of
women, or of *truth?* To this the firft anfwered, *wine* is the ftrongeft; the fecond, that the
king was ftrongeft; and the third, (who was
Zerubbabel) that *women* were ftronger, but above
all things TRUTH beareth the victory.

On the following day the king affembled together the princes and nobility, to hear the
queftion debated; and having placed himfelf upon the royal feat of judgment, he called upon
them to make a public defence of their feveral
opinions; whereupon the firft began upon the
ftrength of wine, as follows:

The Power of Wine.

"O ye princes and rulers, how exceeding strong is wine! it caufeth all men to err that drink it: it maketh the mind of the king and the beggar to be all one; of the bondman and the freeman; of the poor man and of the rich; it turneth alfo every thought into jollity and mirth, fo that a man remembereth neither forrow nor debt; it changeth and elevateth the spirits, and enliveneth the heavy hearts of the miferable. It maketh a man forget his brethren, and draw his fword againft his beft friends. O ye princes and rulers, is not wine the ftrongeft, that forceth us to do thefe things?"

The Power of the King.

Then began the fecond upon the power of kings, and fpoke as follows:

"It is beyond difpute, O princes and rulers, that God has made man mafter of all things under the fun; to command them, to make ufe of them, and apply them to his fervice as he pleafes: but whereas men have only dominion over other fublunary creatures, kings have an authority even over men themfelves, and a right of ruling them by will and pleafure. Now, he that is mafter of thofe who are mafters of all things elfe, hath no earthly thing above him."

The Power of Women and of Truth.

Then began Zerubbabel upon the power of women and of truth, and fpoke as follows:

"O princes and rulers, the force of wine is not to be denied; neither is that of kings, that

unites fo many men in one common bond of allegiance; but the fupereminency of *women* is yet
above all this; for *kings* are but the gifts of women, and they are alfo the mothers of thofe that
cultivate our *vineyards*. Women have the power to make us abandon our very country and
relations, and many times to forget the beft
friends we have in the world, and, forfaking all
other comforts, to live and die with them. But
when all is faid, neither they, nor wine, nor
kings, are comparable to the almighty force of
truth. As for all other things, they are mortal
and tranfient, but truth alone is unchangeable.
and everlafting; the benefits we receive from it
are fubject to no variations or viciffitudes of
time and fortune. In her judgment is no un-
righteoufnefs, and fhe is the ftrength, wifdom,
power and majefty, of all ages. Bleffed be the
God of truth."

When Zerubbabel had finifhed fpeaking, the
princes and rulers cried out,

"Great is truth, and mighty above all things."

Then faid the king to Zerubbabel,

"Afk what thou wilt, and I will give it thee,
becaufe thou art found wifeft among thy companions."

Then faid he to Darius,

"O king, remember thy vow, which thou
haft vowed, to build Jerufalem in the day when
thou fhouldeft come to thy kingdom, and to reftore the holy veffels which were taken away
out of Jerufalem. Thou haft alfo vowed to
build up the temple, which was burned when
Judah was made defolate by the Chaldees. And

now, O king, this is that I defire of thee, that thou make good the vow, the performance whereof with thine own mouth thou haft vowed to the King of Heaven."

Then Darius the king ftood up and embraced him, and gave him paffports and letters to his governors and officers, that they fhould fafely convey both him, and thofe who fhould go with him, to Jerufalem ; and that they fhould not be delayed or hindered from building the city and the temple, until they fhould be finifhed. He alfo reftored all the holy veffels remaining in his poffeffion, that had been taken from Jerufalem, when the children of Ifrael were carried away captive to Babylon, and referved by Cyrus.

Nehemiah iv. 7—21. " But it came to pafs, that when Sanballat, and Tobiah, and the Arabians, and the Ammonites, and the Afhdodites, heard that the walls of Jerufalem were made up, and that the breaches began to be ftopped, then they were very wroth, and confpired all of them together, to come and to fight againft Jerufalem, and to hinder it. Neverthelefs, we made our prayer unto our God, and fet a watch againft them day and night becaufe of them. And Judah faid, The ftrength of the bearers of burdens is decayed, and there is much rubbifh, fo that we are not able to build the wall. And our adverfaries faid, They fhall not know, neither fee, till we come in the midft among them, and flay them, and caufe the work to ceafe. And it came to pafs, that when the Jews, which dwelt by them, came, they faid unto us ten times, From all places whence ye fhall return

unto us, they will be upon you. Therefore set
I in the lower places, behind the wall, and on
the higher places, I even set the people after
their families, with their swords, their spears,
and their bows. And I looked, and rose up,
and said unto the nobles, and to the rulers,
and to the rest of the people, Be not ye
afraid of them: remember the Lord, which
is great and terrible, and fight for your brethren, your sons and your daughters, your
wives and your houses. And it came to pass,
when our enemies heard that it was known unto us, and God had brought their counsel to
nought, that we returned all of us to the wall,
every one unto his work. And it came to pass,
from that time forth, that the half of my servants wrought in the work, and the other half
of them held both the spears, the shields, and
the bows, and the habergeons; and the rulers
were behind all the house of Judah. They
which builded on the wall, and they that bare
burdens, with those that laded, every one with
one of his hands wrought in the work, and with
the other hand held a weapon. For the builders every one had his sword girded by his side,
and so builded; and he that sounded the trump-
et was by me. And I said unto the nobles, and
to the rulers, and to the rest of the people, The
work is great and large, and we are separated
upon the wall, one far from another: In what
place, therefore, ye hear the sound of the trump-
et, resort ye thither unto us: our God shall fight
for us."

Ezra v. "Then the prophets, Haggai the

prophet, and Zechariah the fon of Iddo, prophe-
fied unto the Jews that were in Judah and Jerufalem, in the name of the God of Ifrael, even
unto them. Then rofe up Zerubbabel the fon
of Shealtiel, and Jefhua the fon of Jofadak, and
began to build the houfe of God, which is at Je-
rufaiem : and with them were the prophets of
God helping them. At the fame time came to
them Tatnai, governor on this fide the river,
and Shetharboznai, and their companions, and
faid thus unto them : Who hath commanded you to build this houfe, and to make up
this wall? Then faid we unto them after
this manner : What are the names of the
men that make this building ? But the eye of
their God was upon the elders of the Jews, that
they could not caufe them to ceafe, till the matter came to Darius ; and then they returned anfwer by letter concerning this matter. The copy
of the letter that Tatnai, governor on this fide
the river, and Shetharboznai, and his companions the Apharfachites, which were on this fide
the river, fent unto Darius the king : They fent
a letter unto him, wherein was written : Unto
Darius the king, all peace. Be it known unto
the king, that we went into the province of Judea, to the houfe of the great God, which is
builded with great ftones, and timber is laid in
the walls, and this work goeth faft on, and prof-
pereth in their hands. Then afked we thofe elders, and faid unto them thus : Who commanded you to build this houfe, and to make up thefe
walls ? We afked their names alfo to certify
thee, that we might write the names of the men

that were the chief of them. And thus they returned us anfwer, faying, We are the fervants of the God of heaven and earth, and build the houfe that was builded thefe many years ago, which a great king of Ifrael builded and fet up. But after that our fathers had provoked the God of heaven unto wrath, he gave them into the hand of Nebuchadnezzar the king of Babylon, the Chaldean, who deftroyed this houfe, and carried the people away into Babylon. But in the firft year of Cyrus the king of Babylon, the fame king Cyrus made a decree to build this houfe of God. And the veffels alfo of gold and filver of the houfe of God, which Nebuchadnezzar took out of the temple that was in Jerufalem, and brought them into the temple of Babylon, thofe did Cyrus the king take out of the temple at Babylon, and they were delivered unto one whofe name was Shefhbazzar, whom he made governor ; and faid unto him, Take thefe veffels, go, carry them into the temple that is in Jerufalem, and let the houfe of God be builded in his place. Then came the fame Shefhbazzar, and laid the foundation of the houfe of God which is in Jerufalem : and fince that time even until now hath it been in building, and yet it is not finifhed. Now therefore, if it feem good to the king, let there be fearch made in the king's treafure-houfe, which is there at Babylon, whether it be fo, that a decree was made of Cyrus the king to build this houfe of God at Jerufalem, and let the king fend his pleafure to us concerning this matter."

3. *Ezra* vi. " Then Darius the king made a de-

19*

cree, and fearch was made in the houfe of the
rolls, where the treafures were laid up in Babylon.   And there was found at Achmetha, in the
palace that is in the province of the Medes, a
roll, and therein was a record thus written : In
the firft year of Cyrus the king, the fame Cyrus
the king made a decree concerning the houfe of
God at Jerufalem : Let the houfe be builded, the
place where they offered facrifice, and let the
foundations thereof be ftrongly laid ; the height
thereof threefcore cubits ; and the breadth thereof threefcore cubits ; with three rows of great
ftones, and a row of new timber ; and let the
expenfes be given out of the king's houfe.   And
alfo let the golden and filver veffels of the houfe
of God, which Nebuchadnezzar took forth out
of the temple which is at Jerufalem, and brought
unto Babylon, be reftored and brought again
unto the temple which is at Jerufalem, every
one to his place, and place them in the houfe of
God.   Now therefore, Tatnai, governor beyond
the river, Shetharboznai, and your companions
the Apharfachites, which are beyond the river,
be ye far from thence ; let the work of this houfe
of God alone ; let the governor of the Jews, and
the elders of the Jews, build this houfe of God
in his place.   Moreover, I make a decree what
ye fhall do to the elders of thefe Jews, for the
building of this houfe of God ; that of the king's
goods, even of the tribute beyond the river,
forthwith expenfes be given unto thefe men,
that they be not hindered.   And that which
they have need of, both young bullocks, and
rams, and lambs, for the burnt offerings of the

God of heaven; wheat, falt, wine, and oil, according to the appointment of the priefts which are at Jerufalem, let it be given them day by day without fail; that they may offer facrifices of fweet favours unto the God of heaven, and pray for the life of the king and of his fons. Alfo I have made a decree, that whofoever fhall alter this word, let timber be pulled down from his houfe, and, being fet up, let him be hanged thereon; and let his houfe be made a dunghill for this. And the God that hath caufed his name to dwell there deftroy all kings and people that fhall put to their hand to alter and to deftroy this houfe of God which is at Jerufalem. I Darius have made a decree; let it be done with fpeed. Then Tatnai, governor on this fide the river, Shetharboznai, and their companions, according to that which Darius the king had fent, fo they did fpeedily. And the elders of the Jews builded, and they profpered through the prophefying of Haggai the prophet, and Zechariah the fon of Iddo; and they builded and finifhed it according to the commandment of the God of Ifrael, and according to the commandment of Cyrus, and Darius, and Artaxerxes king of Perfia. And this houfe was finifhed on the third day of the month Adar, which was in the fixth year of the reign of Darius the king," and in the year of the world 3489.

CHAPTER III.

*Observations on the Orders of Knights Templars,
and Knights of Malta.*

ACCORDING to the Abbe-de-Vertot, the order of knights of Malta, who were originally called hofpitallers of St. John of Jerufalem, took its rife about the year 1099; from which time to the year 1118, their whole employment was works of charity, and taking care of the fick.

Some time after the eftablifhment of this order, nine gentlemen (of whofe names two only remain on record, viz. Hugho de Paganis and Godfrey Adelman) formed a fociety to guard and protect the Chriftian pilgrims who travelled from abroad to vifit the holy fepulchre.

Thefe men were encouraged by the Abbot of Jerufalem, who affigned them and their companions a place of retreat in a chriftian church, called the church of the holy temple, from which they were called templars; and not from the temple of Jerufalem, that having been deftroyed by Titus Vefpafian, 982 years before the fociety of Templars was inftituted.

The fociety increafed rapidly, and was much refpected; but had neither habit, order, or mark of diftinction, for the fpace of nine years; when pope Honorius II, at the requeft of Stephen, patriarch of Jerufalem, laid down a rule and manner of life for them; and ordained that they fhould be clothed in white; to which garment pope Eugenius III added a red crofs, to be worn on the breaft, which they promifed by a folemn oath to obferve for ever.

Incited by the example of the *knights templars*, about the year 1118, the *hofpitallers* alfo took up the profeffion of arms, in addition to their original charitable profeffion ; occupying themfelves at one time in attending upon the fick, and at others in acts of hoftility againft the Turks and Saracens. At this time they took the name of *knights* hofpitallers.

Both orders flourifhed and increafed daily ; but that of the templars, though the youngeft of the two, having from its original eftablifhment been wholly employed in the profeffion of arms, was by many efteemed to be the moft honourable ; and therefore many noblemen, princes, and perfons of the higheft diftinction, who thought the fervice of tending the fick too fervile an employment, entered themfelves among the *knights templars*, in preference to the other order.

Both orders, for years, generally took the field together, and as well by themfelves as in conjunction with the troops of the crufaders, won many battles, and performed prodigies of valour. The emulation, however, which fubfifted between them, often occafioned warm difputes, which rofe to fuch a height as produced frequent fkirmifhes between detached parties of the two orders. This occafioned the pope and the refpective grand mafters to interfere ; who in a great meafure fuppreffed thefe quarrels ; but the knights of the different orders ever afterward continued to view each other with jealous eyes.

Some time after these difficulties were thus partially suppressed, the Turks assembled a great force, and drove the whole of the christians out of Palestine. The last fortress they had possession of was that of St. John D'Acre. This was long and bravely defended by the knights templars against their besiegers. The Turks, however, at last forced three hundred knights, being all that remained of the garrison, to take refuge in a strong tower, to which also the women fled for safety. The Turks hereupon set about undermining it, which they in a short time so effectually accomplished, that the knights saw, in case they held out any longer, they must all inevitably perish. They therefore capitulated, stipulating, among other things, that the honour of their women should not be violated. Upon this, the tower being opened, the Turks marched in ; but, in total breach of the terms of capitulation, they immediately began to offer violence to the women. The enraged knights instantly drew their swords, hewed in pieces all the Turks who had entered, shut the gates against those who remained without, and resigned themselves to inevitable death, which they soon met with, by the tower being undermined and thrown down upon their heads.

After this defeat, the two orders found an asylum in the island of Cyprus ; from whence, after some time, the knights templars, finding their number so diminished as to leave no hopes of effecting any thing towards the recovery of the holy land, without new crusades, (which the christian princes did not seem inclined to set on foot) returned to their different commanders in the various parts of chriftendom.

From this time the two orders feparated; the knights hofpitallers remained a while at Cyprus, from whence they afterwards went to Rhodes, and thence to Malta; which name they then affumed. The knights templars difperfed themfelves throughout all Europe, but ftill enjoyed princely revenues, and were extremely wealthy.

Vertot fays, that pope Boniface the VIII, having engaged in a warm difpute with Philip, king of France, the two orders, as had too frequently happened before, took oppofite fides. The knights of Malta declared in favour of king Philip, while the knights templars efpoufed the caufe of the pope. This conduct, Philip, partly from a revengeful difpofition, and partly from the hope of getting poffeffion of the vaft wealth of the knights, never could forgive; but formed, thenceforward, the defign of fuppreffing the order whenever a proper opportunity fhould offer. This however did not occur till after the deceafe of pope Boniface.

Immediately on the death of that pontiff, the cardinals affembled to elect his fucceffor; but party difputes ran fo high in the conclave, that there feemed no probability of again filling the papal chair very fpeedily. At length, through the intrigues and machinations of the friends of Philip, the cardinals were all brought to confent to the election of any prieft that he fhould recommend to them.

This was the darling object the monarch had in view: this being accomplifhed, he immedi-

ately fent for the archbifhop of Bordeaux, whofe
ambition he knew had no bounds, and who
would hefitate at nothing to gratify it; and
communicated to him the power he had received of nominating a perfon to the papal chair,
and promifing he fhould be the perfon, on
his engaging to perform fix conditions. The
archbifhop greedily fnatched at the bait, and
immediately took an oath on the facrament to
the faithful performance of the conditions.
Philip then laid open to him five of the conditions, but referved the fixth until after the archbifhop's coronation as pope; which foon took
place in confequence of the recommendation of
the king to the conclave; and the new pope
took upon himfelf the name of Clement V.

Vertot goes on to fay, that a templar and a
citizen of Beziers, having been apprehended for
fome crime, and committed together to a dun-
geon, for want of a prieft confeffed each other;
that the citizen, having heard the templar's confeffion, in order to fave his own life accufed the
order to king Philip: charging them, on the authority of what his fellow prifoner had told him,
with idolatry, fodomy, robbery, and murder;
adding, that the knights templars, being fecretly
Mahometans, each knight, at his admiffion into
the order, was obliged to renounce Jefus Chrift,
and to fpit on the crofs in token of his abhor-
rence of it. Philip, on hearing thefe accufa-
tions, pardoned the citizen, and difclofed to the
pope his fixth condition, which was, the fup-
preffion of the order of knights templars.

Not only every knight templar muft know to

a certainty the abfolute falfehood of thefe charges ; but every unprejudiced reader of Vertot's
hiftory muft alfo perceive that the whole of their
accufation was the product of Philip's own brain,
in order to accomplifh his long wifhed for object
of fuppreffing the order, and getting poffeffion
of their vaft riches in his dominions. It is therefore evident, that the ftory of the templar's confeffion was all a forgery, and that the citizen
was no other than a tool of Philip, who, to
enfure his own pardon, was prevailed on to make
oath of fuch a confeffion having been made to
him by the templar.

The hiftorian proceeds to fay, that in confequence of this accufation, the knights templars
in France, and other parts of the pope's dominions, were imprifoned by his order, and put to
the moft exquifite tortures, to make them con-
fefs themfelves guilty. They, however, bore
thefe tortures with the moft heroic fortitude,
perfifting to the laft in afferting their own innocence and that of their order.

In addition to thefe proceedings, pope Clement, in the year 1312, iffued his bull for the
annihilation of the order of knights templars,
which he caufed to be publifhed throughout
every country in chriftendom. He at the fame
time gave their poffeffions to the knights of
Malta, which appropriation of the templars' eftates was affented to by moft of the fovereigns
in Europe; and there is now extant, among the
Englifh ftatutes, an act of parliament, whereby,
after fetting forth that the order of templars has
been fuppreffed, their poffeffions in England are
confirmed to the knights of St. John.

Vertot, however, further fays, that in Germany, the hiftorians of that nation relate, that pope Clement having fent his bull for abolifhing the order, to the archbifhop of Metey, for him to enforce, that prelate fummoned all his clergy together, that the publication might be made with greater folemnity : and that they were fuddenly furprifed by the entry of Wallgruffor Count Sauvage, one of the principals of the order, attended by twenty other templars, armed, and in their regular habits.

The count declared he was not come to do violence to any body, but having heard of the bull againft his order, came to infift that the appeal which they made from that decree to the next council and the fucceffor of Clement, fhould be received, read and publifhed. This he preffed fo warmly, that the archbifhop, not thinking it proper to refufe men whom he faw armed, complied. He fent the appeal afterwards to the pope, who ordered him to have it examined in a council of his province. Accordingly a fynod was called, and after a long trial, and various formalities, which were then obferved, the templars of that province were declared innocent of the crimes charged upon them.

Although the templars were thus declared innocent, it does not appear that either their poffeffions or their government, as a diftinct order, were reftored ; but that their eftates in the German empire were divided between the knights of Malta and the Teutonic knights ; to the firft of which orders many knights templars afterwards joined themfelves. This appears altogether probable from the following circumftance, viz. It is unqueftionable, that the habit of the knights templars was originally *white*; but we now obferve they diftinguifh themfelves by the fame colour as the knights of Malta, viz. *black*; which change cannot be accounted for in any other way than by an union with the knights of that order.

MANUAL.

The throne is fituated in the eaft; above are fufpended the arms of the grand patron, between a banner of the emblems of the order, and another of the arms of the grand mafter.

On the right of the throne the deputy grand mafter, and paft grand mafter; or in fubordinate encampments the paft grand commander.

On the left the grand prelate and grand chancellor.

The grand treafurer on the right, and the grand regifter on the left in front.

The knights, who are entitled to feats above the ftandards, are fo arranged as that there fhall be an equal number on each fide the throne. Over the ftall of each is a banner of arms or emblems. Next on each fide is a ftandard bearer with a banner of fky blue filk, on which is a crofs of Malta, in filver, with the motto, "The will of God."

Next below the ftandards two experts, one bearing the fpear and fhield, and the other a battle-axe. Next to them the fword bearer, and crofs bearer; then the knights not in office, concluding with the two ftewards, each with his ftaff. In the fouth-weft the fenior warden; in the north-weft the junior warden

In the weft, between the wardens, a ftall for the initiate; fupported by the mafter of ceremonies, and a herald.

Aprons.

White, with a black border; or black, with a white border. The flap black, and a fkull and crofs bones embroidered in filver thereon.

Drefs.

A full fuit of black, with a rapier and military hat; a broad black fafh on the right fhoulder, acrofs the body to the left fide, ornamented with a filver ftar oppofite to the left breaft, having feven points; the grand mafter or commander, a ftar of nine points; in the centre of the ftar, a crofs and ferpent of gold, furrounded by a circle, on which is engraved or enamelled, "In hoc figno vinces."

The following paffages of fcripture are occafionally rehearfed in encampments of knights templars.

James i. 1—10, 26, 27. " James, a fervant of God and of the Lord Jefus Chrift, to the twelve tribes which are fcattered abroad, greeting. My brethren, count it all joy when ye fall into divers temptations; knowing this, that the trying of your faith worketh patience. But let patience have her perfect work, that ye may be perfect and entire, wanting nothing. If any of you lack wifdom, let him afk of God, that giveth to all men liberally, and upbraideth not; and it fhall be given him. But let him afk in faith, nothing wavering; for he that wavereth is like a wave of the fea, driven with the wind, and toffed. For let not that man think that he fhall receive any thing of the Lord. A double mind-ed man is unftable in all his ways. Let the brother of low degree rejoice in that he is exalt-ed. If any man among you feem to be religious, and bridleth not his tongue, but deceiveth his own heart, that man's religion is vain. Pure religion, and undefiled, before God and the Fa-ther, is this : To vifit the fatherlefs and widows in their afflicion, and to keep himfelf unfpotted from the world."

Exhortation.

1. Let now the brother of low degree rejoice in that he is exalted.

2. Come unto me all ye that are weary and heavy laden, and I will give you reft.

3. Chrift fuffered for us, leaving us an exam-ple, that we fhould follow his fteps.

4. For we were as fheep going aftray, but now are we returned to the fhepherd and bifhop of our fouls.

5. If a brother or fifter be naked, and defti-tute of daily food, and one of you fay, depart in peace, be ye warmed and filled, and ye give them not of thofe things which are needful for the body, what doth it profit ?

6. To do good, and to communicate, forget not, for with fuch facrifices God is well pleafed.

7. May he, who is able, fend you forth into the world, thoroughly furnifhed for every good work, keep you from falling into vice and error, improve, ftrengthen, eftablifh and perfect you.

Matt. xxvii. 24—38. "When Pilate faw that he could prevail nothing, but that rather a tu-mult was made, he took water, and wafhed his

hands before the multitude, faying, I am innocent of the blood of this juft perfon; fee ye to
it. Then anfwered all the people, and faid, His
blood be on us, and on our children. Then re-
leafed he Barabbas unto them : and when he had
fcourged Jefus, he delivered him to be crucified.
Then the foldiers of the governor took Jefus into the common hall, and gathered unto him the
whole band of foldiers. And they ftripped him,
and put on him a fcarlet robe. And when they
had platted a crown of thorns they put it upon
his head, and a reed in his right hand; and
they bowed the knee before him, and mocked
him, faying, Hail, king of the Jews! And they
fpit upon him, and took the reed, and fmote
him on the head. And after that they had
mocked him they took the robe off from him,
and put his own raiment on him, and led him
away to crucify him. And as they came out
they found a man of Cyrene, Simon by name :
him they compelled to bear his crofs. And
when they were come unto a place called Gol-
gotha, that is to fay, a place of a fkull, they
gave him vinegar to drink, mingled with gall :
and when he had tafted thereof he would not
drink. And they crucified him, and parted his
garments, cafting lots : that it might be fulfilled
which was fpoken by the prophet, They parted
my garments among them, and upon my vef-
ture did they caft lots. And fitting down, they
watched him there; and fet up over his head
his accufation written, THIS IS JESUS THE
KING OF THE JEWS."

Matt. xxvi. 14—25 *and* 36—49. " Then one
of the twelve, called Judas Ifcariot, went unto

the chief priefts, and faid unto them, What will
ye give me, and I will deliver him unto you?
And they covenanted with him for thirty pieces of filver. And from that time he fought
opportunity to betray him. Now, the firft day
of the feaft of unleavened bread, the difciples
came to Jefus, faying unto him, Where wilt
thou that we prepare for thee to eat the paffover? And he faid, Go into the city to fuch a
man, and fay unto him, The mafter faith, My
time is at hand; I will keep the paffover at thy
houfe with my difciples. And the difciples did as
Jefus had appointed them; and they made ready
the paffover. Now, when the even was come,
he fat down with the twelve. And as they did
eat, he faid, Verily I fay unto you, that one of
you fhall betray me. And they were exceeding
forrowful, and began every one of them to fay
unto him, Lord, is it I? And he anfwered and
faid, He that dippeth his hand with me in the
difh, the fame fhall betray me. The fon of man
goeth, as it is written of him: but wo unto that
man by whom the fon of man is betrayed! It
had been good for that man if he had not been
born. Then Judas, which betrayed him, anfwered and faid, Mafter, is it I? He faid unto
him, Thou haft faid. Then cometh Jefus with
them unto a place called Gethfemane, and faith
unto the difciples, Sit ye here, while I go and
pray yonder. And he took with him Peter and
the two fons of Zebedee, and began to be forrowful and very heavy. Then faith he unto
them, My foul is exceeding forrowful, even unto death: tarry ye here, and watch with me.
And he went a little farther, and fell on his face,

and prayed, faying, O my Father, if it be poſſible, let this cup paſs from me; neverthelefs, not as I will, but as thou wilt. And he cometh unto the difciples, and findeth them afleep, and faith unto Peter, What! could ye not watch with me one hour? Watch and pray, that ye enter not into temptation : the fpirit indeed is willing, but the fleſh is weak. He went away again the fecond time, and prayed, faying, O my Father, if this cup may not paſs away from me, except I drink it, thy will be done. And he came and found them afleep again ; for their eyes were heavy. And he left them, and went away again, and prayed the third time, faying the fame words. Then cometh he to his difciples, and faith unto them, Sleep on now, and take your reft : behold, the hour is at hand, and the fon of man is betrayed into the hands of finners. Rife, let us be going : behold, he is at hand that doth betray me. And while he yet fpake, lo, Judas, one of the twelve, came, and with him a great multitude, with fwords and ftaves, from the chief priefts and elders of the people. Now he that betrayed him gave them a fign, faying, Whomfoever I fhall kifs, that fame is he : hold him faft. And forthwith he came to Jefus, and faid, Hail, mafter ; and kiffed him."

Acts i. 15—26. "And in thofe days Peter ftood up in the midft of the difciples, and faid, (the number of the names together were about an hundred and twenty,) Men and brethren, this fcripture muft needs have been fulfilled, which the Holy Ghoft, by the mouth of David, fpake before concerning Judas, which was guide

to them that took Jesus. For he was numbered with us, and had obtained part of this miniſtry. Now, this man purchaſed a field with the
reward of iniquity; and, falling headlong, he
burſt aſunder in the midſt, and all his bowels
guſhed out. And it was known unto all the
dwellers at Jeruſalem; inſomuch as that field is
called, in their proper tongue, Aceldama, that is
to ſay, the field of blood. For it is written in
the book of Pſalms, Let his habitation be deſ-
olate, and let no man dwell therein; and, His
biſhoprick let another take. Wherefore, of theſe
men which have companied with us all the time
that the Lord Jeſus went in and out among us,
beginning from the baptiſm of John, unto that
ſame day that he was taken up from us, muſt
one be ordained to be a witneſs with us of his
reſurrection. And they appointed two, Joſeph,
called Barſabas, who was ſurnamed Juſtus, and
Matthias. And they prayed, and ſaid, Thou,
Lord, which knoweſt the hearts of all men, ſhew
whether of theſe two thou haſt choſen, that he
may take part of this miniſtry and apoſtleſhip,
from which Judas by tranſgreſſion fell, that he
might go to his own place. And they gave
forth their lots: and the lot fell upon Matthias;
and he was numbered with the eleven apoſtles."

CHARGE.

Eph. vi. 10—17. " Finally, my brethren, be
ſtrong in the Lord, and in the power of his might.
" Put on the *whole armour* of God, that ye may
be able to ſtand againſt the wiles of the devil.
" For we wreſtle not againſt fleſh and blood,
but againſt principalities; againſt powers; againſt

the rulers of the darknefs of this world; againft fpiritual wickednefs in high places.

" Wherefore take unto you the whole armour of God, that ye may be able to withftand in the evil day, and having done all, to ftand.

" Stand therefore with your *loins girt* about with truth.

" And having on the *breaftplate* of righteouf-nefs.

" And *your feet fhod* with the preparation of the gofpel of peace.

" Above all, taking *the fhield* of faith, where-with ye fhall be able to quench the fiery darts of the wicked.

" And take *the helmet* of falvation,

" And *the fword* of the fpirit, which is the word of God."

CHAPTER IV.

Knights of Malta.

THE following paffages of fcripture are occa-fionally rehearfed in encampments of Knights of Malta.

Acts xxviii. 1—6. " And when they were efcaped, then they knew that the ifland was call-ed Melita. And the barbarous people fhewed us no little kindnefs; for they kindled a fire, and received us every one, becaufe of the pref-ent rain, and becaufe of the cold. And when Paul had gathered a bundle of fticks, and laid them on the fire, there came a viper out of the heat, and faftened on his hand. And when the barbarians faw the venomous beaft hang on his hand, they said among themselves, No doubt this man is a murderer, whom, though he hath escaped the sea, yet vengeance suffereth not to live. And he shook off the beast into the fire, and felt no harm. Howbeit they looked when he should have swollen, or fallen down dead suddenly; but after they had looked a great while, and saw no harm come to him, they changed their minds, and said that he was a god."

St. John xix. 19. "And Pilate wrote a title, and put it on the cross. And the writing was, JESUS OF NAZARETH, THE KING OF THE JEWS."

St. John xx. 24—28. "But Thomas, one of the twelve, called Didymus, was not with them when Jesus came. The other disciples, therefore, said unto him, We have seen the Lord. But he said unto them, Except I shall see in his hands the print of the nails, and put my finger into the print of the nails, and thrust my hand into his side, I will not believe. And after eight days, again his disciples were within, and Thomas with them. Then came Jesus, the doors being shut, and stood in the midst, and said, Peace be unto you. Then saith he to Thomas, Reach hither thy finger, and behold my hands: and reach hither thy hand, and thrust it into my side; and be not faithless, but believing. And Thomas answered, and said unto him, My Lord, and my God."

CHAPTER V.

THE order of *Knights* of the *Holy Sepulchre* was instituted in the year 1219. Their uniform was a red crofs, and their oath to defend the fepulchre of Chrift. Upon the extinction of this order, many of them joined the Knights of Malta.

The *Knights* of *Tutons*, or *Allemagne*, wore a white garment with a black crofs.

The *Knights* of *Calatrava*, a black garment, with a red crofs on the breaft.

The *Knights* of *Alcantara*, a green crofs.

The *Knights* of the *Redemption* wore a white garment, with a black crofs.

The *Knights* of *Chrift* wore a black garment with a double crofs.

The *Knights* of the *Mother* of *Chrift*, a little red crofs, reflected with gold.

The *Knights* of *Lazarus* wore a green crofs on the breaft.

The *Knights* of the *Star* wore a ftar on their hats.

The *Knights* of the *Band* wore a band of three fingers width, faftened on the left fhoulder, and brought over the breaft, under the right arm.

The *Knights* of the *Annunciation* of the *Virgin Mary* wore a collar made of plates of gold and filver, with a picture of the Virgin Mary pendent thereto.

The *Knights* of *St. Michael* wore a chain of gold, woven like little fhells, and a picture of St. Michael pendent thereto.

The *Knights* of *St. Stephen* wore a black garment, with a red crofs.

The *Knights* of the *Holy Ghoft* wore a dove on the middle of a crofs.

FREEMASON'S MONITOR.

PART FIRST.

BOOK IV.

ON ENCAMPMENTS OF KNIGHTS IN AMERICA.

CHAPTER I.

Grand Encampment of Knights Templars, and the Appendant Orders, for the ſtates of Maſſachuſetts and Rhode-Iſland.

A GRAND convention of Knights Templars was holden in Providence, R. I. on the 6th day of May, A. D. 1805; when the following meaſures were propoſed, and adopted unanimouſly, viz.

"Reſolved, as the sense of this convention, that the formation and establishment of a grand encampment of knights templars would tend to promote the honour and interests of the orders of knighthood, and of masonry.

"Resolved, that a committee be appointed to devise and report a form of constitution, explanatory of the principles upon which a grand encampment shall be opened.

"Resolved, that the convention be adjourned until Monday, the 13th instant, then to meet again in Masons' Hall, in Providence."

Monday, 13th May, A. D. 1805.

The convention met, agreeably to adjournment, to take into confideration the report of the committee appointed on the fixth inftant, for devifing and preparing a form of conftitution; which being read and amended was unanimoufly approved and adopted.

The convention then proceded to a choice of officers, who were inftalled in ample form. At an affembly of this grand encampment, holden in Bofton, in the month of May, A. D. 1816, it was refolved that three delegates be appointed on the part of this grand encampment to meet a general grand convention to be holden in the city of Philadelphia, or the city of New York, in the month of June, A. D. 1816, for the purpofe of forming a general grand encampment of knights templars for the United States, and a conftitution for the government of the fame; and the M. E. Thomas Smith Webb, M. E. Henry Fowle, and M. E. John Snow, were appointed accordingly.

The delegates proceeded to the city of New-York, where a convention affembled confifting of the reprefentatives of nine encampments and councils.

The convention, after mature deliberation, formed and adopted a conftitution, and opened a general grand encampment of knights templars, and the appendant orders, for the United States.

CHAPTER II.

CONSTITUTION

OF THE

General Grand Encampment

OF

KNIGHTS TEMPLARS

AND THE

APPENDANT ORDERS,

FOR THE

UNITED STATES OF AMERICA.

ARTICLE I.

OF THE GENERAL GRAND ENCAMPMENT.

SECT. 1. There shall be a General Grand Encampment of Knights Templars, and the Appendant Orders, for the United States of America, which shall consist of a general grand master, deputy general grand master, general grand generalissimo, general grand captain general, general grand prelate, general grand senior warden, general grand junior warden, general grand treasurer, general grand recorder, general grand warder, general grand standard bearer, general grand sword bearer, all past general grand masters, deputy general grand masters, general grand generalissimos, and general grand captain generals of this general grand encampment; the grand masters, deputy grand masters, grand generalissimos, and grand captain generals of all such state grand encampments as may be instituted or holden by virtue of this constitution; and the said enumerated officers, or their proxies, shall be the only members and voters in the said general grand encampment.

SECT 2. The general grand encampment shall be instituted and opened on the 22d day of June, A. D. 1816; it shall meet on the third Thursday in September, A. D. 1819, and septennially thereafter, for the choice of officers, and other business, on the third Thursday in September, at such place as may from time to time be appointed.

SECT. 3. A special meeting of the general grand encampment shall be called whenever any two of the first four general grand officers may deem it necessary; and also whenever it may be required by a majority of the grand encampments of the states aforesaid; provided such requisition be made known, in writing, by the said grand encampments respectively, to either of the before mentioned general grand officers.

SECT. 4. The general grand master, deputy general grand master, g. g. generalissimo, and g. g. captain general, are severally hereby authorized and empowered, to visit and preside in any and every assembly of knights of the red cross, knights templars, and of Malta, throughout the jurisdiction of the general grand encampment, and to give such instructions and directions as the good of the institution may require; always adhering to the ancient landmarks.

SECT. 5. In all cases of the absence of any officer from any assembly instituted or holden by virtue of this constitution, the officer next in rank shall succeed his superior; unless through courtesy such officer should decline in favour of a past superior officer present. And in case of the absence of all the officers, the members present, according to seniority and abilities, shall fill the several offices.

SECT. 6. In every assembly of knights, all questions (except upon the admission of members or candidates) shall be determined by a majority of votes; the presiding officer for the time being, shall be entitled to a vote, if a member; and in case the votes should be equally divided he shall also give the casting vote.

SECT. 7. The general grand encampment shall be competent, on concurrence of two thirds of its members present, at any time hereafter, to revise, amend, and alter this constitution.

SECT. 8. In case any casualty should at any time hereafter prevent the septennial election of officers, the several general grand officers shall sustain their respective offices until successors shall be duly elected and qualified.

SECT. 9. The general grand master, deputy general grand master, g. g. generalissimo, and g. g. captain general, shall severally have power and authority to institute new councils of knights of the red cross, and encampments of knights templars, and of Malta, in any state or territory wherein there is not a grand encampment regularly established. The fees for instituting a new Council and Encampment, in manner aforesaid, shall be ninety dollars, exclusive of such compensation for executing the letters of dispensation, or charter, as may be deemed reasonable.

SECT. 10. The general grand master, and deputy general grand master, are severally authorized to appoint a general grand visitor, or more than one if necessary, to superinted and perform such distant business, and to communicate such instructions as may come within the cognizance of the said grand officers respectively, conformably to the duties and prerogatives of their respective offices.

ARTICLE II.

OF STATE GRAND ENCAMPMENTS.

SECT. 1. Whenever there shall be three or more encampments instituted or holden under this constitution in any one state, a Grand

Encampment may be formed in such state, after obtaining the approbation and consent of the general grand master, the deputy general
grand master, or the general grand encampment.

SECT. 2. The state grand encampments shall severally consist of
a grand master, deputy grand master, grand generalissimo, grand captain general, grand prelate, grand senior warden, grand junior warden, grand treasurer, grand recorder, grand warder, grand standard
bearer, and grand sword bearer ; all past grand masters, deputy grand
masters, grand generalissimos, and grand captain generals, of any
state grand encampment, wheresoever they may reside ; the grand
commander, generalissimo, and captain general for the time being of
the encampments over which they shall respectively preside ; and all
past grand commanders of such encampments ; and the said enumerated officers, or their proxies, shall be the only members and voters
in the said state grand encampments respectively.

SECT. 3. The state grand encampments shall be holden at least
once in every year, at such times and places as they shall respectively direct, and the grand or deputy grand masters respectively may
call special meetings when they may deem the same necessary.
Their officers shall be chosen annually, by ballot.

SECT. 4. The several state grand encampments (subject to the
provisions of this constitution) shall have the sole government and
superintendence of the several councils of knights of the red cross,
knights templars and knights of Malta, within their respective jurisdictions ; to assign their limits, and settle controversies that may happen between them ; and shall have power, under their respective
seals, and the sign manual of their respective principal grand officers,
attested by their respective secretaries, to constitute new councils
and encampments of the above mentioned orders, within their respective jurisdictions.

SECT. 5. The grand and deputy grand masters severally shall
have the power and authority (during the recess of the grand encampment of which they are officers) to grant letters of dispensation
under their respective hands and private seals to a competent number of petitioners, residing within their respective jurisdictions, (possessing the constitutional qualifications) empowering them to form
and open a council and encampment, for a certain specified term of
time, not extending beyond the next meeting of the grand encampment. And in all cases of such dispensations, the officer granting the
same shall make report thereof at the next meeting of the grand encampment, who may either continue or recall the same, or may
grant the petitioners a charter.

SECT. 6. The several state grand encampments shall possess authority, upon the institution of new councils and encampments, within their respective jurisdictions, to require the payment of such fees
as they may deem expedient, which said fees shall be advanced and
paid before a charter or letters of dispensation shall be issued.

SECT. 7. The state grand encampments severally shall have power to require from the several councils and encampments within their
respective jurisdictions, such reasonable proportion of sums received
by them for the promotion of candidates, and such certain annual

sums from their respective members, as may be necessary for supporting the grand encampment with propriety and respectability; which said dues shall be made good, and paid over, by the councils and encampments respectively at such times as the said grand encampments may direct.

SECT. 8. No charter shall be issued for constituting a council of knights of the red cross excepting upon the petition of at least seven knights of that order; nor for constituting an encampment of knights templars and knights of Malta, excepting upon the petition of nine knights of those orders; and the petitioners must be recommended by the council or encampment in the same state, nearest the place where the new council or encampment is to be established.

SECT. 9. The grand recorders shall severally make an annual communication to each other, and also to the general grand recorder, containing a list of grand officers, and all such other matters as may be deemed useful for the mutual information of the several grand encampments. And the said state grand recorders shall also regularly transmit to the general grand recorder a copy of all their by-laws and regulations.

SECT. 10. The jurisdiction of the several state grand encampments shall not extend beyond the limits of the state in which they shall respectively be holden; excepting any case wherein, before the formation of this constitution, a grand encampment had been formed by an united representation of the encampments in two adjoining states.

ARTICLE III.

OF SUBORDINATE COUNCILS AND ENCAMPMENTS.

SECT. 1. All regular assemblies of knights of the red cross are called *Councils*; and all regular assemblies of knights templers, and knights of Malta, are called *Encampments*. Every council and encampment ought to assemble at least quarterly, for business and improvement. Every encampment shall consist of a grand commander, generalissimo, captain general, prelate, senior warden, junior warden, treasurer, recorder, warder, standard bearer, sword bearer, and as many members as may be found convenient.

SECT. 2. No encampment shall confer the orders of knighthood for a less sum than twenty dollars, nor upon any one who shall not have regularly received the several degrees of entered apprentice, fellow craft, master mason, mark master, past master, most excellent master, and royal arch mason. The rule of succession in conferring the orders of knighthood shall be as follows, viz. knight of the red cross, knight templar, and knight of Malta.

SECT. 3. Every council and encampment shall have a charter or warrant, from the grand encampment of the state in which they may respectively be holden, or from one of the first four general grand officers. And no council or encampment that may hereafter be formed and opened shall be deemed legal, without such charter or warrant; and communication is hereby interdicted and forbidden, between any council or encampment under this jurisdiction, or any member of either of them, and any council, encampment or assembly, that may be so formed, opened or holden, without such charter or warrant, or any or either of their members, or any person introduced into such illegal assembly.

SECT. 4. The grand commander of every encampment and council has it in special charge to see that the by laws of his council or encampment are duly observed, as well as the general constitution, and the regulations of the grand encampment; that accurate records are kept, and just accounts rendered; that regular returns are made to the grand encampment, and to the general grand recorder, annually, and that the annual dues are promptly paid; he has authority to call special meetings at pleasure; and it is his duty, together with his second and third officers, to attend all meetings of the grand encampment, in person or by proxy.

SECT. 5. It shall not be deemed regular for any encampment, or council, to confer the orders of knighthood upon any sojourner whose fixed place of abode is within any state in which there is an encampment regularly established; and in case any encampment shall confer the said orders, contrary to this section, such encampment shall, on demand, pay over to the encampment situated nearest the candidate's fixed place of abode, the whole amount of fees received for his admission.

SECT. 6. The officers of every council and encampment under this jurisdiction, before they enter upon the exercise of their respective offices, and also the members of all such councils and encampments, and every candidate, upon his admission into the same, shall take the following obligation, viz. "I A. B. do promise and swear, that I will support and maintain the Constitution of the United States' General Grand Encampment of Knights Templars and the Appendant Orders."

I hereby certify, that the foregoing is a true copy of the Constitution of the United States' General Grand Encampment, adopted and ratified in convention at the city of New-York, on the 21st day of June, A. D. 1816.   J. J. LORING,
General Grand Recorder.

————◆————

List of General Grand Officers, elected June 21st, A. D. 1816; to continue in office until the third Thursday in September, A. D. 1819.

M. E. and Hon. DEWITT CLINTON, Esq. of New-York, *General Grand Master.*
THOMAS SMITH WEBB, Esq. of Boston, *Deputy General Grand Master.*
HENRY FOWLE, Esq. of Boston, *G. G. Generalissimo.*
EZRA AMES, Esq. of Albany, *G. G. Captain General.*
Rev. PAUL DEAN, of Boston, *G. G. Prelate.*
MARTIN HOFFMAN, Esq. of New-York, *G. G. Senior Warden.*
JOHN CARLILE, Esq. of Providence, (R. I.) *G. G. Junior Warden.*
PETER GRINNELL, Esq. of Providence, (R. I.) *G. G. Treasurer.*

J. J. LORING, Esq. of Boston, *G. G. Recorder.*
THOMAS LOWNDES, Esq. of New-York, *G. G. Warder.*
JOHN SNOW, Esq. of Providence, (R. I.) *G. G. Standard Bearer.*
JONATHAN SCHIEFFELIN, Esq. of N. York, *G. G. Sword Bearer.*

CHAPTER III.

LIST OF ENCAMPMENTS.

Maſſachuſetts.

Encampment of K. T. Boſton.
Encampment of K. T. Newburyport.
Council of K. R. C. at Portland.

Rhode-Iſland.

St. John's encampment of K. R. C.—K. T. and K. of M. meets at Maſons' Hall in Providence, on the firſt Monday evenings in March, June, September and December.

Newport encampment of K. R. C.—K. T. and K. of M. meets at Newport.

New-York.

The old encampment, city of New-York.
Jeruſalem encampment,   do.
Montgomery encampment,   Stillwater.
Temple encampment,   Albany.

END OF PART FIRST.

RULES

CHRISTIAN FREEMASONS.

I. Worship and adore the Most High, by whose order every thing that exists had its origin; by whose unremitting operations every thing is preserved. Bow thy knees before the incarnate word, and praise Providence that caused thee to be born in the bosom of christianity. Confess this divine religion every where, and let none of its duties go unfulfilled. Let every one of thy actions be distinguished by enlightened piety, without bigotry or fanaticism.

II. Remember always that Man is the master-piece of the creation, because God himself animated him with his breath. Be sensible of the immortality of thy soul; and separate from this heavenly, unperishable being, all that is foreign to it.

III. Thy first homage thou owest to the Deity; the second to the authority of civil society. Honour the Father of the State; love thy country; be religiously scrupulous in the fulfilling of all the duties of a good citizen. Consider that they are become sacred by the voluntary masonic vow, and that the violation of them, which in a profane man would be weakness, in thee would be hypocrisy and criminality.

IV. Love affectionately all those, who, as offspring of the same progenitor, have like thee the same form, the same wants, and an immortal soul. The mother country of a Mason is the world. All that concerns mankind is contained within the circle of his compass. Honour the Order of Freemasons, which has extended itself as far as enlightened reason, and come to our temples to do homage to the sacred rites of humanity.

V. God suffers Man to partake of the unlimited eternal happiness which he found from eternity in himself. Strive to resemble this divine Original by making all mankind as happy as thou canst. Nothing good can be imagined, that is not an object of thy activity. Let effectual and universal benevolence be the plumb rule of thy actions. Remain not insensible to the cries of the miserable. Detest *avarice* and ostentation. Do not look for the reward of virtue in the plaudits of the multitude, but in the innermost recesses of thine own heart; and if thou canst not make as many happy as thou wishest, reflect on the sacred tie of benevolence that unites us, and exert thyself to the utmost at our fruitful labours.

VI. Be affable and serviceable; kindle virtue in every heart. Rejoice at thy neighbour's prosperity, and never embitter it with envy. Forgive thy enemy, and if thou wouldst revenge thyself on him, do it by benevolence. Fulfil by that means one of the most exalted commands of religion, and pursue the career of thy original dignity.

VII. Scrutinize thy heart to discover its most secret dispositions. Thy soul is the rough ashler which thou must polish. Offer up to the Deity regular inclinations and restrained passions. Let thy course of life be without blemish, and chaste; thy soul, penetrated with love of truth, candid and modest. Beware of the dismal consequences of pride; it was pride that first caused the degradation of man. Study the meaning of our emblems; under their veil important satisfactory truths are concealed.

VIII. Every Freemason, without any consideration to what sect of religion he belongs, where he was born, or what rank he holds, is thy brother, and has a claim upon thy assistance. Honour in human society the adopted gradations of rank; in our assemblies we acknowledge only the preference of virtue to vice. Be not ashamed before the world of an honest man, whom thou hast acknowledged as a brother. Haste to his assistance; offer thy hand to lift up the fallen; and let not the sun set before thou art reconciled with thy brother, if thou hadst any difference with him. It is only by unanimity that our labours can prosper.

IX. Be faithful in fulfilling all that thou hast engaged in as a Freemason. Revere and obey thy superiors, for they speak in the name of the law. Keep always in sight the vow of secrecy; shouldst thou ever violate it, thou wouldst find the torturer in thine own heart, and become the horror of all thy brethren.

These are the rules by which every Freemason *ought* to live ; and if he does so, we may with confidence hope, that he will find a happy entrance into the supreme Celestial Lodge, where the ineffable brightness of the great and adorable ARCHITECT of the Universe is the only light, and where the most extatic pleasures are continually flowing for evermore.

THE

FREEMASON'S MONITOR;

OR

Illustrations of Masonry:

IN TWO PARTS.

BY THOMAS SMITH WEBB,

PAST GRAND MASTER OF THE GRAND LODGE OF
RHODE ISLAND, &c.

———◆———

PART SECOND.

CONTAINING

AN ACCOUNT OF THE INEFFABLE DEGREES OF
MASONRY;

AND THE

HISTORY OF FREEMASONRY IN AMERICA.

════════

SALEM:
PUBLISHED BY CUSHING AND APPLETON.
————
Ezra Lincoln, Printer, Boston.
1818.

PREFACE.

————

THE Ineffable Degrees of Masonry, the history and charges of which are contained in the following pages, are as ancient (it is alleged) as the time of king Solomon; the proof of which is probably known only to those who are professors of the degrees.

The general design of this part of the work is to preserve the history and charges of the several ineffable degrees from falling into oblivion; with which they have been long threatened, as well from the small number of conventions of masons who possess them, as from the little attention that has been paid to their meetings of late years.

It will also serve to convince masons who possess the degrees treated of in the first part of this work, that there is a total difference between those and the ineffable degrees; for it is a circumstance necessary to be known, that there is no part of these degrees that have any resemblance to the fourth, fifth, sixth, or seventh degrees before mentioned, or that have any reference or allusion to any of the circumstances on which those degrees were founded. But, notwithstanding this difference, it will clearly appear, from the account here given of the ineffable degrees, that much ingenuity is displayed in their formation ; that their design is noble, benevolent and praiseworthy ; and that the institution was intended for the glory of the Deity and the good of mankind.

FREEMASON'S MONITOR.

PART SECOND.

BOOK I.

CHAPTER I.

Observations on the Degree of Secret Master.

THE lodge of Secret Masters is spread with black. The master represents Solomon coming to the temple to elect seven experts. He is styled, Most Powerful.

There is only one warden, who is called Adoniram, after him who had the inspection of the workmanship done at Mount Libanus. He was the first made secret master.

Solomon holds a sceptre in his hand, standing in the East, before a triangular altar, upon which is a crown, and some olive and laurel leaves. Adoniram, the inspector, stands in the West.

The first officer is decorated with a blue ribbon, from the right shoulder to the left hip, to which hangs a triangle. The second officer is decorated with a white ribbon, bordered with black, in a triangular form, and an ivory key suspended therefrom, with a figure of Z upon it.

All the other brethren are decorated in the same manner, with white aprons and gloves, the strings of the aprons black; the flap of the apron is blue, with a golden eye upon it. This lodge should be enlightened by eighty-one candles, distributed by nine times nine.

A candidate, after being strictly examined by the inspector, who must vouch for his qualifications, is thus addressed by the M. P.

"BROTHER,

"You have hitherto only seen the thick veil that covers the S. S. of God's temple; your fidelity, zeal and constancy have gained you this favour I now grant you, of shewing you our treasure, and introducing you into the secret place."

He is then invested with the ribbon, the crown of laurels and olives, by the M. P. who thus addresses him:

"MY BROTHER,

"I receive you as secret master, and give you rank among the Levites. This laurel, the emblem of victory, is to remind you of the conquest you are to gain over your passions. The olive is the symbol of that peace and union, which ought to reign among us. It belongeth to you to deserve the favour, that you may be enabled one day to arrive in the secret place, to contemplate the pillar of beauty. I decorate you with the ivory key hung to a white and black ribbon, as a symbol of your fidelity, innocence and discretion.

"The apron and gloves are to be marks of the candour of all S. M. in the number of which you have deserved to be introduced. In this quality, my brother, you are to become the faithful guardian of the S. S. and I put you in the number of seven, to be one of the conductors of the works which are raising to the divinity. The eye upon your apron is to remind you to have a careful watch over the conduct of the craft in general."

The lodge is closed by the mysterious number.

CHAPTER II.

Observations on the Degree of Perfect Master.

THE lodge of perfect masters is hung with green tapestry, on eight columns, four on each side, placed at equal distances; to be illuminated with sixteen lights, placed at the four cardinal points. A table before the canopy covered with black. The R. W. and respectable master represents the noble Adoniram, being the first that was elected S. M. because S. chose him the first of the seven. He commanded the works of the temple before H. A. arrived at Jerusalem, and afterwards had the inspection of the works at Mount Libanus. He is decorated with the ornaments of perfection, and is a prince of Jerusalem, with those decorations. He occupies the place of S. in the east under the canopy.

There is only one warden, who represents Stockin, in the function of an inspector, with the ornaments of his highest degrees, which he received in the west.

The assistants, being at least perfect masters, ought to be decorated with a large green ribbon hung to the neck, with a jewel suspended thereto, being a compass extended to 60 degrees.

The brethren all have aprons of white leather with green flaps; on the middle of the apron must be embroidered a square stone, surrounded by three circles, with the letter P in the centre.

After a candidate is duly examined in the proficiency he has made in the foregoing degree, he is regularly introduced, and is thus addressed by the M. P.

"MY BROTHER,

"It is my desire to draw you from your vicious life, and, by the favour I have received from the most powerful of kings, I raise you to the degree of perfect master, on condition that you strictly adhere to what shall be presented to you by our laws."

The ceremonies, &c. of this degree, were originally established as a grateful tribute of respect to the memory of a departed worthy brother.

The lodge is closed by four times four.

CHAPTER III.

Observations on the Degree of Intimate Secretary.

THE lodge of I. S. is furnished with black hangings, and represents the hall of audience of Solomon. It should be enlightened with twenty seven lights, in three candle-sticks of nine branches each, placed E. W. and S.

This lodge consists of two persons only ; who represent S. and H. K. of T. They are covered with blue mantles, lined with ermine, with crowns on their heads, sceptres in their hands, and seated at a table, on which are placed two naked swords, a roll of parchment and a death's head.

All the rest of the brethren are considered only as perfect masters, and are termed the guards. They should have white aprons, lined and embroidered with a blood colour, with strings of the same ; and ribbons of the same colour round their necks, to which must be suspended, hanging on the breast, a solid triangle.

Charge to a new made Intimate Secretary.

"MY BROTHER,

" I receive you an Intimate Secretary, on your promise to be faithful to the order in which you have just now entered. We hope, brother, that your fidelity will be proof to every trial ; and that this sword, with which we arm you, will defend you from the attacks of those, who may try to extort from you those secrets which we are now about to confer upon you."

History.

Solomon had agreed with the king of Tyre, in return for the materials taken from Mount Lebanon, and those drawn from the quarries of Tyre, made use of in con-structing the temple (in part payment of which, he had already furnished him with a measure of oil, honey and wheat) to have given him a province in Galilea, of thirty. cities, immediately after the temple was completed.

A year bad elapsed before this was complied with on the part of Solomon; and when Hiram went to visit this newly acquired territory, he found the lands poor, the people rude, uncultivated, and of bad morals; and that the keeping of it would be attended with more expense than profit. He therefore went in person to Solomon, to complain of the deceit. Being arrived, he made his entry through the guards in the court, and went hastily to the king's apartment. —

The countenance of the king of Tyre was so expressive of anger, as he entered, that one of Solomon's favourites, named Joabert, perceived it, and, apprehensive of the consequence, followed him to the door to listen. Hiram, observing him, ran and seized upon him, and delivered him into the custody of the guards; however, by the intercession of Solomon (who represented that Joabert was, of all those about the temple, most attached to him, and that his intentions could not have been evil) Hiram agreed to pardon him; and before they parted, renewed their former friendship, and concluded a treaty of perpetual alliance, which was signed by them, and to which Joabert was Intimate Secretary.

This lodge is closed by three times nine.

CHAPTER IV.

Observations on the Degree of Provost and Judge.

THIS lodge is adorned with red, and lighted by five great lights; one in each corner, and one in the centre. The master is placed in the east, under a blue canopy, surrounded with stars, and is styled, thrice illustrious. He represents Tito Prince Harodim, the eldest of the P. M. and I. S. first grand warden, and inspector of the three hundred architects; whose office was, to draw plans for the workmen.

After the candidate is introduced in due form, the master thus addresses him:

"RESPECTABLE BROTHER,

"It gives me joy, that I am now about to re-compense your zeal and attachment to the institution of masonry, by appointing you provost and judge, over all the works of this lodge; and, as we are well assured of your prudence and discretion, we without the least hesitation entrust you with a most important secret. We expect you will do your duty in the degree to which you will now be elevated, as you have done in those already taken."

He is then decorated with a golden key suspended by a red ribbon, and an apron with a pocket in its centre.

The intention of Solomon in forming this degree, was, to strengthen the means of preserving order among such a vast number of craftsmen. Joabert, being honoured with the intimate confidence of his king, received this new mark of distinction.

Solomon first created Tito Prince Harodim, Adoniram and Abda his father, provosts and judges, and gave them orders to initiate Joabert, his favourite, into the secret mysteries of this degree, and to give him the keys of all the building.

Lodge is closed by four and one.

CHAPTER V.

Observations on the Degree of Intendant of the Buildings, or Master in Israel.

THIS lodge is decorated with red hangings, and illuminated with twenty seven lights, distributed by three times nine round the lodge. There must be also five other great lights on the altar before the most puissant, who represents Solomon seated with a sceptre in his hand.

The first warden, called inspector, represents the most illustrious Tito Harodim: second warden represents Adoniram, the son of Abda; all the rest are arranged angularly. The most puissant, and all the brethren, are decorated with a large red ribbon, from the right shoulder to the left hip, to which is suspended a triangle fastened by a small green ribbon. On one side of the triangle are engraved the words, *Benchorin, Achard, Jachinai;* on the reverse, *Judea, Ky, Jea.* The aprons are white, lined with red, and bordered with green; in the centre, a star, with nine points, above a balance; and on the flap a triangle, with these letters, B. A. I. on each angle.

A candidate, after being previously prepared and having gone through the ceremonies, is thus addressed:

"My Brother,

"Solomon, willing to carry to the highest degree of perfection the work he had begun in Jerusalem, found it necessary, from a circumstance with which you are acquainted, to employ the five chiefs of the five orders of architecture: and gave command over them to Tito, Adoniram, and Abda his father; being well assured that their zeal and abilities would be exerted to the utmost in bringing to perfection so glorious a work. In like manner we expect you will do all that lies in your power to promote the grand design of masonry."

This lodge is closed by five, seven, and fifteen.

———

CHAPTER VI.

Observations on the Degree of Elected Knights, called a Chapter.

This chapter represents the audience chamber of Solomon, and is to be decorated with white and red hangings—the red with white flames.

There are nine lights in the east, and eight in the west. The master represents Solomon, seated in the east, with a table before him, covered with black, and is styled, Most Potent.

There is only one warden, in the west, who represents Stockin, with seven brethren round him. All the brethren must be dressed in black, and their hats flapped, with a broad black ribbon from the left shoulder to the right hip, on the lower part of which are nine red roses, four on each side, and one at the bottom, to which is suspended a poniard. The aprons are white, lined with black, speckled with blood; on the flap a bloody arm with a poniard, and on the area a bloody arm holding by the hair a bloody head.

History of this Degree.

In the reign of Solomon, several of the workmen had been guilty of some crime of an enormous nature, and made their escape from Jerusalem. A great assembly of masters had sat in consultation on the best means of discovering and apprehending them. Their deliberations were interrupted by the entrance of a stranger, who demanded to speak to the king in private. Upon being admitted, he acquainted Solomon that he had discovered where Akirop, one of the traitors, lay concealed; and offered to conduct those whom the king should please to appoint, to go with him. This being communicated to the brethren, one and all requested to be partakers in the vengeance due to the villain. Solomon checked their ardour, declaring that only nine should undertake the task; and to avoid giving any offence, ordered all their names to be put into an urn, and that the first nine that should be drawn, should be the persons to accompany the stranger.

At break of day, Joabert, Stockin, and seven others, conducted by the stranger, travelled onwards, through a dreary country. On the way, Joabert found means to learn from the stranger, that the villain they were in quest of had hidden himself in a cavern not far from the place where they then were; he soon found the cavern, and entered it alone, where, by the light of the lamp, he discovered the villain asleep, with a poniard at his feet. Enflamed at the sight, and actuated by an impatient zeal, he immediately seized the poniard, and stabbed him, first in the head, and then in the heart: he had only time to ery *Vengeance is taken*, and expired. When the other eight arrived and had refreshed themselves at the spring, Joabert severed the head from the body, and taking it in one hand and his poniard in the other, he, with his brethren, returned to Jerusalem. Solomon was at first very much offended, that Joabert had put it out of his power to take vengeance himself, in presence of, and as a warning to the rest of the workmen to be faithful to their trust; but, by proper intercession, was again reconciled.

Joabert became highly favoured of Solomon, who conferred upon him, and his eight companions, the title of *Elected Knights*.

The chapter is closed by eight and one.

CHAPTER VII.

Observations on the Degree of Elected Grand Master, or Illustrious Elected of Fifteen.

THIS lodge represents Solomon's apartment, and is to be decorated in the same manner as that of the *Nine Elect*. There are two wardens; the senior is called inspector.

This lodge should consist of only fifteen members; but should there be more at a time of reception, they must attend in the antichamber.

The apron peculiar to this degree is white, and bordered with black; and on the flap three heads or spikes in form of a triangle; the jewel is the same as that of the *Nine Elect*, only on that part of the black ribbon which crosses the breast, there should be the same device as upon the apron.

History of this Degree.

About six months after the execution of the traitor mentioned in the preceding degree of elected Knights, Bengabee, an intendant of Solomon, in the country of Cheth, which was tributary to him, caused diligent inquiry to be made if any person had lately taken shelter in those parts, who might be supposed to have fled from

B

Jerusalem : he published at the same time a particular description of all those traitors who had made their escape : shortly after, he received information that several persons answering his description had lately arrived there, and, believing themselves perfectly secure, had begun to work in the quarry of Bendaca.

As soon as Solomon was made acquainted with this circumstance, he wrote to Maacha, king of Cheth, to assist in apprehending them, and to cause them to be delivered to persons that he should appoint, to secure them, and have them brought to Jerusalem, to receive the punishment due to their crimes.

Solomon then elected fifteen masters, in whom he could place the highest confidence, and among whom were those, who had been in the cavern, and sent them in quest of the villains, and gave them an escort of troops. Five days were spent in the search, when, Terbal, who bore Solomon's letter to Moriha and Eleham, discovered them, cutting stone in the quarry; they immediately seized them and bound them in chains. When they arrived at Jerusalem, they were imprisoned in the tower of Achizer, and the next morning a punishment was inflicted on them adequate to their crimes.

Lodge is closed by three times five.

CHAPTER VIII.

Illustrious Knights, or Sublime Knights elected.

THIS lodge is called a grand chapter; Solomon presides, and of course is to be decorated with a sceptre. In place of two wardens, there are a grand inspector, and grand master of ceremonies.

The jewel worn in this lodge is a sword, intended to represent a sword of justice, hung to a large black ribbon; on the part crossing the breast, must be an inflamed heart; which is also to be painted on the flap of the apron. The chapter is illuminated by twelve lights.

History of this Degree.

After vengeance had been fully taken on the traitors mentioned in the foregoing degrees, Solomon instituted this, both as a reward for the zeal and integrity of the grand masters elect of fifteen, and also by their preferment to make room for raising other worthy brethren from the lower degrees to that of grand master elect of fifteen. He accordingly appointed twelve of the fifteen, chosen by ballot, to constitute a grand chapter of illustrious knights, and gave them command over the twelve tribes. He expressed a particular regard for this order, and shewed them the precious things in the tabernacle.

Here follow the names of the twelve illustrious knights, with the tribes over which they respectively presided:

1. Joabert, who presided over the tribe of Judah.
2. Stockin, ... Benjamin.
3. Terrey, ... Simeon.
4. Morphey, ... Ephraim.
5. Alycuber, ... Manasseh.
6. Dorson, ... Zebulun.
7. Kerim, ... Dan.
8. Berthemar, ... Asher.
9. Tito, ... Naphtali.
10. Terbal, ... Reuben.
11. Benachard, ... Issachar.
12. Taber, ... Gad.

The illustrious knights gave an account to Solomon, every day, of the work that was done in the temple by their respective tribes, and received their pay.

This chapter is closed by twelve.

CHAPTER IX.

Observations on the Degree of Grand Master Architects.

This chapter is painted white, with red flames; by which is signified the purity of heart and zeal, that should be the characteristic of every grand master architect. It must have in it a delineation of the five orders of architecture; together with a representation of the north star, with seven small stars round it, which signify, that as the north star is a guide to mariners, so ought virtue to be the guide of grand master architects. The Jewel is a gold medal, on both sides of which are engraved the five orders of architecture, suspended by a broad, dark, stone-coloured ribbon, from the left shoulder to the right hip.

Every grand master architect must be furnished with a case of mathematical instruments.

Address to a candidate on his admission to this degree.

"BROTHER,

"I have elevated you to this degree from an expectation that you will so apply yourself to geometry, to which you are now devoted, as will procure you knowledge sufficient to take away the veil from before your eyes, which yet remains there, and enable you to arrive at the perfect and sublime degree."

History.

Solomon established this degree with a view of forming a school of architecture for the instruction of the brethren employed in the temple of God, and animating them to arrive at perfection in the royal art. He was a prince equally famed for his justice, as for his wisdom and foresight; he was therefore desirous of rewarding the talents and virtues of the faithful, in order to make them perfect, and fit to approach the throne of God. He accordingly cast his eyes upon the chiefs of the twelve tribes, as persons extremely proper to fulfil the promise made to Enoch, to Moses, and to David, that with great zeal, in fulness of time, the bowels of the earth should be penetrated.

This chapter is closed by one and two.

CHAPTER X.

Observations on the Degree of Knights of the Ninth Arch.

To form a lodge of this degree, five persons at least must be present.

1st. The most potent grand master, representing Solomon, in the east, seated in a chair of state, under a rich canopy, with a crown on his head, and a sceptre in his hand. He is dressed in royal robes of yellow, and an ermined vestment of blue satin, reaching to the elbows; a broad purple ribbon from the right shoulder to the left hip, to which is hung a triangle of gold.

2d. The grand warden representing the king of Tyre, on his left hand, seated as a stranger, clothed in a purple robe and a yellow vestment.

3d. The grand inspector, representing G——, in the west, with a drawn sword in his hand.

4th. The grand treasurer, representing Joabert, in the north, with a golden key to his fifth button hole, and upon it the letters I. V. I. L. *Juvenis verbum intre Leonis.*

5th. The grand secretary, representing Stockin, in the south.

The four last mentioned officers to be ornamented with the same ribbon and jewel as the M. P. and to sit covered. The three last to have robes of blue without vestments.

No person can be admitted to this degree without having previously taken all the preceding degrees.

History and Charge of this Degree.

"MY WORTHY BROTHER,

" It is my intention at this time to give you a clearer account, than you have yet been acquainted with, of masonry ; of which at present you barely know the elements.

" In doing this it will be necessary to explain to you some circumstances of very remote antiquity.

B 2

" Enoch, the son of Jared, was the sixth son in descent from Adam, and lived in the fear and love of his Maker.

" Enoch, being inspired by the Most High, and in commemoration of a wonderful vision, built a temple under ground, and dedicated the same to God. Methuselah, the son of Enoch, constructed the building, without being acquainted with his father's motives.

" This happened in that part of the world which was afterwards called the land of Canaan, and since known by the name of the Holy Land.

" Enoch caused a triangular plate of gold to be made, each side of which was a cubit long ; he enriched it with the most precious stones, and encrusted the plate upon a stone of agate, of the same form. He then engraved upon it the ineffable characters, and placed it on a triangular pedestal of white marble, which he deposited in the deepest arch.

" When Enoch's temple was completed, he made a door of stone, and put a ring of iron therein, by which it might be occasionally raised ; and placed it over the opening of the arch, that the matters enclosed therein might be preserved from the universal destruction impending. And none but Enoch knew of the treasure which the arches contained.

" And, behold the wickedness of mankind increased more and became grievous in the sight of the Lord, and God threatened to destroy the whole world. Enoch, perceiving that the knowledge of the arts was likely to be lost in the general destruction, and being desirous of preserving the principles of the sciences, for the posterity of those whom God should be pleased to spare, built two great pillars on the top of the highest mountain, the one of brass, to withstand water, the other of marble, to withstand fire ; and he engraved on the marble pillar, hieroglyphics, signifying that there was a most precious treasure concealed in the arches under ground, which he had dedicated to God. And he engraved on the pillar of brass the principles of the liberal arts, particularly of masonry.

" Methuselah was the father of Lamech, who was the father of Noah, who was a pious and good man, and beloved by God. And the Lord spake unto Noah, saying, 'Behold I will punish the sins of mankind with a general deluge ; therefore build an ark, capable of containing thyself and family, as also a pair of every living creature upon earth, and those only shall be saved from the general destruction, which I am about to inflict for the iniquities of the people.'

" And God gave unto Noah a plan by which the ark was to be constructed. Noah was one hundred years in building the ark ; he was six hundred years old when it was finished, and his son Seth was ninety nine. His father Lamech had died a short time before, aged 777 years. There was not at this time any of the ancient patriarchs living save Methuselah the grandfather of Noah, who was about 969 years old, and it is supposed that he perished in the general ruin.

" The ark being finished, Noah, agreeable to the instructions he had received from the Most High, went into it with his family, and took with him such things as he was commanded.

" The flood took place in the year of the world
1656, and destroyed most of the superb monuments of antiquity. The marble pillar of Enoch
fell in the general destruction ; but by divine per-
mission, the pillar of brass withstood the water, by
which means the ancient state of the liberal arts,
and particularly masonry, has been handed down
to us.

" We learn from holy writ, the history of succeeding times, till the Israelites became slaves to
the Egyptians ; from which bondage they were
freed under the conduct of Moses. The same
sacred book informs us that Moses was beloved
of God, and·that the Most High spoke to him on
Mount Sinai. To Moses God communicated his
divine law, written on tables of stone ; with many
promises of a renewed alliance. He also gave
him the true pronunciation of his sacred name :
and God gave a strict command unto Moses, that
no one should pronounce it ; so that in process of
time the true pronunciation was lost.

" The same divine history particularly informs
us of the different movements of the Israelites,
until they became possessed of the land of promise, and of the succeeding events until the Divine
Providence was pleased to give the sceptre to David ; who, though fully determined to build a temple to the Most High, could never begin it ; that
honour being reserved for his son.

" Solomon, being the wisest of princes, had
fully in remembrance the promises of God to Moses, that some of his successors, in fulness of time,
should discover his holy name ; and his wisdom
inspired him to believe, that this could not be ac-

●omplished until he had erected and consecrated a temple to the living God, in which he might deposit the precious treasures.

"Accordingly, Solomon began to build, in the fourth year of his reign, agreeably to a plan given to him by David his father, upon the ark of alliance.

" He chose a spot for this purpose, the most beautiful and healthy in all Jerusalem.

" The number of the grand and sublime elected, were at first three, and now consisted of five ; and continued so until the temple was completed and dedicated ; when king Solomon, as a reward for their faithful services, admitted to this degree the twelve grand masters, who had faithfully presided over the twelve tribes ; also one other grand master architect. Nine ancient grand masters, eminent for their virtue, were chosen knights of the royal arch, and shortly afterwards were admitted to the sublime degree of perfection.

" You have been informed in what manner the number of the grand elect was augmented to twenty seven, which is the cube of three : they consisted of two kings, three knights of the royal arch, twelve commanders of the twelve tribes, nine elected grand masters, and one grand master architect."

This lodge is closed by the mysterious number.

CHAPTER XI.

Perfection, or Grand Elect, Perfect and Sublime Mason.

THE lodge of perfection, or ultimate degree of ancient masonry, should represent a subterraneous vault painted red, and adorned with many colours, and columns of a flame colour. Behind the master must be a light to shine through a triangular sun; and before him there must be a pedestal appearing to be broken. There ought to be several other lights, arranged numerically, according to the different stages of masonry.

The most perfect grand elect and sublime master in this degree, is to represent Solomon, seated in the east, dressed in royal robes, and having a crown and sceptre placed on a pedestal before him. The two grand wardens are seated in the west. On the right hand of the most perfect sits the grand treasurer, having a table before him, upon which must be placed some perfumes, with a small silver hod, and a trowel of gold. On his left hand sits the grand secretary, with a table also before him, on which must be seven loaves of shew bread, with a cup of red wine for libation, and also jewels for the candidates at their reception.

The jewels appertaining to this degree are a crowned compass, extended to ninety degrees; or a quadrant, a sun in the centre; and on the reverse a blazing star, enclosing a triangle, hung to a broad flame coloured ribbon, of a triangular form, round the neck; and also, a gold ring with this motto, " Virtue unites what death cannot part."

The apron must be flamed with red, a blue ribbon round the edge, and the jewel painted on the flap. The brethren must be dressed in black, with swords in their hands.

Prayer at Opening.

" Almighty and Sovereign Architect of heaven and earth, who by thy divine power dost ultimately search the most secret recesses of thought ; purify our hearts by the sacred fire of thy love ; guide us by thine unerring hand, in the path of virtue, and cast out of thy adorable sanctuary all impiety and perverseness ; we beseech thee that our thoughts may be engaged in the grand work of our perfection, which, when attained, will be an

ample reward for our labour ; let peace and charity link us together in a pleasing union, and may
this lodge exhibit a faint resemblance of that happiness which the elect will enjoy in thy kingdom.
Give us a spirit of holy discrimination, by which
we may be able to refuse the evil and choose the
good : and also that we may not be led astray by
those who unworthily assume the character of the
grand elect. Finally be pleased to grant, that all
our proceedings may tend to thy glory, and our
advancement in righteousness. Bless us and prosper our works, O Lord ! Amen."

When a candidate is introduced, after certain solemn
forms, the master of the ceremonies says,

" I impress you, my brother, with an ardent
zeal for the honour of the Grand Architect of the
Universe ; to the end that you may live always in
his adorable presence with a heart disposed to every thing that is pleasing to him."

The most perfect then presents the candidate with the
bread and wine, saying,

" Eat of this bread with me, and drink of the
same cup, that we may learn thereby to succour
each other in time of need by a mutual love and
participation of what we possess."

He then presents to him a gold ring, saying,

" Receive this ring, and let it be remembered by
you as a symbol of the alliance you have now con-
tracted with virtue and the virtuous. You are
never, my dear brother, to part with it while you
live ; nor to bequeath it at your death, except to
your wife, your eldest son, or your nearest friend."

When this part of the ceremony is ended, the brethren
make a libation, according to ancient usage.

The most perfect then decorates the candidate according to the ornaments of the order, saying,

" I now with the greatest pleasure salute you, my brother, as a grand elect, perfect and sublime mason, which title I now confer on you, and grace you with the symbols thereof. Receive this ribbon, the triangular figure of which, is emblematical of the divine triangle. The crown upon your jewel is a symbol of the royal origin of this degree. The compass, extended to ninety degrees, denotes the extensive knowledge of the grand elect. These jewels, suspended on your breast, should make you attentive to your duty and station."

Charge.

" Thus, my venerable brother, by your unblamable conduct, assiduity, constancy and integrity, you have at last attained the title of grand elect, perfect and sublime mason, which is the summit of ancient masonry, and upon your arrival to which, I most sincerely congratulate you.

" I must earnestly recommend to you the strictest care and circumspection in all your conduct, that the sublime mysteries of this degree be not profaned or disgraced.

" As to what remains of completing your knowledge in the ancient state of masonry, you will find it by attending to the following

" History.

" When the temple of Jerusalem was finished, the masons, who were employed in constructing that stately edifice, acquired immortal honour.

Their order became more uniformly established and regulated than it had been before. Their delicacy in admitting new members of their order, brought it to a degree of respect ; as the merit of the candidate was the only thing they then paid attention to. With these principles instilled into their minds, many of the grand elect left the temple after its dedication, and dispersed themselves among the neighbouring kingdoms, instructing all who applied, and were found worthy, in the sublime degrees of ancient craft masonry.

" The temple was finished in the year of the world 3000.

" Thus far the wise king of Israel behaved worthy of himself, and gained universal admiration ; but in process of time, when he had advanced in years, his understanding became impaired ; he grew deaf to the voice of the Lord, and was strangely irregular in his conduct. Proud of having erected an edifice to his Maker, and much intoxicated with his great power, he plunged into all manner of licentiousness and debauchery, and profaned the temple, by offering that incense to the idol Moloch, which only should have been offered to the living God.

" The grand elect and perfect masons saw this, and were sorely grieved ; being fearful that his apostacy would end in some dreadful consequences, and perhaps bring upon them their enemies, whom Solomon had vainly and wantonly defied. The people, copying the follies and vices of their king, became proud and idolatrous, neglecting the true worship of God for that of idols.

c

"As an adequate punishment for this defection, God inspired the heart of Nebuchadnezzar, king of Babylon, to take vengeance on the kingdom of Israel. This prince sent an army, with Nebuzarádan, captain of the guards, who entered Judah with fire and sword, took and sacked the city of Jerusalem, razed its walls, and destroyed that superb model of excellence, the temple. The people were carried captive to Babylon, and the conquerors carried with them all the vessels of gold and silver, &c. This happened 470 years, 6 months and 10 days after its dedication.

"When the time arrived that the christian princes entered into a league to free the holy land from the oppression of the infidels, the good and virtuous masons, anxious for so pious an undertaking, voluntarily offered their services to the confederates, on condition that they should have a chief of their own election, which was granted; accordingly they accepted their standard and departed.

"The valour and fortitude of those elected knights were such, that they were admired by, and took the lead of, all the princes of Jerusalem, who, believing that their mysteries inspired them with courage and fidelity to the cause of virtue and religion, became desirous of being initiated; upon being found worthy, their desires were complied with, and thus the royal art, meeting the approbation of great and good men, became popular and honourable, and was diffused to the worthy, throughout their various dominions, and has continued to spread, far and wide, through a succession of ages, to the present day."

FREEMASON'S MONITOR.

PART SECOND.

BOOK II.

SKETCH OF THE HISTORY OF FREEMASONRY IN AMERICA.

CHAPTER I.

General Remarks.

A GRAND Lodge consists of the master and wardens of all the regular lodges of master masons, within its jurisdiction, with the grand master at their head, the deputy grand master on his left, and the grand wardens and deacons in their proper places; attended also by the grand secretary, grand treasurer, grand chaplain, grand sword bearer, grand marshal, and also the past grand and deputy grand masters, and past masters of regular lodges while members of a lodge within the jurisdiction.

In England, until the year 1717, a sufficient number of masons met together, had ample power to make masons, and discharge every duty of masonry by inherent privileges, vested in the fraternity at large, without a warrant of constitution. But at the meeting of the grand lodge of England, on St. John the Baptist's day, in that year, the following regulation was adopted:

"The privilege of assembling as masons, which has hitherto been unlimited, shall be vested in certain lodges of masons, convened in certain places; and every lodge hereafter convened, shall be legally authorized to act by a warrant from the grand master for the time being, granted to certain individuals by petition, with the consent and approbation of the grand lodge in communication; and without such warrant, no lodge shall hereafter be deemed regular or constitutional."

CHAPTER II.

Commencement of Masonry in America.

On application of a number of brethren residing in Boston, a warrant was granted by the right honourable and most worshipful Anthony, Lord Viscount Montague, grand master of masons in England, dated the 30th of April, 1733, appointing the right worshipful Henry Price grand master in North America, with full power and authority to appoint his deputy, and other masonic officers necessary for forming a grand lodge ; and also to constitute lodges of free and accepted masons, as often as occasion should require.

In consequence of this commission, the grand master opened a grand lodge in Boston,* on the 30th of July, 1733, in due form, and appointed the right worshipful Andrew Belcher deputy grand master, the worshipful Thomas Kennelly and John Quann, grand wardens.

The grand lodge being thus organized, under the designation of *St. John's Grand Lodge*, proceeded to grant warrants for instituting regular lodges in various parts of America; and from this grand lodge originated the first lodges in Massachusetts, New-Hampshire, Rhode-Island, Connecticut, New-Jersey, Pennsylvania, Maryland, Virginia, North-Carolina, South-Carolina, Barbadoes, Antigua, Newfoundland, Louisburgh, Nova-Scotia, Quebec, Surinam, and St. Christopher's.

There was also a grand lodge holden at Boston, upon the *ancient* establishment, under the designation of " *The Massachusetts Grand Lodge*," which originated as follows :

In 1755, a number of brethren residing in Boston, who were *ancient* masons, in consequence of a petition to the grand lodge of Scotland, received a deputation, dated Nov. 30, 1752, from Sholto Charles Douglas, *Lord Aberdour*, then grand master, constituting them a regular lodge under the title of *St. Andrew's Lodge*, No. 82, to be holden at Boston.

This establishment was discouraged and opposed by the St. John's grand lodge, who thought their privileges

* Sometimes called " The grand lodge of *modern masons*."

infringed by the grand lodge of Scotland ; they therefore, refused to have any intercourse with St. Andrew's lodge, for several years.

The prosperous state of St. Andrew's lodge soon led its members to make great exertions for the establishment of an ancient grand lodge in America ; which was soon effected in Boston, by the assistance of travelling lodges, belonging to the British army, who were stationed there.

Dec. 27, 1769. The festival of the evangelists was celebrated in due form.   When the brethren were assembled, a commission from the right honourable and most worshipful George, Earl of Dalhousie, grand master of masons in Scotland, dated the 30th of May, 1769, appointing Joseph Warren to be grand master of masons in Boston, and within one hundred miles of the same, was read, and he was, according to ancient usage, duly installed into that office. The grand master then appointed and installed the other grand officers, and the grand lodge was at this time completely organized.

Between this period and the year 1791, this grand lodge granted warrants of constitution for lodges to be holden in Massachusetts, New-Hampshire, Connecticut, Vermont and New-York.

In the year 1773, a commission was received from the right honourable and most worshipful Patrick, Earl of Dumfries, grand master of masons in Scotland, dated March 3, 1772, appointing the right worshipful Joseph Warren, Esq. grand master of masons for the *continent of America.*

In 1775, the meetings of the grand lodge were suspended, by the town of Boston becoming a garrison.

At the battle of Bunker's hill, on the 17th of June, this year, masonry and the grand lodge met with a heavy loss, in the death of grand master Warren, who was slain contending for the liberties of his country.

Soon after the evacuation of Boston by the British army, and previous to any regular *communication*, the brethren, influenced by a pious regard to the memory of the late grand master, were induced to search for his body, which had been rudely and indiscriminately buried in the field of slaughter. They accordingly repaired to the place, and, by direction of a person who was on the ground at the time of his burial, a spot was found where the earth had been recently turned up. Upon removing the turf, and opening the grave, which was on the brow of a hill, and adjacent to a small cluster of sprigs, the remains were discovered, in a mangled condition, but were easily ascertained;* and, being decently raised, were conveyed to the state house in Boston; from whence, by a large and respectable number of brethren, with the late grand officers, attending in procession, they were carried to the stone chapel, where an animated eulogium was delivered by brother Perez Morton. The body was then deposited in the silent vault, "without a sculptured stone to mark the spot; but as the whole earth is the sepulchre of illustrious men, his fame, his glorious actions, are engraven on the tablet of universal remembrance; and will survive marble monuments or local inscriptions."

1777, *March* 8. The brethren, who had been dispersed in consequence of the war, being now generally collected, they assembled to take into consideration the state of masonry. Being deprived of their chief by the melancholy death of their grand master, as before mentioned, after due consideration they proceeded to the formation of a grand lodge, and elected and installed the most worshipful Joseph Webb, their grand master.

1783, *January* 3. A committee was appointed to draft resolutions explanatory of the power and authority of this grand lodge. On the 24th of June following, the committee reported as follows, viz.

" The committee appointed to take into consideration the conduct of those brethren who assume the powers and prerogatives of a grand lodge, on the ancient establishment, in this place, and examine the extent of their authority and jurisdiction, together with the powers of any other ancient masonic institution within the same, beg leave to report the result of their examination, founded on the following facts, viz.

" That the commission from the grand lodge of Scotland, granted to our late grand master Joseph Warren, Esq. having died with him, and of course his deputy, whose appointment was derived from his nomination, being no longer in existence, they saw themselves without a

---

* By an artificial tooth.

head, and without a single grand officer; and of consequence it was evident, that not only the grand lodge, but all the particular lodges under its jurisdiction, must cease to assemble, the brethren be dispersed, the pennyless go unassisted, the craft languish, and *ancient* masonry be extinct in this part of the world.

"That in consequence of a summons from the former grand officers to the masters and wardens of all the regular constituted lodges, a grand communication was held, to consult and advise on some means to preserve the intercourse of the brethren.

" That the political head of this country having destroyed all connexion and correspondence between the subjects of these states and the country from which the grand lodge originally derived its commissioned authority, and the principles of the craft inculcating on its professors submission to the commands of the civil authority of the country they reside in : the brethren did assume an elective supremacy, and under it chose a grand master and grand officers, and erected a grand lodge, with independent powers and prerogatives, to be exercised however on principles consistent with and subordinate to the regulations pointed out in the constitutions of ancient masonry.

" That the reputation and utility of the craft, under their jurisdiction, has been most extensively diffused, by the flourishing state of *fourteen* lodges constituted by their authority, within a shorter period than that in which *three only* received dispensations under the former grand lodge.

" That in the history of our craft we find, that in England there are two grand lodges independent of each other ; in Scotland the same ; and in Ireland their grand lodge and grand master are independent either of England or Scotland. It is clear that the authority of some of their grand lodges originated in assumption ; or otherwise, they would acknowledge the head from whence they derived.

" Your committee are therefore of opinion, that the doings of the present grand lodge were dictated by principles of the clearest necessity, founded in the highest reason, and warranted by precedents of the most approved authority."

This report was accepted, and corresponding resolutions entered into by the grand lodge, and recorded.

1791, *Dec. 5.*   A committee was appointed, agreeably to a vote of the second of March, 1790, "to confer with the officers of St. John's grand lodge upon the subject of a complete masonic union throughout this commonwealth."

On the 5th of March, 1792, the committee brought in their report, and presented a copy of the laws and constitution for associating and uniting the two grand lodges, as agreed to by St. John's grand lodge, which, being read and deliberately considered, was unanimously approved of.

June 19, 1792. The officers and members of the two grand lodges met in conjunction, agreeable to previous arrangements, and installed the most worshipful John Cutler grand master ; and resolved, "that this grand lodge, organized as aforesaid, shall forever hereafter be known by the name of *The Grand Lodge of the Most Ancient and Honourable Society of Free and Accepted Masons for the Commonwealth of Massachusetts.*"

In addition to the powers vested by charter in the two grand lodges before mentioned, for instituting subordinate lodges, the grand lodge of England appointed *provincial grand masters* in several of the states, and invested them also with authority to grant warrants for holding lodges.

The revolution, which separated the American States from the government of the mother country, also exonerated the American lodges from their allegiance to foreign grand lodges : because the principles of masonry inculcate obedience to the governments under which we live. The lodges, in the several States, therefore, after the termination of the war, resorted to the proper and necessary means of forming and establishing independent grand lodges, for the government of the fraternity in their respective jurisdictions.

CHAPTER III.

Grand Lodge of New-Hampshire.

The Grand Lodge of New-Hampshire was first formed the eighth of July, A. L. 5789. A number of Lodges in this state had received warrants from Massachusetts, which united in the establishment of this grand lodge, and came under its jurisdiction. Its meetings are holden at Portsmouth, in January, April, July and October.

Subordinate Lodges.

St. John's, No. 1, Portsmouth.

Columbian, No. 2, Nottingham. *Cancelled.*

Rising Sun, No. 3, Keene. *Surrendered.*

Jerusalem, No. 4, Walpole and Westmoreland.

Franklin, No. 6, Hanover.

Benevolent, No. 7, Amherst.

North Star, No. 8, Lancaster.

Hiram, No. 9, Claremont.

Union, No. 10, Haverhill.

Blazing Star, No. 11, Concord.

Faithful, No. 12, Charlestown.

Washington, No. 13, Exeter.

King Solomon's, No. 14, New-London.

Mount Vernon, No. 15, Washington.

Olive Branch, No. 16, Plymouth.

Morning Star, No. 17, Moultonborough.

Charity, No. 18, Fitzwilliam.

Sullivan, No. 19, Deerfield.

Centre, No. 20, Sandbornton.

Humane, No. 21, Rochester.

Bethel, No. 22, New Ipswich.

CHAPTER IV.

Grand Lodge of Massachusetts.

THE first grand lodge in America was holden at Boston, on the 30th July, A. D. 1733, known by the name of *St. John's* Grand Lodge, and descended from the grand master of England.

The *Massachusetts* Grand Lodge (also holden at Boston) was first established on the 27th Dec. A. D. 1769, and descended from the grand master of Scotland.

On the 19th of June, A. D. 1792, a grand masonic union was formed by the two grand lodges, and all distinctions between ancient and modern masons abolished.

Subordinate Lodges.

St. John's Lodge, Boston.

Rising States, do.

Lincoln, Wiscasset.

Old Colony, Hingham.

Portland, Portland.

Tyrian, Gloucester.

Massachusetts, Boston.

St. Peter's, Newburyport.

Trinity, Lancaster.

Warren, Machias.

Unity, Ipswich.

King Solomon's, Charlestown.

Friendship, Williamstown.

Essex,   Salem.
Kennebeck,   Hallowell.
Fayette,   Charlestown.
Harmony,   Northfield.
Union,   Dorchester.
Thomas,   Monson.
Bristol,   Norton.
Jerusalem,   Williamsburg.
St. Paul's,   Groton.
Fellowship,   Bridgewater.
Corinthian,   Concord.
Montgomery,   Franklin.
Olive Branch,   Oxford.
Meridian Sun,   Brookfield.
Adams,   Wellfleet.
Hiram,   Lexington.
Meridian,   Watertown.
King Solomon's Lodge of
    Perfection, Holmes' Hole.
Mount Moriah,   Reading.
Maine,   Falmouth.
Social,   Ashby.
Eastern Star,   Rehoboth.
Philanthropic, Marblehead.
Tuscan,   Columbia.
K. David's,   Taunton.
Rising Star,   Stoughton.
Mount Zion's,   Hardwich.
Fraternal,   Barnstable.
Mount Lebanon,   Boston.
Pacific,   Leverett.
Aurora,   Leominster.
Eastern,   Eastport.
Federal,   Blandford.
Morning Star,   Worcester.
Hancock,   Penobscot.
Franklin,   Cheshire.
Republican,   Greenfield.
Middlesex,   Framingham.
Columbian,   Boston.
Evening Star,   Lenox.
Cincinnatus, N. Marlboro'.

King Hiram's,   Truro.
Washington,   Roxbury.
St. John's, Demerara(W.I.)
Amity,   Camden.
Rural,   Randolph.
Sumner's,   Dennis.
Sincerity,   Patridgefield.
Corner Stone,   Duxbury.
United,   Topsham.
Union, No. 5,   Nantucket.
American Union, Marietta.
Constellation,   Dedham.
Charity,   Mendon.
Cincinnatus,G't Barrington.
Cumberland, New Glouces-
    ter.
Harris,   Athol.
Hancock,   Castine.
Forefathers' Rock, Ply-
    mouth.
Jerusalem,   South Hadley.
Merrimack,   Haverhill.
Pythagorean,   Fryeburg.
Rising Virtue,   Bangor.
St. John's,   Newburyport.
St. Mark's,   do.
Sheffield,   Sheffield.
Saco,   Pepperelborough.
Wisdom, West Stockbridge.
Washington Remembered,
    New-Bedford.
Mount Carmel,   Lynn.
Amicable, Cambridgeport.
Oxford,   Paris.
Ancient Landmark, Port-
    land.
Rising Sun,   Sandisfield.
Jordan,   Danvers.
Orient,   Thomastown.
St. George's,   Warren.
Mountain,   Rowe.
Ionic,   Steuben.

MountVernon,Belchertown. Maine, Farmington.
Pautucket, Chelmsford. Fredonia, Northborough.
Sylvian, Southwick. Mystic, Lanesborough.
Mount Pleasant, Middle St. John, Stabrock, Deme-
Grenville. rara.
Felicity, Buckstown.

CHAPTER V.

Grand Lodge of Rhode-Island.

THE Grand Lodge of Rhode-Island was organized on the 25th of June, A. L. 5791, agreeably to a plan previously proposed and adopted by St. John's lodge, No. 1, of Newport, and St. John's lodge, No. 2, of Providence, which were the only lodges in the State at that time.

Subordinate Lodges.

St. John's, No. 1, Newport.
St. John's, No. 2, Providence.
Washington, No. 3, Warren.
Mount Vernon, No. 4, Providence.
Washington, No. 5, County of Washington.
St. Alban's, No. 6, Bristol.
Friendship, No. 7, Gloucester.
Mount Moriah, No. 8, Springfield.
Harmony, No. 9 Pawtuxet.
King Solomon's, No. 10, Greenwich.
Union, No. 11, Pawtucket.
Morning Star, No. 12, Cumberland.
Manchester, No. 13, Coventry.

The quarterly communications are holden in Providence, on the last Monday in February, May, August and November.

The annual meeting for the choice of officers is on the anniversary of St. John the Baptist.

CHAPTER VI.

Grand Lodge of Connecticut.

THE Grand Lodge of Connecticut was constituted on the 8th day of July, A. D. 1789, by fifteen lodges, which then existed in the State. These lodges were instituted by virtue of charters derived from the grand lodges of Massachusetts and New-York, but chiefly from the former.

The grand communications are holden semi-annually, in the months of May and October. The members of the grand lodge consist of all past and present grand officers, and the master and wardens of all the lodges under its jurisdiction, or their proxies.

Subordinate Lodges.

No.
1, Hiram lodge, New-Haven.
2, St. John's, Middletown.
3, St. John's, Bridgeport.
4, St. John's, Hartford.
5, Union, Greenwich.
6, St. John's, Norwalk.
7, K. Solomon's, Woodbury.
8, St. John's, Stratford.
9, Compass, Wallingford.
10, Wooster, Colchester.
11, St. Paul's, Litchfield.
12, King Hiram, Derby.
13, Montgomery, Salisbury.
14, Frederick, Farmington.
15, Moriah, Canterbury.
16, Temple, Cheshire.
17, Federal, Watertown.
18, Hiram, Newtown.
19, Washington, Huntington.
20, Harmony, Berlin.
21, St. Peter's, New Milford.
22, Hart's, Woodbridge.
23, St. James's, Preston.
24, Uriel, Tolland.
25, Columbia, Weathersfield.
26, Columbia, East Haddam.

No.
27, Rising Sun, Washington.
28, Morning Star, East Windsor.
29, Village, West Simsbury.
30, Day Spring, Hampden.
31, Union, New-London.
32, Meridian Sun, Warren.
33, Friendship, Southington.
34, Somerset, Norwich.
35, Aurora, Harwinton.
36, St. Mark's, Granby.
37, Western Star, Norfolk.
38, St. Alban's, Guilford.
39, Ark, Western.
40, Union, Danbury.
41, Federal, Brookfield.
42, Harmony, Waterbury.
43, Trinity, Killingworth.
44, Eastern Star, Lebanon.
45, Pythagoras, Lyme.
46, Putnam, Pomfret.
47, Morning Star, Oxford.
48, St. Luke's, Kent.
49, Jerusalem, Bridgefield.
50, Warren, Andover.
51, Warren, Chatham.
52, Mount Olives, Saybrook.
53, Widow's Son, North Stonington.

CHAPTER VII.

Grand Lodge of Vermont.

THE Grand Lodge of the State of Vermont was constituted at Rutland, on the 14th day of October, A. D. 1794. Its annual meetings are holden on the Monday preceding the second Thursday of October, annually, at 9 o'clock, A. M. at Windsor and Vergennes alternately. Its members are all past and present grand officers, and the masters and wardens of the several subordinate lodges.

Subordinate Lodges.

Vermont Lodge,	Windsor.	Morning Sun,	Bridport.
North Star,	Manchester.	Cement,	West Haven.
Dorchester,	Vergennes.	Friendship,	Charlotte.
Temple,	Bennington.	Washington,	Brandon.
Union,	Middlebury.	Lively Stone,	Darby.
Centre,	Rutland.	Warren,	Woodstock.
Washington,	Burlington.	George Washington, Chel-	
Hiram,	Paulet.	sea.	
Aurora,	Montpelier.	Rainbow,	Middletown.
Franklin,	St. Albans.	Morning Star,	Poultney.
Olive Branch,	Chester.	Rising Sun,	Royalton.
Newton,	Arlington.	Tabernacle,	Bennington.
Golden Rule,	Putney.	Farmer's,	Danby.
Harmony,	Danville.	St. John's,	Springfield.
Federal,	Randolph.	Blazing Star,	New Fane.
Mount Moriah,	Wardsbo-	Charity,	Newbury.
rough.		Green Mountain,	Ludlow.
Meridian Sun,	Greensbo-	United Brethren,	Norwich.
rough.		Mount Vernon, Hyde Park.	

CHAPTER VIII.

Grand Lodge of New-York.

THE Grand Lodge of New-York was first constituted by a warrant from the Duke of Athol, dated London, 5th September, A. D. 1781.

In conformity to the example which had been set by the grand lodges of several States after the revolutionary con-

D

test, on the 5th September, A. D. 1787, the masters and wardens of the several lodges within the state, having been duly notified, assembled in the city of New-York; and the late provincial grand lodge having been closed *sine die*, formed and opened an independent grand lodge, and elected and installed their grand officers.

Subordinate Lodges.

St. John's, No. 1, New-York.
St. John's, No. 6, do.
Hiram, do.
St. Andrew's, do.
Trinity, do.
Temple, do.
Phœnix, do.
Washington, do.
Holland, do.
Albion, do.
Abram's, do.
Adelphi, do.
Warren, do.
L'Unité Americaine, do.
Clinton, do.
Erin, do.
Mount Moriah, do.
Morton, do.
Benevolent, do.
Woods, do.
New Jerusalem, do.
L'Union Française, do.
La Sincerité, do.
Howard, do.
Temple Lodge, Albany.
Union Lodge, do.
Mount Vernon, do.
Whites, do.
Master's Lodge, do.
Bern, do.
Morning Star, do.
Solomon's, Poughkeepsie.
St. George's, Schenectady.
St. Patrick's, Johnstown.

Fortitude, Brooklyn.
Temple Lodge, North East Precinct.
Washington, Fort Edward.
St. Simon and St. Jude, Fishkill.
Hudson Lodge, Hudson.
Jamaica, Jamaica.
Hiram Lodge, Lansingburg.
Unity Lodge, Canaan.
Steuben, Newburg.
St. John's, Warwick.
La Fayette, Armenia.
Washington, Clermont.
St. John's, Florida.
Livingston, Kingston.
Montgomery, Stillwater.
Amicable, Whitestown.
Ontario Lodge, Canandaigua.
Aurora, Hampton.
Huntington, Huntington.
Paine Lodge, Armenia.
Livingston, Kingsbury.
Freehold Lodge, Freehold.
Union, Newton, Long Island.
Harmony, Catskill.
Rural, Cambridge.
Federal, Hoosick.
Courtlandt, Courtlandt.
Amicable, Herkimer.
Columbus, South East.
Franklin, Ballstown.
Columbus, Frederickstown.

Otsego,	Cooperstown.	Horizontal,	Frederick.
Montgomery,	Broadalbin.	Roman,	Rome.
Patriot,	Pittstown.	Herschel,	Hartford.
Canaan,	Canaan.	Hiram,	Aurelius.
Orange,	Waterford.	Morton,	Schenectady.
Orange,	Goshen.	Asylum,	Coeymans.
St. Andrew's,	Stanford.	Selected Friends,	Camillus.
Westchester,	Westchester.	Western Star,	Scipio.
Beekman,	Beekmantown.	Sylvan,	Sempronius.
Apollo,	Troy.	Western Star,	Sheldon.
Coxsackie,	Coxsackie.	Moriah,	De Ruyter.
North Star,	Salem.	Rising Sun,	Adams.
Schoharie Union,	Schoharie.	Gilboa,	Blenheim.
Aurora,	Fairfield.	Northern Constellation, Malone.	
Liberty,	Granville.		
United Brethren,	Cazenovia.	Harmony,	Chazy.
Western Star,	Unadilla.	St. John's,	Greenfield.
Suffolk,	Smithtown.	Morning Star,	Pittsford.
Morton,	Hempstead, Long Island.	Delhi,	Delhi.
		Genesee,	Honeydye.
Bath,	Bath.	Sullivan,	Lenox.
St. Paul's,	Conajoharie.	Homer,	Homer.
Morton,	West Chester.	St. John's,	Wilmington.
St. James's,	Middletown.	Friendship,	Oswego.
Tioga Lodge,	Union.	Ark,	Geneva.
Moriah,	Marbletown.	Champion,	Champion.
Montgomery,	Rhinebeck.	St. Laurence,	Kortright.
Homer,	Schaticoke.	Harmony,	Tompkins.
Adoniram,	Franklin.	Village,	Marcellus.
Genoa Lodge,	Cayuga.	Aurora,	Meredith.
Sharon Felicity,	Sharon.	Harmony,	Riga.
Montgomery,	Montgomery.	Richfield,	Richfield.
Schodach,	Schodach.	Hamilton,	Eaton.
Hiram,	Mount Pleasant.	Olive Branch,	Litchfield.
Federal,	Paris.	Farmer's Lodge,	Easton.
Morton,	Bedford.	Meridian Sun,	Butternuts and N. Lisbon.
Salem,	North Salem.		
St. Alban's,	Brooklyn.	Western Light,	Lisle.
Franklin,	Charlestown.	Solomon's, Mark Master's, 49 N. East.	
Tioga,	Union.		
Walton,	Duanesburg.	Warsaw,	Warsaw.
Village Lodge,	Marcellus.	Sanger,	Sangerfield.

Northern Light,	Dekalb.	Rising Sun,	Trenton.
Western Star,	Bridgewater.	Genesee,	Richmond.
Scipio,	Aurora.	Morton,	Walton.
Hampton, Sag Harbour, Long Island.		Sincerity,	Phelps.
		Hiram,	Huntington.
Genesee,	Avon.	Steuben,	Steuben.
Eastern Light, Watertown.		Rensselaer, Rensselaerville.	

CHAPTER IX.

Grand Lodge of New-Jersey.

A CONVENTION of free and accepted masons of the State of New-Jersey was holden, agreeable to previous notice, on the 18th December, A. D. 1786, at the city of New-Brunswick, when a grand lodge for the said State was duly constituted, and the Hon. David Brearly, Esq. chief justice of the State, was elected first grand master.

Subordinate Lodges.

Solomon's Lodge, Somersville.		Salem,	Salem.
		Trinity, Middletown Point.	
St. John's,	Newark.	Union,	Orange.
Trenton,	Trenton.	Friendship, Port Elizabeth.	
Unity,	Amwell.	Augusta,	Frankford.
Harmony,	Newton.	United,	Sandyston.
Brearly,	Bridgetown.	Hiram,	Flemington.
Nova Cæsarea,	Cincinnati.	Hope Lodge,	Hope.
Woodbury,	Woodbury.	Mount Meriah, New Brunswick.	
Washington, N. Brunswick.			
Patterson,	Patterson.	St. Tammany, Morristown.	
Farmer's,	Sussex county.	Independence, Hackett's Town.	
Federal,	Hopewell.		
Olive Branch, Phillipsburgh.		Princeton,	Princeton.
		Mansfield, New Hampton.	
Cincinnati,	Montville.	Sharp Town, Sharp Town.	
Mount Holly, Mount Holly.		Chatham,	Chatham.

The annual meeting of the grand lodge is holden on the second Tuesday in November at Trenton.

CHAPTER X.

Grand Lodge of Pennsylvania.

On the 24th of June, 1734, upon the petition of several brethren residing in Philadelphia, a warrant of constitution was granted by the grand lodge of Boston, for holding a lodge in that place; appointing the Rt. Worshipful Benjamin Franklin their first master; which is the beginning of masonry in Pennsylvania.

The grand lodge of England granted a grand warrant, bearing date the 20th June, A. D. 1764, to the M. W. William Bell and others, authorizing them to form and hold a grand lodge for the State of Pennsylvania.

The grand officers, together with the officers and representatives of a number of regular lodges under their jurisdiction, at a communication holden in the grand lodge room in the city of Philadelphia, on the 25th day of September, 1786, after mature and serious deliberation, unanimously resolved, " That it is improper that the grand lodge of Pennsylvania should remain any longer under the authority of any foreign grand lodge." And the said grand lodge did then close, *sine die*.

The grand convention thus assembled did then and there *unanimously resolve*, that the lodges under the jurisdiction of the grand lodge of Pennsylvania, aforesaid, lately holden as a provincial grand lodge, under the authority of the grand lodge of England, should, and they did form themselves into a grand lodge, to be called " *The Grand Lodge of Pennsylvania and masonic jurisdiction thereunto belonging*," to be held in the said city of Philadelphia.

Subordinate Lodges.

No.		No.	
2	Philadelphia.	11	Loudon Grove.
3	do.	12	Winchester.
4	do.	14	Wilmington, D.
5	Cantwell's Bridge.	17	Chester Mills.
7	Chestertown.	18	Dover.
8	Norristown.	18	British 7th Regt.
9	Philadelphia.	19	Philadelphia.

No.
21 Lancaster.
23 Sunbury.
24 Reading.
25 Bristol.
26 Carlisle.
33 Newcastle, D.
35 Joppa.
43 Lancaster.
44 Duck Creek.
45 Pittsburgh.
46 Church Town.
47 Port au Prince.
48 Bedford.
50 Chester County.
51 Philadelphia.
52   do.
54 Washington.
55 Huntingdon County.
56 Carlisle.
57 Newton.
58 Army U. S.
59 Philadelphia.
60 Fort Burd.
61 Wilkesbarre.
62 Reading.
64 Greensburg.
65 Susquehannah.
66 Robinson.
67 Philadelphia.
68 Mifflin.
69 Chester.
70 Tyoga Point.
71 Philadelphia.
72   do.
73   do.
74 Franklin County.
75 Pughtown.
76 Neuville.
77 Trinidad.
78 Old Mingo.
79 Chambersburgh.

No.
80 Salisbury.
81 Germantown.
82 Mitford.
83 Upper Smithfield.
84 Somerset.
85 Alexandria.
86   do.
87 St. Domingo.
88 St. Marque.
89 Aux Cayes.
90 New-Orleans.
91 Union township.
92 Philadelphia.
93 New-Orleans.
95 St. Domingo.
96 Newcastle, D.
97 St. Domingo.
99   do.
100 Bloomsbury.
101 Palms Town, Dauphin County.
102 Jerusalem, Joppa.
103 Le Temple des Vertus Theologales, Havana.
104 Philanthropic, Leacock township.
105 Lodge of Amity, Zaneville.
106 Williamsport, Lycoming County.
107 Western Star, Kaskaskias.
108 Union, Wysox and Orwell.
109 Lousiana, St. Genevieve.
110 Youghrogania, Counelsville.
111 St. Louis, Louisiana.
112 The Desired Reunion, New-Orleans.

No.
114 ——, Philadelphia.
115 St. John's, Philadelphia.
116 Amicitia, Elizabethtown, Lancaster Co.
117 Lodge la Concorde, New-Orleans.
118 Lodge la Perseverance, do.
119 Town of Clifford, Luzerne County.
120 Liberty Lodge, Tioga township.
121 Union, Philadelphia.
122 Harmony, New-Orleans.
123 St. John's, Borough of York.
124 Borough of Erie, Erie County.
125 Herman's, (a German Lodge) Philadelphia.

No.
126 Rising Star, Philadelphia.
127 Philanthropy, do.
128 Temple, do.
129 L'Etoile, Polaire, New-Orleans.
130 Phœnix, Philadelphia.
131 Industry, do.
132 Brandywine, Brandywine township.
133 St. James, Beaver.
134 Franklin, Philadelphia.
135 Roxborough, Roxborough.
136 Friendship, Abington.
137 Bedford Bath, Bedford.
138 Schuylkill, Orwigsburgh.
139 Rising Sun, Philadelphia.

CHAPTER XI.

Grand Lodge of Delaware.

At a grand communication of a majority of the lodges, established in the State of Delaware, at the Town Hall, in the borough of Wilmington, on Friday, June 6, A. D. 1806, A. L. 5806, it was

Resolved unanimously, " That the several lodges of ancient masons in the State of Delaware, here represented by deputies properly authorized, consider it as a matter of right, and for the general benefit of masonry, that they ought to form a grand lodge within the said State; and do now proceed to form and organize themselves into a grand lodge accordingly, to be known and distinguished by the name of *The Grand Lodge of Delaware.*

Subordinate Lodges.

No.
1 Washington, Wilmington.
2 St. John's, Newcastle.
3 Hiram, Newark.
4 Hope, Laureltown.
5 Cantwell's Bridge, Newcastle County.

No.
6 Hiram, Buck Tavern, Newcastle County.
7 Union, Dover.
8 Union, Port Penn.
9 Temple, Milford.

CHAPTER XII.

Grand Lodge of Maryland.

THE Grand Lodge of Maryland was constituted on the 17th day of April, A. D. 1787, and is holden in the city of Baltimore.

Subordinate Lodges.

Amanda, Annapolis.
Amicable, Baltimore.
Bellair, Hartford.
Benevolent, Baltimore.
Columbia, Port Tobacco.
Concordia, Baltimore.
Columbia, Georgetown.
Federal, Washington City, vacated.
Federal, Baltimore.
Harmony, Salisbury.
St. John's, Cambridge.
St. John's, Baltimore.
Spiritual, do.
Veritas St. Johannis, do. vacated.
Zion, Havre de Graec.
Washington, Fell's Point, Baltimore.
Temple, Rayster's town.

Hiram, Leonard's town.
Hiram, Fredericktown.
Union, Elkton.
Orange, Vienna.
Mount Moriah, Hagerstown.
Hope, Sussex, Delaware.
No. 2, Chestertown.
No. 6, Easton.
Somerset, Princess Ann.
No. 44, Mount Ararat, Slate Ridge, Harford county.
Philadelphos, Taney-town.
Cassia, Baltimore.
Door to Virtue, Pipe Creek.
Philanthropic, Newmarket.
Warren, Baltimore.
Harmony, West Nottingham.
Corinthian, Baltimore.
Worcester, Worcester co.
Phœnix, Baltimore.

CHAPTER XIII.

Grand Lodge of Virginia.

THE Grand Lodge of Virginia began its operations October 30, A. D. 1778. It meets annually, at the city of Richmond, on the second Monday in December. The mode of address is, " The Secretary of the Grand Lodge of Virginia, Richmond."

Subordinate Lodges.

1 Norfolk, Norfolk Boro'.
2 Killwining Cross, Port-Royal.
3 Blandford, Blandford.
4 Fredericksburg, Fredericksburg.
5 Dormant.
6 Williamsburg, Willia.'
7 Botetourt, Gloucester.
8 Suspended.
9 Dormant.
10 Richmond, Richmond.
11 Northampton, dormant.
12 Kempsville, Princess Anne.
13 Staunton, Augusta.
14 Manchester, Chesterfield.
15 Petersburg, dormant.
16 La Sagesse, Norfolk.
17 Charlotte, dormant.
18 Smithfield Union, Isle of Wight.
19 Richmond Randolph, Richmond.
20 Extinct.
21 Hiram, Winchester.
22 Alexandria, Alexandria.
23 Dinwiddie, Dinwiddie.
24 Pittsylvania, dormant.
25 Now under the G. L. of Kentucky.

26 Washington, dormant.
27 Rockingham, dormant.
28 Suspended.
⁎ No Lodge, No. 29.
30 Solomon's, Nansemond.
31 Columbia, dormant.
32 George, Warminster.
33 Warren, Albemarle.
34 Benevolent, dormant.
35 Now under the G. L. K.
36 St. John's, Richmond.
37 Hicks' Ford, Greensville.
38 Buckingham Union, dormant.
39 Marshall, Lynchburg.
40 Stevensburgh, Culpepper.
41 Lebanon, dormant.
42 Bath Union, Bath.
43 Fairfax, Culpepper.
44 Door to Virtue, dormant.
45 Aberdeen, dormant.
46 Now under the G. L. K.
47 Brooke, Alexandria.
48 Abingdon, Washington.
49 Greenbrier, Greenbrier.
50 Dumfries, Prince Wm.
51 Painville, dormant.
52 Brunswick, Brunswick.
53 Chuckatuck, Nansemond.
54 Jerusalem, Richmond.
55 Fraternal, Wythe.

56 Naphtali, Norfolk.
57 Now under the G. L. K.
58 Day, Louisa, *dormant.*
59 Hiram, Westmoreland.
60 Widow's Son's, Albemarle, Milton.
61 Chester, Frederick, *dormant.*
62 Harmony, Amelia, *dormant.*
63 Fredericksburg American, Fredericksburg.
64 Madison, Madison.
65 Jefferson, Surry.
66 Winchester Union, Winchester.
67 Haymarket, Centerville.
68 Rockbridge, Lexington.
69 Warrington, Fauquier county.
70 Cartersville, *dormant.*
71 Way to Happiness, Patrick county.
72 No Lodge of this number.
73 Ark, *dormant.*
74 Friendship, Lovingston.
75 Loudon, *dormant.*
76 Center, Southampton co.
77 Franklin, Mecklenburg.
78 Washington, *dormant.*
79 Farnham, Richmond co.
80 Moorfield, Hardy co.
81 Salem, Paris.
82 Portsmouth, *dormant.*
83 Concord, Lunenburg.
84 Sycamore, King and Queen co.
85 Astrea, Sussex co.
86 Preston, King George co.
87 N. Glasgow Union, Amherst co.
88 Lancaster Union, Lancaster co.
89 Mount Horeb, Martinsburg, Berkley co.
90 Charlottesville, Charlottesville.
91 Mount Nebo, Shepherdstown.
92 Rockfish Harmony, Nelson co.
93 Morgantown Union, Monongalia county.
94 P. E. Providence, Prince Edward county.
95 Liberty Lodge, Bedford county.
96 Halifax Hiram Lodge, Halifax county.

CHAPTER XIV.

Grand Lodge of North-Carolina.

THE Grand Lodge of North-Carolina was first constituted by virtue of a charter from the grand lodge of Scotland, A. D. 1771. It convened occasionally at Newbern and Edenton, at which latter place the records were deposited previous to the revolutionary war. During the contest, the records were destroyed by the British army, and the meetings of the grand lodge suspended.

The members of the craft convened at Hillsborough in this State, A. D. 1787, and compiled certain regulations for the government of the grand lodge, and again set to work. In the same year they appointed a committee to form a constitution for their future government, which was accordingly done, and in the year following, the said constitution was formally adopted and ratified, at the city of Raleigh, at which place the grand lodge meets annually.

Subordinate Lodges.

St. John, Wilmington.
Royal White Hart, Halifax.
St. John, Newbern.
St. John, Kingston.
Royal Edwin, Windsor.
Phoenix, Fayetteville.
Old Cone, Salisbury.
Johnston Caswell, Warrenton.
St. John, Dublin county.
Washington, Beaufort do.
St. Tammany, Martin do.
American George, Murfreesborough.
King Solomon, Jones co.
Hiram, Williamsborough.
Pansophia, Moore county.
Davie, Glasg. Greene do.
Mount Moriah, Iredell do.
Columbia, Wayne do.
Harmony, No. 1, of Tennessee, Nashville in the State of Tennessee.
St. Tammany, Wilmington.
Phalanx, Charlotte, Mecklenburg county.
Stakes, Cabarrus do.
Freeland, Rowan do.
Unanimity, Rockford.
Jerusalem, Carteret county.
Friendship, Fort Barnwell.
Wm. R. Davie, Lexington.

Rising Sun, Morganton.
Davie, Bertie county.
Hiram, city of Raleigh.
Tennessee, No. 2, of the State of Tennessee, Knoxville.
Federal, Pitt county.
Greenville, Greenville, Tennessee.
Williams, Johnstonville.
Liberty, Wilkesborough.
Social, Pittsborough.
Orange, Lincoln county.
Taylor, Beaufort.
No. 49, surrendered.
Newport No. 4, of Tennessee, Newport.
Rogerville, Tennessee.
Town of Gallatin, do.
Indian Town, Carrituck co.
Edenton.
Town of Franklin, Tennessee.
Northampton Court House.
Louisburg, Franklin co.
Tarborough.
Plymouth, Washington co.
Union, Waynesborough.
Camden, Jonesborough.
Kilwinning, Wadesborough.
Friendship, St. Stephen's, M. T.

CHAPTER XV.

Grand Lodge of South-Carolina.

THE Grand Lodge of the State of South-Carolina was instituted and established at Charleston on the 24th day of March, A. D. 1787.

The general grand communication is holden in Charleston annually, on St. John the Evangelist day ; and the quarterly communications on the last Saturday in March, June, and September, and on the next Saturday but one preceding St. John the Evangelist's day.

Subordinate Lodges.

No.		No.	
1	Charleston.	24	Rocky Creek.
2	do.	25	Union County.
3	do.	26	Jacksonborough.
4	do.	27	Salem Court House.
5	do.	28	Chester County.
6	Waynesborough.	29	New-Orleans.
8	Charleston.	30	St. Augustine, E. F.
9	do.	31	Charleston.
10	Columbia.	32	Yorkville.
11	Charleston.	33	Lancaster County.
12	Orangeburgh.	34	Edisto Island.
13	*Extinct.*	35	Edgefield County.
14	Charleston.	36	Chester do.
15	Little River.	37	Statesburgh.
16	Georgetown.	38	Newbury County.
17	Greenville.	39	Coosawatchie.
18	Broad River.	40	Cambridge.
19	Laurens County.	41	Beaufort.
20	Greensborough, Georgia.	42	St. Helena Island.
21	Black Mingo.	43	Newbury County.
22	Little Pedee.	44	Laurens do.
23	Georgetown.		

CHAPTER XVI.

Grand Lodge of Georgia.

THE Grand Lodge of Georgia is holden " by virtue, and in pursuance of, the right of succession, legally derived from the most noble and most worshipful Thomas Thyne, lord viscount Weymouth, grand master of England, by his warrant directed to the right worshipful Roger Lacey; and by the renewal of the said power by Sholto Charles Douglas, lord Aberdour, grand master of Scotland, for the years 1755 and 1756; and grand master of England for the years 1757 and 1758; as will appear in his warrant, directed to the right worshipful Grey Elliot."

On the 16th day of December, A. D. 1786, a convention of the several lodges holden in the state assembled at Savannah, when the permanent appointments which had been heretofore made by the grand master of England were solemnly relinquished, by the right worshipful Samuel Elbert, grand master, and the other officers of the grand lodge; and certain regulations adopted, by which the grand officers are now elected annually by the grand lodge.

Subordinate Lodges.

No.
1 Solomon's, Savannah.
2 Hiram, do.
3 Columbia, Augusta.
4 St. Louis, Washington.
5 Washington, do.
6 St. John's, Sunbury.
7 Little River, Little River.
8 St. Patrick's, Waynesborough.
9 St. George's, Kiokas.
10 Union, Savannah.
11 Georgetown, Georgetown.
12 Elbert, Elberton.
13 St. Tammany, Green County.

No.
14 Forsyth's, Augusta.
15 Amity, Lake Ferry.
16 Camden, St. Mary's.
17 Stith, Sparta.
18 Social, Augusta.
19 Haustoun, Effingham.
20 Stephens, Waynesborough.
21 Petersburgh, Petersburgh.
22 La Constance, Savannah.
23 Harmony, Darien.
24 Franklin, Warrenton.
25 Royal, Bourke.
28 San Fernando, Fernandina.
29 ——, Elberton.

E

CHAPTER XVII.
Grand Lodge of Kentucky.

THE Grand Lodge of Kentucky was established on the 13th of October, A. D. 1800, and holds its commmunications in the town of Lexington.

Subordinate Lodges.

No.
1 Lexington, in Lexington.
2 Paris, Paris.
3 Georgetown, Georgetown.
4 Hiram, Frankfort.
5 Solomon's, Shelbyville.
6 Washington, Bairdstown.
7 Harmony, Natchez, M. T.
8 Abraham's, Louisville.
9 Jerusalem, Henderson.
10 Unity, Millersburgh.
11 St. John's, Flemings-
burgh.
12 Philanthropic, David-
son, Kentucky.
13 Cincinnati, Cincinnati,
Ohio.
14 Mount Vernon, George-
town.

No.
15 Vincennes, Vincennes,
I. T.
16 Paris Union, Paris.
17 Russelville, Russelville.
18 St. Andrews, Cinthiana.
19 Washington, Washing-
ton.
20 Winchester, Winchester.
21 Madison, Huntsville.
22 Davies, Lexington.
23 Montgomery, Mt. Ster-
ling.
24 Allen, Glasgow.
25 Richmond, Richmond.
26 Maysville, Maysville.
27 Columbia, Columbia.
28 Union, Madison T.

CHAPTER XVIII.
Grand Lodge of Ohio.

THE Grand Lodge of Ohio was instituted by a convention of delegates from all the lodges within the State, assembled at Chillicothe, on the first Monday of January, A. D. 1808, and elected their grand officers on the 7th of the said month. The first communication of the grand lodge was holden at Chillicothe on Monday, the 2d day of January, A. D. 1809.

Subordinate Lodges.

No.
1 American Union, Marietta.
2 N. E. Harmony, Cincinnati.
3 Erie, Warren.

No.
4 New-England, Worthing-
ton.
5 Amity, Zanesville.

No.

6 Scioto, Chillicothe.
7 Morning Dawn, Gallipolis.
8 Harmony, Urbana.
9 Mount Zion, Clinton.
10 Meridian Orb, Paines-
ville.
11 Centre Star, Granville.
12 Unity, Ravenna.
13 St. John's, Dayton.
14 Franklin, Troy.
15 Concord, Cleaveland.
16 Belmont, St. Clairsville.
17 Washington, Hamilton.
18 Hiram, Delaware.
19 Jerusalem, Vernon.
20 Farmers, Belpre.
21 Western Star, Canfield.

No.

22 Rising Sun, Ashtabula.
23 Pickaway, Circleville.
24 Army.
25 Paramuthia, Athens.
26 Lebanon, Lebanon.
27 Morning Star, Spring-
field.
28 Temple, Harpersfield.
29 Clermont Social, Wil-
liamsburgh.
30 Ohio, Columbus.
31 Golden Rule, Fairfield.
32 Friendship, St. Clairsville, Co. of Adams.
33 Ebenezer, Wooster.
34 Middlebury, Middlebury.
35 Mansfield, Mansfield.

CHAPTER XIX.

Grand Lodge of Tennessee.

Subordinate Lodges.

No.

2 Tennessee, Knoxville.
3 Greenville, Greenville.
4 Newport, Newport.
5 Overton, Rogersville.

No.

6 King Solomon's, Gallatin.
7 Hiram, Franklin.
8 Cumberland, Nashville.
9 Western Star, Port Royal.

CHAPTER XX.

Grand Lodge of Upper-Canada.

M. W. William Jarvis, Esq. grand master.
R. W. Robert Kerr, Esq. deputy grand master.

Subordinate Lodges.

No.

1 Newark, Niagara.
2 Queenstown.
3 York.
4 Newark, Niagara.
5 ———
6 ———

No.

7 ———
8 ———
9 Bertie, Fort Erie.
10 Barton.
11 Mohawk Village.
12 Stamford.

The grand lodge meets at Newark, Niagara.

CHAPTER XXI.

Grand Lodge of Lower-Canada.

M. W. His Royal Highness Prince Edward, &c. &c. G. M.
R. W. George Lewis Hamilton, D. G. M.

Subordinate Lodges.

No.
9 In the 4th Bat. R. Artillery, at Quebec.
40 Quebec.
241 Do. These three on the Registry of England.
1 Glengary Lodge, in the 2d Bat. R. C. Volunteers.
2 Royal Rose in the 7th Regt. of foot.
3 St. John's, Lower-Canada.
4 2d Bat. 60th Reg.
5 Royal Edward, Edwardsburg, U. C.
6 Richlieu, at William Henry, L. C.

No.
7 Fidelity, 7th Reg. of foot.
8 Union, Montreal.
9 Select Surveyors, at Missisquoui Bay.
10 Zion, Detroit.
11 Chambly.
12 St. Paul's, Montreal.
354 Quebec, 49th Reg. of foot, Registry of Ireland.
816 98th Reg. do.
14 Nelson Lodge, Caldwell Manac, Lake Champlain.
15 Rural Lodge, Ascot, Eastern townships.

CHAPTER XXII.

Grand Lodge of Nova Scotia, &c.

M. W. John George Pike, Esq. grand master.
R. W. Hon. Andrew Belcher, deputy grand master.

Subordinate Lodges.

No.
1 Union, Halifax.
2 Virgin, do.
3 Parr, Shelburne.
6 Digby, Digby.
7 Temple, Guysborough.
9 Chester, Chester.
11 St. George, Cornwallis.
19 St. George, Maugerville.
21 Sion, Sussex Vale.
22 Solomon's, Frederickt'n.
25 Annapolis, Royal.
26 St. John's, Charlottetown, Prince Edward Island.

No.
27 Hibernia, Liverpool.
28 Harmony, Sydney, Island of Cape Breton.
29 St. John, St. John's, N. B.
31 Midian, Kingston, do.
32 Wentworth, Yarmouth.
33 Royal Welch Fusiliers, 23d Reg.
34 Orphan's Friend, St. Stephen's, N. B.
35 New Caledonia, Picton.
155 St. Andrew's, Halifax.
211 St. John's, do. Registry of England.

MASONIC SONGS.

MOST EXCELLENT MASTER'S SONG.

BY BROTHER T. S. WEBB.

To be sung when one is received into that degree.

ALL hail to the morning
    That bids us rejoice;
The temple's completed,
    Exalt high each voice;
The cape-stone is finish'd,
    Our labour is o'er;
The sound of the gavel
    Shall hail us no more.
To the Power Almighty, who ever has guided
  The tribes of old Israel, exalting their fame,
To him who hath govern'd our hearts undivided,
  Let's send forth our voices, to praise his great name.

Companions, assemble
    On this joyful day,
(Th' occasion is glorious)
    The key-stone to lay;
Fulfill'd is the promise,
    By th' ANCIENT OF DAYS,
To bring forth the cape-stone,
    With shouting and praise.

x 2

Ceremonies.

There's no more occasion for level or plumb-line,
  For trowel or gavel, for compass or square;
Our works are completed, the ark safely seated,
  And we shall be greeted as workmen most rare.

Now those that are worthy,
  Our toils who have shar'd,
And prov'd themselves faithful,
  Shall meet their reward.
Their virtue and knowledge,
  Industry and skill,
Have our approbation,
  Have gain'd our good will.
We accept and receive them most excellent masters,
  Invested with honours, and power to preside;
Among worthy craftsmen, wherever assembled,
  The knowledge of masons to spread far and wide.

ALMIGHTY JEHOVAH,
  Descend now, and fill
This lodge with thy glory,
  Our hearts with good will!
Preside at our meetings,
  Assist us to find
True pleasure in teaching
  Good will to mankind.
Thy wisdom inspired the great institution,
  Thy strength shall support it, till nature expire;
And when the creation shall fall into ruin,
  Its beauty shall rise, through the midst of the fire!

MASTER'S SONG.

BY BROTHER T. S. WEBB.

[TUNE—" *Greenwich Pensioner.*"]

I SING the mason's glory,
  Whose prying mind doth burn,
Unto complete perfection
  Our mysteries to learn;

Not those who visit lodges
 To eat and drink their fill,
Not those who at our meetings
 Hear lectures 'gainst their will:
Chor. But only those whose pleasure,
 At every lodge, can be
 T' improve themselves by lectures,
  In glorious masonry.
     Hail! glorious masonry!

The faithful, worthy brother,
 Whose heart can feel for grief,
Whose bosom with compassion
 Steps forth to its relief,
Whose soul is ever ready,
 Around him to diffuse
The principles of masons,
 And guard them from abuse;
Chor. These are thy sons, whose pleasure,
 At every lodge, will be,
 T' improve themselves by lectures
  In glorious masonry.
     Hail! glorious masonry!

King Solomon, our patron,
 Transmitted this command—
"The faithful and praise-worthy
 True light must understand;
And my descendants, also,
 Who're seated in the East,
Have not fulfill'd their duty,
 Till light has reach'd the West."
Chor. Therefore, our highest pleasure,
 At every lodge, should be,
 T' improve ourselves by lectures
  In glorious masonry.
     Hail! glorious masonry!

The duty and the station,
 Of master in the chair,
Obliges him to summon
 Each brother to prepare;

.That all may be enabled,
     By slow, though sure degrees,
To answer in rotation,
     With honour and with ease.
Chor.   Such are thy sons, whose pleasure,
     At every lodge, will be,
     T' improve themselves by lectures
     In glorious masonry.
                 Hail ! glorious masonry!

SENIOR WARDEN'S SONG.

BY BROTHER T. S. WEBB.

[TUNE—" *When the hollow drum doth beat to bed.*"]

WHEN the Senior Warden, standing in the West,
Calls us from our labours to partake of rest,
     We unite, while he recites
         The duties of a mason.
         On the level meet,
         On the square we part,
         Repeats each worthy brother.
         This rule in view,
         We thus renew
            Our friendship for each other.
Chorus.   When the Senior, &c.

When our work is over, implements secure,
Each returning homeward, with intentions pure,
     Our wives we kiss, give sweethearts bliss,
         Which makes them both love masons ;
         And thus we may
         Enjoy each day,
            At home, and at our meetings :
         Our sweethearts eas'd,
         Our wives well pleas'd,
            Saluted with such greetings.
Chorus.   When the Senior, &c.

JUNIOR WARDEN'S SONG.

BY BROTHER T. S. WEBB.

[TUNE—" *Faint and wearily, &c.*"]

WHEN the Junior Warden calls us from our labours,
When the sun is at meridian height,
Let us merrily unite most cheerily,
With social harmony new joys invite.
 One and all, at his call,
  To the feast repairing,
 All around joys resound,
  Each the pleasure sharing.
Chorus. When the Junior Warden, &c.

Mirth and jollity, without frivolity,
Pervade our meetings at the festive board ;
Justice, temperance and prudence govern us,
There's nought but harmony among us heard.
 One and all, at the call,
  To the feast repairing,
 All around joys resound,
  Each the pleasure sharing.
Chorus. Mirth and jollity, &c.

Thus we ever may enjoy the pleasant moments
Given unto us from the master's chair,
Till the sun an hour has past meridian,
And then each brother to his work repair.
 One and all hear the call,
  From the feast repairing,
 All around gavels sound,
  Each the labour sharing.
Chorus. Thus we ever may, &c.

SENIOR WARDEN'S TOAST.

FREEMASONS all
Attend the call ;

'Tis by command
You are all warn'd
To fill up a bumper and keep it at hand,
    To drink to " *The mother of masons.*"
Let each give the word to his brother,
To prove that we love one another:
    Let's fill to the dame
    From whom we all came ;
And call her " *Of masons the mother.*"
Chor. The stewards have laid foundations,
To prove that we love our relations,
    By toasting the dame
    From whom we all came ;
We'll call her " *The mother of masons.*"

In days of yore
Freemasons bore
A flask of wine,
Of mirth the sign,
And often they fill'd with the liquor divine,
    To drink to " *The mother of masons.*"
'Twas on these joyful occasions,
All charged stood firm to their stations,
    And toasted the dame
    From whom we all came,
Repeating, " *The mother of masons.*"
Chor. The stewards have laid, &c.

Be all prepar'd,
Each motion squar'd,
And at the nod,
With one accord,
In strictest rotation we'll pass round the word,
    Drink, drink, to " *The mother of masons.*"
Have a care, right and left, and make ready,
Be all in your exercise steady,
    And fill to the dame
    From whom we all came,
" *The mother of masons,*" the lady.
Chor. The stewards have laid, &c.

PAST MASTER'S SONG.

[Tune—" *Rule Britannia.*"]

WHEN earth's foundation first was laid,
By the Almighty Artist's hand,
'Twas then our perfect, our perfect laws were made,
Established by his strict command.

Chor. Hail, mysterious—hail, glorious Masonry !
That makes us ever great and free.

In vain mankind for shelter sought,
In vain from place to place did roam,
Until from heaven, from heaven he was taught
To plan, to build, to fix his home.

Illustrious hence we date our Art,
And now in beauteous piles appear,
Which shall to endless, to endless time impart,
How worthy and how great we are.

Nor we less fam'd for every tie,
By which the human thought is bound ;
Love, truth, and friendship, and friendship socially,
Join all our hearts and hands around.

Our actions still by virtue blest,
And to our precepts ever true,
The world admiring, admiring shall request
To learn, and our bright paths pursue.

ANTHEM.

" Let there be light !" the Almighty spoke ;
Refulgent streams from chaos broke,
To illume the rising earth !
Well pleas'd the Great Jehovah stood ;
The Power Supreme pronounc'd it good,
And gave the planets birth !

In choral numbers masons join,
To bless and praise this light divine.

Parent of light! accept our praise!
Who shedd'st on us thy brightest rays,
   The light that fills the mind:
By choice selected, lo! we stand,
By friendship join'd, a social band!
   That *love*, that *aid* mankind!
     In choral numbers, &c.

The widow's tear, the orphan's cry,
All wants our ready hands supply,
   As far as power is given;
The naked clothe, the pris'ner free;
These are thy works, sweet charity!
   Reveal'd to us from heaven.
     In choral numbers masons join,
     To bless and praise this light divine.